INSIGHT GUIDES

Created and Directed by Hans Höfer

WASHINGTON D.C.

Edited and Produced by Martha Ellen Zenfell
Photography by Catherine Karnow

Editorial Director: Brian Bell

Houghton Mifflin

APA PUBLICATIONS

ABOUT THIS BOOK

Ever since George Washington chose the site for America's federal city, the US capital has been the object of a curious blend of praise and imprecation. It's "the most beautiful city in the world." It was also the "murder capital of America" for many years. Washington isn't a city, said Dylan Thomas, it's an abstraction.

Coming to grips with this abstraction was the perfect challenge for Apa Publications' Insight Guides, the 190-strong award-winning travel series. Each book is edited in the belief that, without insight into a destination's people and culture, travel narrows the mind rather than broadens it.

Putting the philosophy into practice for this book was the job of project editor **Martha Ellen Zenfell,** who is editor-in-chief of the company's many North American titles. Zenfell knew from editing Insight Guides to New York City and New Orleans that Apa's formula of combining hard-hitting text with superb photographs would give scope for the in-depth coverage Washington needed. Her knowledge of the city was local, as she spent much of her childhood in Shenandoah National Park.

Zenfell

"In those days Virginians used to leave home to discover Washington; now Washingtonians have discovered my part of rural Virginia," she says. The big, wooden-frame homes in her remote mountain town have been bought by weekending politicians, who have spruced them up, installed jacuzzis and "improved the look of the town no end." Zenfell is living proof that you *can* go home again, providing you can afford the house prices.

Among the most important aspects of an Insight Guide are the pictures. Several Apa photographers live in the Washington area ("because communications and airports are so good"), so the choice was difficult. In the end, the assignment went to **Catherine Karnow,** responsible for many of the bold images used in *Insight Guide: Los Angeles* and *Insight Guide: New York City.* She worked round the clock and over several seasons to take the pictures reproduced here. The daughter of local Pulitzer Prize-winning historian Stanley Karnow, she alternated between the family home in Potomac and a calm apartment in lively Adams Morgan while doing this work.

Karnow

Immersing himself in the history of this "City of Magnificent Distances" was **John Gattuso,** who majored in English and anthropology in college. These useful subjects were brought to bear not only on this book but also on other projects for Apa: editing *Insight Guide: Native America, Insight Guide: Philadelphia, Insight Guide: The Wild West,* and two Insight Guides to America's national parks.

Gattuso

The job of being a foreign correspondent is to cast a fresh eye over familiar terrain, and to make sense of it for their readers. This is the daily work of **Martin Walker,** DC bureau chief of London's *The Guardian,* who wrote the essays about politics and Washington's power elite. Educated at Oxford and Harvard universities, the winner of "Reporter of the Year" awards, and a commentator on CNN and the BBC, Walker first dipped his toes into political waters by serving on the staff of Senator Ed Muskie in 1970–1971.

Arriving straight from four years as bureau chief in Moscow, Walker was startled by the similarities between the

Walker

two very different cities. "Life in Washington is sweet, if you are employed, live in a safe white suburb and have enough disposable income to enjoy it," he says. "But below the ruling class, uncannily similar discontents are seething to those which led to Russia's *perestroika*: the economy stagnates, drug addiction and ethnic tensions are rampant, and only one American in two bothers to vote."

This foreign perspective is also shared by Walker's journalist wife, **Julia Watson**, who began her publishing career at Penguin Books, and has contributed to many periodicals. For this book, she cast an eye over the capital's cultural affairs, and compiled Travel Tips. Watson, like Dylan Thomas, was struck by the city's abstract quality. "Like other cities that were invented to specific purpose rather than evolving naturally, it seems Washington still struggles for a personality. Old-timers assure newcomers baffled by what precisely Washington is that it really has come a long way in the past 10 years. The town does offer much to seduce, however."

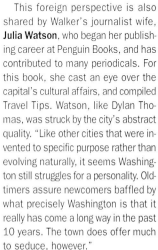
Watson

The genial ways of the city are something that second-generation Washingtonian and confirmed capital-lover **Maria Mudd** knows all about. "I love Washington for its green spaces – its woodland parks, gardens, vest-pocket parks and tree-lined streets," she says. This enthusiasm is evident in all of Mudd's "Places" chapters, as she shares her insider's knowledge of museum shops and farmers markets, revealing at the same time a sound understanding of the workings of Capitol Hill. Mudd's work has appeared in *National Geographic Traveler* magazine, *Islands* and the *Washington Post*.

Mudd

Another agreeable guide was **Alison Kahn**, who "came to Washington by default and stayed by choice." Formerly on the staff at *National Geographic* magazine and now a freelance writer and folklorist, Kahn's trained eye and expert research skills, honed at the Smithsonian, made her the perfect choice to write about Washington's museums and monuments, as well as the city's varied neighborhoods, including her own.

The short piece on the C&O Canal was written by **Elaine Koerner**, who grew up in neighboring Maryland and after several exotic sojourns, ended up in a pretty apartment in DC's Cleveland Park. Many thanks for her hospitality and late-night conferences. "How the American Government Works" in the Travel Tips section was penned by **B. Claiborne Edmunds**, whose sophisticated grasp of the political system, coupled with a knack for simple definition, made this complex subject fathomable.

Kahn

Carol Bluestone, trained as a city planner, combines her love of Washington with a rare talent for making touring fun for kids, most notably as co-author of *Washington, D.C. Guidebook for Kids*, published by Noodle Press. "The history that is studied in class really does come to life here," she says. "Plus, so much is geared to the child traveler that parents get to enjoy the trip, too."

In Insight Guides' editorial office, **Terri Paddock** brought her long-term knowledge of Washington to bear on the manuscript, **Jill Anderson** steered the copy through a variety of Macintosh computers, and **Mary Morton** proofread and indexed the book.

Bluestone

CONTENTS

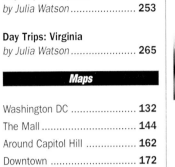

Maps

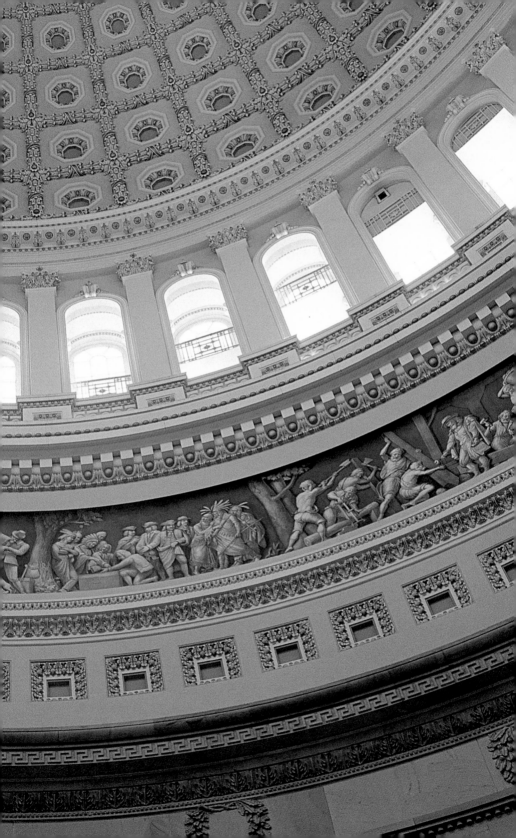

Susan Butler
Miss Nation's Capital

A CAPITAL IDEA

"Washington has only politics; after that, the second biggest thing is white marble," said an East Coast notable some years ago. It's certainly true that politics is much in evidence in Washington, and that the white marble monuments are striking signature images. But to sum up the capital of the United States by its most obvious facets is to ignore the undercurrents of an intricate city.

For instance, Washington is neither Southern nor Northern. It retains characteristics of both but remains aloof from each. The city has more black residents than white (although tourists can rarely tell), and more lawyers than it does doctors. Compared to other established East Coast cities there's little "old money" around, just new administrations every four years. It's a town of meetings and agendas, of ethnic groups and power struggles, both in the board-rooms and on the streets. Its boulevards are tree-lined and shady. In Washington, even some of the ghettos are attractive, their low-rise buildings of architectural significance. Yet, despite its beauty, Washington has one of the highest murder rates in America.

The "public face" of DC can slip in a matter of minutes. Taxis, for instance, are allowed to pick up more than one passenger at a time. On a sweltering summer's day, squashed in a cab with an Ethiopian driver, four stony-faced, perspiring strangers and a broken-down air-conditioning system, the cool corridors of Washington can feel very like a Third-World *barrio*.

The capital is not known for its restaurants, yet the variety of food is both excellent and expanding. Nor is it known for its cultural activities. A number of small museums, however, offer first-rate concerts, lectures and films, not to mention the events held in the grand museums on the Mall.

The city has a hot, sticky climate, but cool bathing beaches are only an hour's drive away. You can go hiking in the mountains, sailing in the bay, swimming in the ocean, or boating on the canal. This, in a town more noted for its indoor accomplishments than its outdoor pursuits.

Politics does propel Washington; it provides the impetus for achievement and its power residents with a job and a *raison d'être*. On moonlit nights, when strolling along the Mall with the Lincoln Memorial to the left, the Capitol to the right and the Washington Monument soaring high above, it does seem as if the city were composed of white marble.

But to dismiss the nation's capital in such a narrow way is like calling the president of the United States a public official. It's true – but it's not the whole story.

Preceding pages: painted patriots; classic statue; 4th of July frolics; DC's breathtaking "reciprocity of sight," the Jefferson Memorial; the Federal City's realized "seat of empire;" inside the Capitol dome; the Reading Room of the Library of Congress. <u>Left</u>, capital gains.

HONI · SOIT · QUI · MAL · Y · PENSE

A Scale of English Miles
10   20   30   40

VIRGI

The Falls

CAROLINA

PART OF

Henrico C.

The Falls

City C.

Randolphe R.

Charles

Pomkitchan R.

The Marrowes of York. R.

Chichahoma. R.

NewKent

Manskin Indian

Indian iand

Pumasomuck Indians

NIA

Mattopin R.

Rappahanock R.

Weft

Rappahanock

Doegs Indi

Blackwater Sweme

Marchant's hope

Elites c

Upper Chisapak

Planters

Black Waters

Nautemond

Surry C.

Crayes c

Isle of Weight C.

Onaure

Idle

Mold

Clayborn

Mantapke

Dragon Swamp

Pescataway

Middlesex Cardin.

Corotomen River

Check tanck

North

Toliksy C.

Wacomoco

Lancaster

Tindolls Point

Redman R.

Rackahiak

Maskdomak

Selmon cr

Wycomiks R.

Albemarle C

Powels pt

Whits Willowbies I

Albemarle River

Naussom cr

Lower Norfolk C.

Pigmn cr

Elizabeth R.

James R.

Lyons

Warwick c

Newports News

Eliza

Boeth

Pokoson

Green Spring

James Town

Yorke Neck C.

Loster C.

Porton bay

Great Swamp

Ferry God

Cheesake

James R.

York

Vacomeco

River

St Marys

Appomatox

Britt

Piankatanck River

Patowmeck

CHES

Carotuk C.

Willowbies pt

Lin haven

Point Comfort

Cape Henry

Masken Inlett

Carotuk Inlet

Goulden Inlet

N River

Cape Charles

Smiths I

Hungars

Goulden quarters

Northampton C.

Accomac C.

Philips

Smiths Ifle

Tredions pt

Scharburghs Gargophrst

Gughq

Swansecut c

Matshapuncke

Matsapreack

Ar Scharburghs

Tetches I

Chingotecg I.

Benito R. R.

elias Pocomoke R.

Matfhapunke

THE NORTH SEA.

Washington, DC was hacked out of the wilderness with one purpose in mind: to serve as the nation's capital. Appropriately, the whole thing started with a political deal.

The architects of this deal were Thomas Jefferson and Alexander Hamilton, the nation's first Secretary of State and Secretary of Treasury and two of the young republic's savviest political operators. The year was 1790, about one year after George Washington's presidental inauguration; the place was Philadelphia, temporary headquarters of the fledgling US government.

Despite months of bitter debate, Congress had still not agreed on a permanent location for the nation's capital. Northern delegates wanted to keep the capital in the North. Southern delegates wanted to move it to the South. And neither side seemed willing to compromise.

Northerners and Southerners were deadlocked over a second issue, too: namely, Alexander Hamilton's plan to consolidate federal finances by assuming the states' Revolutionary War debts. Again, the argument fell along regional lines: Northerners were in favor of the plan. Southerners were against it. Hamilton's plan "produced the most bitter and angry contest ever known in Congress," Jefferson wrote, noting with particular concern that some delegates were talking of "secession and dissolution." Convinced that the survival of the Union was at stake, Jefferson organized a meeting with Hamilton, Washington and several key members of Congress in the hope of striking a compromise.

The deal they came up with was simple: In exchange for the necessary Southern votes in favor of Hamilton's financial plan, the Northerners agreed to vote for a federal capital farther south than they previously wished for, ie, on the banks of the Potomac River. It was a classic case of one hand

washing the other. Within a year, President Washington was authorized by Congress to select a site, and the 10-mile-square District of Columbia was ceded to the federal government by the states of Maryland and Virginia. The president, a no-nonsense businessman, went to Suter's Tavern in Georgetown to negotiate personally with landowners to purchase the land on which the new "seat of empire" would stand.

Tidewater colony: More than 180 years ear-

lier, in 1608, the first European to chart the inland waterways of the tidewater region described the "Patawomeck" flowing "downe a low pleasant valley overshadowed in manie places with high rocky mountains; from whence distill innumerable sweet and pleasant springs." The man was Captain John Smith, a founding member of Jamestown, Virginia, the first permanent English colony in North America, located about 150 miles south of present-day Washington. Smith was hoping to find gold along the Potomac or, failing that, a shortcut to the South Seas. What he found instead were

Preceding pages: area map *circa* 1675. **Left,** the city was to embody the highest ideals. **Right,** President Washington was the site negotiator.

several Indian villages, many of them willing to trade for much-needed provisions.

As Smith already knew, most of the villages in this region were members of a loose Indian confederacy led by Chief Wahunsonacoock, known to the English as King Powhatan. Several months earlier, Smith had had the unexpected pleasure of meeting Powhatan after he and a few of his men were captured by an Indian hunting party. According to legend – and most of it is probably true – Powhatan's daughter, Pocahontas, begged the old chief to spare Smith's life. It seems Powhatan took a liking to the brash young captain and even offered to exchange

corn and meat for English trade goods.

Despite the Indians' help, life in the early years of the colony was a constant struggle for survival. During the dreadful winter of 1609–10, known to the English as the "starving time," only 60 of the 500 colonists survived. "So great was our famine," a colonist reported, "that a Salvage [Savage] we slew and buried, the poorer sort tooke him up again and eat him." The same grisly report tells of an English settler who killed his wife, "powdered [salted] her, and had eaten part of her before it was knowne." To which the writer adds this gastronomical note: "now whether shee was better roasted, boyled or carbonado'd, I know not; but of such a dish as powdered wife I never heard."

The arrival of several hundred new colonists in 1610 put the wretched little settlement back on its feet and, thanks to the tyrannical leadership of the new governor, Sir Thomas Dale, who employed whipping, burning at the stake and exile to motivate slackers, Jamestown finally sunk roots into the tidewater's marshy soil. Relations with the Indians ran hot and cold during these years. "Blessed Pocahontas" was kidnapped by the English and married to a prominent colonist named John Rolfe. Rolfe later brought Pocahontas back to England where she became an immediate sensation in London society, only to die of smallpox several months later.

Rolfe was also responsible for introducing a strain of West Indian tobacco that was particularly well-suited to the tidewater's climate and soil. The "precious herb" was much in demand in England at the time, and it rapidly became Virginia's most profitable crop. But if tobacco was a blessing to the English, it was a curse to the Indians. As the number of colonists multiplied and the demand for land increased, the tidewater tribes were forced off their traditional homeland in greater and greater numbers.

Hostilities broke out in 1675 when a group of vigilantes launched a bloody campaign against the Nanticoke and Susquehannock Indians, violating the explicit orders of colonial Governor William Berkeley who apparently was uninterested in stirring up more trouble. The leader of the vigilantes was Nathaniel Bacon, Berkeley's younger cousin, who felt that their struggle was as much against the Indians as it was against the privileged and wealthy "Parasites whose tottering Fortunes have bin repaired and supported at the Publique Chardg."

Bacon's makeshift army marched on Jamestown and set it on fire. Before the rebellion could escalate into all-out war, however, the young rebel died suddenly of the "bloody phlux," (probably tuberculosis), putting rather an anticlimatic finish on what some historians claim to be the first fitful steps toward American independence.

L'Enfant's city: The American Revolution came and went with little military impact on the Potomac, although the British blockade of Chesapeake Bay virtually shut down the tobacco trade out of Georgetown and Alexandria. After the British defeat at Yorktown, General George Washington had hoped to retire to his Mount Vernon estate near the Potomac, but destiny had different plans. In 1789, Washington accepted his election to the new office of president, and several weeks later took the oath of office.

Even before the Revolutionary War, George Washington had high expectations for the development of the Potomac River.

Fellow Virginian Thomas Jefferson shared Washington's enthusiasm for the region, and when the search began for a permanent federal capital it seemed only natural to them that the Potomac be placed at the top of the list. To design the federal city, Washington selected Major Pierre Charles L'Enfant.

Several years earlier, at the age of 22, L'Enfant had left the French court of Versailles and arrived in America to serve as a private in the Continental Army. As a member of the Corps of Engineers, he endured the brutal winter of 1777–78 with General George Washington at Valley Forge, then distinguished himself at the battles of Savannah

He saw the Potomac as a gateway to the resources and markets of the Ohio and Mississippi valleys, which he felt were in imminent danger of falling to the Spanish or British, or, almost as bad, to the merchants of New York City. Immediately after the war, he undertook a 600-mile survey trip in order to assess the Potomac's commercial potential, and then helped create the Potomac Company to make the upper river navigable.

Left, Pocahontas begs her father to spare John Smith. **Above**, a 1793 street map showing Pierre L'Enfant's city plan.

and Charleston. After the Revolutionary War, L'Enfant supervised an extensive renovation of Federal Hall in New York City, site of Washington's first inauguration and temporary seat of the infant US government.

When talk of a new capital reached L'Enfant, he wrote President Washington requesting (in rather tangled English) to be involved in the city's founding. "The late determination of Congress to lay the foundation of a Federal City which is to become the Capital of this vast Empire, offers so great an occasion for acquiring reputation... that Your Excellency will not be surprised that my ambition and the desire I have of becoming a useful citizen should lead me to wish to share in the undertaking."

L'Enfant was hired to lay plans for the capital in 1791. With memories of Versailles lingering in his mind and Thomas Jefferson (a masterful architect in his own right) inspiring him toward grandeur, L'Enfant conceived a city of broad boulevards, sweeping vistas and stately public buildings on the monumental scale of classical Greece or Rome. "No nation had ever before the opportunity offered them of deliberately deciding on the spot where their Capital City should be fixed," L'Enfant wrote to Washington.

"The plan should be drawn on such a scale as to leave room for the aggrandizement and embellishment which the increase of the wealth of the nation will permit it to pursue at any period, however remote."

On Jenkin's Hill, the city's highest prominence, L'Enfant placed the Capitol, seat of the Congress, the very embodiment of the young nation's democratic principles. On the banks of the Potomac, commanding a view of Alexandria, L'Enfant placed the Executive Mansion, known later as the White House. Between these two hubs stretched Pennsylvania Avenue, one of several broad thoroughfares that sliced diagonally through the street grid, connecting the various departments of government and affording a breathtaking "reciprocity of sight."

Unfortunately, what L'Enfant possessed in architectural skill he lacked in social grace. Arrogant, impetuous, and utterly incapable of subordinating himself to authority, the Frenchman immediately ran afoul of his superiors, a commission of prominent landowners who were authorized to oversee the project. In one particularly damning incident, L'Enfant demolished a house owned by a commissioner's uncle because it stood in the path of one of his streets.

Hearing of L'Enfant's behavior, Thomas Jefferson advised Washington that the architect "must know there is a line beyond which he will not be suffered to go." The president, perhaps feeling a bit paternal, first tried to appease the commissioners. But when L'Enfant demanded that the landowners be dismissed, Washington put his foot down. Less than 12 months after he started, L'Enfant was discharged.

Congress offered the architect $2,625 and a plot of land in "a good part of the City," but the Frenchman, apparently insulted, refused. L'Enfant accepted a number of commissions after designing Washington, but never enough to keep him from poverty in his latter years. "Daily through the city stalks the picture of famine, L'Enfant and his dog," wrote fellow architect Benjamin Henry Latrobe. The ill-fated Frenchman became a common sight in the capital, his shabbily dressed figure pacing the avenues of a city that, only years before, existed solely in his imagination. He died in 1825 and was buried in a modest Maryland cemetery. It wasn't until the early 1900s, when the city's original plan was revived and expanded, that L'Enfant's talent was properly acknowledged. In 1909, the architect's remains were re-interred in Arlington National Cemetery at a site overlooking the capital, his greatest and most embittering achievement.

Fourteen years after the signing of the Declaration of Independence (right), a compromise plan for the siting of the nation's capital was organized by Thomas Jefferson (left).

BUILDING A NATION

In the summer of 1800 John Adams, second president of the United States, traveled by coach from Philadelphia to the nation's new seat of government, Washington City. Surveying the unfinished capital from a crest above the Potomac, the urbane Bostonian might well have felt a mixture of wonder and disappointment.

Not that the setting was unpleasant. The Potomac flowed gently below; dense woods and tobacco fields spread from the riverbanks; farmhouses were tucked into the valley, and tobacco boats sailed across the water. But in its incomplete state, the nation's capital must have seemed a remote and primitive place. The major government buildings, the great structures that were to embody the highest ideals of the young republic, were little more than rough skeletons surrounded by workmen's shacks and scattered debris.

Swamp city: Pennsylvania Avenue, the grand boulevard that was to connect the Capitol Building and the White House, was a tangle of elder bushes and tree stumps. A few rows of boarding houses were complete, but the streets, the few that existed, were little more than muddy lanes. Compared to the great European capitals Adams had visited in the past, Washington was little more than an unkempt backwoods town.

Several months later Adams's wife, Abigail, put into words what her husband was perhaps too politic to express: "Washington City was not a city at all." Although she was pleased with the White House's riverfront location, Abigail complained that "not one room or chamber is finished of the whole." Moreover, the nearby port of Georgetown was "the very dirtyest hole I ever saw." Ever the pragmatic New Englander, she used the White House's "great unfinished audience room" in which to hang the President's laun-

dry. Other new arrivals concurred with the First Lady. Sir Augustus John Foster, a British diplomat, found the new capital "scarce any better than a swamp." Congressman Gouverneur Morris quipped: "We want nothing here but houses, cellars, kitchens, well-informed men, amiable women, and other little trifles of this kind, to make our city perfect."

By 1809, Thomas Jefferson's last year as president, Washington was still a frontier town, criss-crossed with rutted trails, littered with debris and surrounded by wilderness. Work had proceeded at a snail's pace over the intervening years and neither the White House nor the Capitol building were complete. The nation's 106 delegates huddled in the House of Representatives – known derisively as "the oven" because of its poor design – while construction continued on the remainder of the building.

When President James Madison led the country into a second war against the British, in 1812, Washington was still so undeveloped that many people were unconcerned, even though enemy warships were cruising Chesapeake Bay. Washingtonians had great confidence in Secretary of War John Armstrong, who assured the president that the British would not waste their time attacking the "sheep walk on the Potomac" when Baltimore, a far richer target, was also within easy reach.

When 4,500 British soldiers landed on the Patuxent River about 35 miles south of the capital, however, it became tragically clear that Armstrong had misjudged the British Navy. As residents and government workers fled into the countryside, American militiamen rushed to the capital's defense at Bladensburg on the District's border. But when the Redcoats attacked on August 24, 1814, the Americans beat a hurried retreat back to the city – one of the less glorious episodes in American history and known derisively as the "Bladensburg races."

By evening, the British were torching public buildings throughout the city, including

Preceding pages: Lincoln's second inauguration, 1865; John Wilkes Booth and two co-conspirators are allegedly in the photo. **Left,** constructing the Washington Monument, 1860.

the Capitol and the White House. Only hours before, Dolley Madison had managed to save a few prized possessions from the White House, including Gilbert Stuart's famous portrait of George Washington.

When the British pulled out two days later, the capital was in ruins. "I do not suppose the Government will ever return to Washington," wrote Margaret Bayard Smith. "All those whose property was invested in that place will be reduced to poverty... The consternation about us is general. The despondency still greater." With the city in shambles and the government in disarray, a visiting Virginian feared that the republic might also

crumble: "The appearance of our public buildings is enough to make one cut his throat," he wrote. "The dissolution of the Union is the theme of almost every private conversation."

But with American forces rallying against the British outside Baltimore and later at New Orleans, anxiety over the capital's and the country's future began to fade. With news of Yankee victories arriving daily in Washington, Congress reconvened in the cramped quarters of the Post Office, the only public building left undamaged, and voted to stay in Washington.

"A great[er] benefit could not have accrued to this city than the destruction of its principal buildings by the British," wrote Benjamin Henry Latrobe, one of Washington's leading architects after the War of 1812. From the city's blackened ruins came a renewed determination to make Washington the national showcase envisioned by Jefferson, Washington and L'Enfant. While President Monroe took temporary quarters at the Octagon House, Latrobe and his successor, renowned Boston architect Charles Bulfinch, supervised the reconstruction of the White House and the Capitol. Construction began on several new federal buildings as well, including the magnificent neo-classical Treasury Building, Patent Office and Post Office, all designed by a newcomer, Robert Mills.

Up from the ashes: Washington was expanding in other areas, too. The short-lived Chesapeake & Ohio Canal, thought to be the key to Washington's commercial success, opened for business in 1830, but was quickly superseded by the Baltimore & Ohio Railroad. Georgetown University, founded in 1789, was joined by Columbian College (later George Washington University) in 1822. A grant bequeathed by eccentric British scientist James Smithson in 1829 was finally discharged for the use of the Smithsonian Institution, housed in a medieval-style "castle" on the Mall. And in 1859, C.C. Corcoran began construction of the handsome Corcoran Gallery to house his much-coveted art collection.

Unfortunately, the city's problems were growing as fast as its buildings. Washington's notorious alleys were already filled with shacks and shanties and crowded with an ever increasing population of poor people. Vacant lots – many of them squeezed between the city's finest buildings – were heaped with trash and overgrown with weeds. Sanitation, never very sophisticated, was woefully inadequate.

Even the Washington Canal, the "miasmatic swamp near the Presidential Mansion," was choked with sewerage, silt and garbage, as were other marshy areas around the White House. An active slaughterhouse near the Mall added to the stench. As one army wife put it, "I was never in such a place for smells."

Crime was also becoming a major concern. "Riot and bloodshed are a daily occurrence," a Senate Committee reported in 1858. "Innocent and unoffending persons are shot, stabbed, and otherwise shamefully maltreated, and not unfrequently the offendor is not even arrested." And violence was hardly limited to the streets. More than once, congressional debates degenerated into bare-knuckle brawls.

Dueling pistols: Abolitionist Charles Sumner was nearly caned to death by a South Carolinian delegate in 1856. Congressman

a "sleepy country town," still tentative and only partially realized. During his visit in 1842, Charles Dickens expressed his delight at the casual grace of the nation's political elite, but couldn't help detecting a certain civic immaturity.

Washington "is sometimes called the City of Magnificent Distances," Dickens wrote, "but it might with greater propriety be termed the City of Magnificent Intentions." Its leading features were "Spacious avenues, that begin in nothing, and lead nowhere; streets, milelong, that only want houses, roads and inhabitants; public buildings that need but a public to be complete; and orna-

Daniel Sickles was acquitted for the admitted murder of his wife's lover in 1859. And political squabbles were regularly settled with dueling pistols. Add to this the usual round of gambling, drinking and whoring in which members of Congress routinely engaged, and it's not difficult to see why one righteous soul denounced the "unparalleled depravity of Washington society."

But for all of Washington's urban problems, the nation's capital still had not come of age as a major American city. It was still

Left, Capitol capers. Above, Georgetown in 1864.

ments of great thoroughfares, which only lack great thoroughfares to ornament."

Like other visitors, Dickens was especially disturbed by the presence of slavery, which he found all the more loathsome in the capital of a nation supposedly built on and dedicated to life, liberty and the pursuit of happiness. "Their are many kinds of hunters engaged in the Pursuit of Happiness," he wrote. Some "take the field after their Happiness equipped with cat and cartwhip, stocks, and iron collar, and to shout their view halloa!... to the music of clanking chains and bloody stripes."

Although some Washingtonians tried to shut their eyes to it, slavery was impossible to ignore. At the time of Dickens' visit, there were approximately 3,000 slaves in the District of Columbia. Prominent slave traders advertised in local newspapers; public slave auctions were held on a regular basis; and slaves could be seen on the streets marching in chains or being held for sale in slave pens across from the Smithsonian Institution.

In 1849 a little-known Illinois representative named Abraham Lincoln introduced legislation outlawing slavery in the District of Columbia, but the bill was quickly defeated. Instead, Congress adopted Henry Congress battled furiously over the Fugitive Slave Law and the extension of slavery into Nebraska and "bleeding Kansas." Northerners were inflamed by the Supreme Court's pro-slavery Dredd Scott decision. And Southerners were thrown into a panic by John Brown's unsuccessful attempt to incite a slave insurrection at Harper's Ferry, Virginia. The conflict reached the boiling point during the fractious presidential campaign of 1860.

On November 8, 1860, Abraham Lincoln was elected president without a single Southern electoral vote and on a minority of the popular vote. South Carolina immedi-

Clay's Compromise of 1850, which, among other measures, abolished the slave trade in the District of Columbia but did not outlaw slave ownership.

At best, Clay's compromise was a stopgap measure, slowing but not stopping the movement toward a major confrontation. Abolitionists were becoming more influential in the North and secessionists more militant in the South. The nation was headed for war with itself and the battle lines were being drawn in Washington.

"A house divided": Sectional tensions escalated in Washington throughout the 1850s. ately seceded, and six other states followed.

On March 4, 1861, Lincoln was inaugurated under the watchful eyes of sharpshooters patroling nearby rooftops. In his inaugural address he spoke directly to the newly formed Confederacy: "In your hands, my dissatisfied fellow-countrymen, and not in mine is the momentous issue of civil war. We are not enemies, but friends... Though passion may have strained, it must not break our bonds of affection!"

But Lincoln's appeal fell on deaf ears. About a month later, on April 12, Confederate canons fired at Fort Sumter. Virginia seceded two weeks later, following Arkansas, North Carolina and Tennessee. Robert E. Lee, formerly superintendent at West Point and never a supporter of slavery or secession, nevertheless declared allegiance to his home state, Virginia, and assumed the command of the Army of Northern Virginia. After agonizing debate, Maryland, Washington's other slave-owning neighbor, agreed to remain neutral.

Washington was in a perilous situation. It was a Northern capital in a Southern city, nearly half of its population hailing from, or sympathetic to, the Confederate states. As Southern soldiers resigned their posts and

other livestock were corralled in the Mall.

When a showdown between Union and Confederate troops developed at Bull Run, Virginia, Washington's society people turned out in their finest carriages, fully expecting a glorious Union victory. The horror and humiliation of the Union defeat, and the panicked retreat of soldiers and civilians back into the capital, convinced even the most cocksure that this was to be a long and bloody fight. With Confederate troops looming just beyond the district's borders, a massive effort was made to ring the city with fortifications and secure the surrounding countryside. Soldiers continued to flood the

joined the Confederate Army, Lincoln called for 75,000 volunteers to come to the Union's defense. Thousands of troops poured into a capital that was little prepared to receive them. By the end of April 1861, soldiers were being quartered in the Capitol, Treasury, Patent Office, and at Georgetown University. The unfinished Corcoran Gallery was commandeered by the Union's quartermaster; a bakery was established in the basement of the Capitol; Army horses, mules and

Left, 15th and Pennsylvania in 1865. **Above**, the same view 36 years later.

city, swelling the population from 61,000 to more than 1 million in a single year.

As the fighting raged at the Second Battle of Bull Run, Antietam, Fredericksburg and Chancellorsville, some 50,000 wounded men filled makeshift hospitals in churches and public buildings scattered throughout the capital. At night, carts loaded with dead soldiers rumbled through the streets, many of them headed across the Potomac River to the former estate of Confederate commander Robert E. Lee, which is now part of Arlington National Cemetery.

Troubled by crime before the war, the city

was now hopelessly overrun. "Every possible form of human vice and crime, dregs, offscourings and scum had flowed into the capital and made of it a national catch-basin of indescribable foulness," one newspaperman reported. Aptly named neighborhoods like Murder Bay were rife with gambling dens, whiskey joints, gangs and crooks. But with so many soldiers in town, the boom industry was prostitution. Captain Joseph Hooker tried to limit the trade to a red-light district called "Hooker's Division," inadvertently lending the women his name.

In April 1862, President Lincoln freed slaves in the District of Columbia and then, several months later, isolating the bulk of the Confederate Army in central Virginia. Surrounded by Union forces, General Robert E. Lee surrendered to General Ulysses S. Grant at Appomattox Courthouse on April 9, 1865.

Five days later, Lincoln reluctantly agreed to attend a play, *Our American Cousin*, at Ford's Theater on 10th Street. While Lincoln sat in the balcony, John Wilkes Booth, a well-known actor and Confederate conspirator, crept behind the President, shot him, and then leapt to the stage below, crying "*Sic semper tyrannis!* The South is avenged!", breaking his leg in the fall. Fatally wounded, Lincoln was rushed to a

in January of the following year, issued the Emancipation Proclamation, abolishing slavery in the Confederate states. In July 1864, Confederate general Jubal Early sent Washingtonians into a panic with a brief but terrifying assault on the District of Columbia. It was the Confederates' last stab at the capital. After Union victories at Gettysburg and Vicksburg and the loss of Confederate power in the West, the tide of war turned decisively in the Union's favor.

In September 1864, Union general William Tecumseh Sherman delivered the *coup de grâce* at Atlanta. Richmond fell

nearby boarding house and died the following morning. A frenzied manhunt was organized, which turned up Booth two weeks later in a Virginia barn. The barn was set on fire and Booth was killed.

As Washington mourned, the assassination seemed to take on a sense of inevitability, as if Lincoln sacrificed his own life for the life of the Union. The country was at last one entity, but deeply scarred. Washington, and the nation, lay in ruins.

Since Washington's streets were "a sea of mud," washday (underline: above) was important.

TRACING YOUR ROOTS

The National Archives are best known for their original copies of the Declaration of Independence and the Constitution, kept in special bronze and glass cases filled with helium that can be lowered instantly into a fireproof and shock-proof safe. But Americans can also trace their family history here, sifting through over 3 billion documents of the nation's history for priceless ancestral footprints.

Passenger lists for immigrant ships, the national census back to 1790 (which includes the names of heads of households), military and naturalization records, passport applications, pensions and land grants – the Archives contain the country's principal data base for family histories and other uses. There is a free booklet available which is basically a guide to the collection; the pamphlet does, however, contain the warning phrase "the staff is unable to make extensive searches but, given enough identifying information, will try to find a record about a specific person."

What this means in practice is that family research has to start at home, so you should arrive at the Archives with a list of ancestral names, approximate dates of birth and places of residence and military details, as far back as you can go. Look in the attic, interview older relatives and check out the boxes which have been in storage for years. The more information the better. Armed with these clues, the Archives staff can be extraordinarily helpful – given that many of the records have no index organized by name.

A serious search really requires an investment in the National Archives' paperback book *Guide to Genealogical Research*, which offers a step-by-step procedure on how to go about research on the flimsiest of details, like "great-great grandfather Abner Smith who moved to Indiana sometime after the Civil War." The point is that even in pre-computer days, it was not easy to inhabit the US without leaving a paper trace in the Archives. Military records (including the Confederate forces), seamen's certificates and pension files and land grants are useful, but the heart of the collection is the census data.

For ancestors born before 1861, it is much easier to start with the (free) males of the household. The 1790–1840 census lists give the head of household only; other family members are listed

without age or sex. For the 1850 and 1860 censuses, separate schedules list slave owners and the age, sex and color (but not the name) of each slave. These same lists do, however, give details of each free person in a household.

The 1880 census is even more useful, since there is a microfilm version of a card index which gives entries to each household that included a child aged 10 or less, including details of every household member. The card indexes are organized by state, and then alphabetically by the first letter of each last name, and then by the first letter of the Christian name of each head of household. Most of the 1890 census was lost in a fire in 1921; only 6,160 names remain.

If your 18th-century ancestor came from the

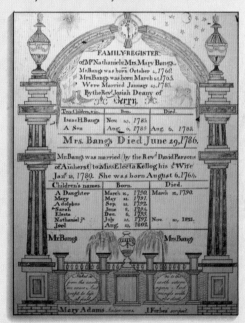

states of Delaware, Georgia, Kentucky, New Jersey, Tennessee or Virginia, you may be unlucky. The census data for these states was burned by the British in the War of 1812. The Virginia government has since painfully rebuilt the census for about half the state's population in 1790, using mainly tax and property lists.

Ironically, since they lost their land as the white immigrants poured through the country, some of the best data concerns Native Americans. The school class lists from 1910 to 1939 are one place to start, but there is a near-census quality data bank for those Indians, mainly from the Cherokee, Chickasaw, Choctaw and Creek tribes, who moved west between 1830 and 1846. ∎

<u>Right</u>, tree of life.

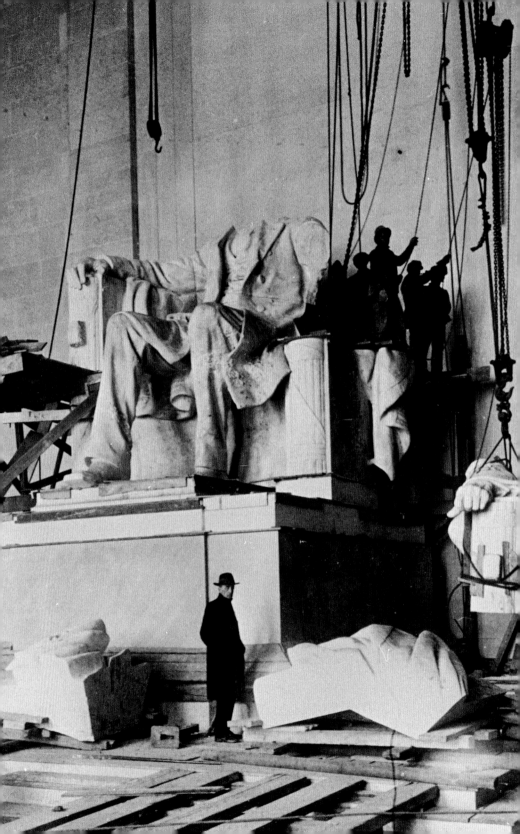

The Civil War left Washington a less provincial, less Southern and, all things considered, a less agreeable place to live. The Army of the Potomac had turned public buildings into a shambles and the streets into a "sea of mud." The city's slums were swollen with former slaves and discharged soldiers. Disease and squalor were evident in every neighborhood. "Crime, filth and poverty seem to vie with each other in a career of degradation and death," the Police Chief reported. A relief worker described "a cloud of darkness, poverty, rags, hunger, cold and suffering" in Washington's alleyways.

As before, there were those who wanted to relocate the capital to a more suitable place, a western city perhaps, where the country was still young and growing. But Congress was not yet ready to give up on Washington and, more importantly, Washingtonians were not ready to give up on themselves.

Big spender: The first effort to rebuild Washington started in the early 1870s with the appointment of Alexander "Boss" Shepherd to the newly constituted Board of Public Works. A single-minded, energetic bull of a man, Shepherd ran herd over the local blue bloods and the District government in his efforts to make the "Federal City worthy of being in fact, as well as in name, the Capital of the nation." Shepherd's swaggering, big-spending style made him as many enemies as friends in Washington, but despite his heavy-handedness, he got things done.

Shepherd also managed to drive the city directly into bankruptcy, tallying up a $20 million deficit, more than three times the city's debt in its entire 70-year history. Although exonerated of any criminal wrongdoing by two Congressional probes, Shepherd's "negligent, careless, improvident [and] unjust" management of public funds hounded him all the way to Mexico.

Shepherd's civic facelift ushered in a period of good feelings. Despite the national

depression of 1893–94 and the unexpected arrival of the "Army of the Unemployed" – some 3,000 jobless men seeking government relief – Washington society managed to recapture the "extraordinarily easy and pleasant life" of the antebellum years. Tired of war, weary of politics, Washington became, in Henry James's words, "a city of conversation," blithely attending the business of society balls and teas and letting the government take care of itself. "The social side of Wash-

ington was to be taken for granted as three-fourths of existence," Henry Adams wrote. "Politics and reform became the detail, and waltzing the profession."

A second wave of civic improvements was launched at the turn of the century by Michigan Senator James McMillan, who commissioned some of the leading lights in architecture, including Daniel Burnham, Charles McKim and Frederick Law Olmsted, Jr, to create "a well-considered general plan covering the entire District of Columbia." At the heart of the McMillan Commission's proposal was a plan to sweep away the run-

<u>Left</u>, Lincoln's memorial nears completion. <u>Right</u>, Ulysses S. Grant, president from 1869 to 1877.

down buildings, roads and railways that had cluttered the Mall for years, to build a bridge connecting the Mall to Arlington National Cemetery, and to erect two new monuments, one to Abraham Lincoln, the other to Thomas Jefferson.

It was an expansive time for Washington as well as for the nation. The Spanish-American War came to a swift end, catapulting Teddy Roosevelt and his Rough Riders into the national spotlight and giving the US its first colonial possessions abroad. Roosevelt joined President William McKinley's re-election bid as the vice-presidential candidate, and found himself in the Oval Office

Patent Office and technology-minded legislators. Electric lights made an illuminating debut in the 1880s, and by the late 1910s motor cars were chugging through the streets and terrorizing unsuspecting pedestrians.

America's entry into world politics brought new responsibilities to Washington. When war broke out in Europe in 1914, the Allies looked to the United States to exercise its newfound military muscle. Although President Woodrow Wilson was an early advocate of "peace without victory" in Europe, Germany's persistent attacks on American ships forced his hand toward war. In a special address to Congress on April 2,

after McKinley's assassination only four months later.

With the industrial revolution in full bloom, a new breed of "social Darwinists" gravitated toward the capital, housing their families in extravagant Victorian mansions in the West End, particularly on Massachusetts Avenue (now "Embassy Row"). Inventors such as Alexander Graham Bell, the Wright Brothers and Herman Hollerith (founder of the Tabulating Machine Company, forerunner of IBM) came too, drawn by the intellectual and commercial opportunities offered by the Smithsonian Institution,

1917, Wilson dubbed Germany's U-boat campaign "warfare against mankind." Congress took its cue and declared war against Germany four days later.

Almost overnight, the "city of conversation" was transformed into the hub of an international war machine. "Life seemed suddenly to acquire a vivid scarlet lining," Helen Nicolay remembered. "Old prejudices gave way to passionate new beliefs. Old precedents were wrecked in an endeavor to live up to the duty of the hour." As thousands of Americans passed through the capital en route to the trenches of the Argonne, the city was swept into the war effort. Military advisers, scientists, intellectuals, industrialists and clerks poured into the city; the federal government expanded dramatically; government housing was hastily erected; and boxy "tempos" were thrown up along the Mall to use as office space. Once a "sleepy country town," Washington suddenly became a major player in global politics.

The US military tipped the balance of power in Europe and within two years peace negotiations were underway at Versailles. In 1919, Washingtonians cheered as President Wilson and General John "Black Jack" Pershing led triumphant American soldiers

whiskey, suffragettes, shiny new Fords or extravagant parties. The nation's outlook seemed so rosy, in fact, that President Herbert Hoover could confidently announce at his 1929 inauguration: "The poorhouse is vanishing among us. We in America today are nearer to the final triumph of poverty than ever before in the history of the land."

It was a particularly unfortunate prediction. On Black Thursday, October 24, 1929, only seven months after Hoover uttered those words, the stock market crashed, the economy took a nose-dive, and the Great Depression was on. The hardships of the Depression were slow to reach Washington,

down Pennsylvania Avenue. The "war to end all wars" was over, a new decade was on the horizon and Americans were ready to enjoy the fruits of victory.

Good times, bad times: Prohibition kicked off the Roaring Twenties on a rather dreary note, but somehow the taboo on liquor made the good times seem even better. And although Washington couldn't boasts the likes of F. Scott Fitzgerald, Eugene O'Neill or Al Capone, there was no shortage of bootleg

Left, the Roaring Twenties reaches Glen Echo.
Above, ice skating on the Reflecting Pool.

but when they hit, they hit hard. City-wide income was slashed by nearly half; unemployment soared to 25 percent, 50 percent among blacks. People lost their jobs, their homes, their dignity. Ramshackle "Hoovervilles" sprang up in vacant lots, and breadlines stretched along sidewalks. Hundreds of "hunger marchers" trickled into the city seeking relief from the federal government, and protests erupted daily in front of the White House and the Capitol.

In the spring of 1932, some 20,000 World War I veterans marched into Washington from all parts of the US demanding early payment of a cash bonus due in 1945. The self-proclaimed Bonus Expeditionary Force, or Bonus Army, was allowed to occupy several condemned buildings on Pennsylvania Avenue and to set up a large shantytown – known as Camp Marks – on the Anacostia Flats. "The arrival of the bonus army seems to be the first event to give the inhabitants of Washington any inkling that something is happening in the world outside of their drowsy sun parlor," author John Dos Passos noted wryly. As far as President Herbert Hoover was concerned, however, the Bonus Army was strictly a "local problem." He promised to veto any

Eisenhower and an infantry unit under General George Patton. Leading the column was General Douglas MacArthur, decked out in full military regalia.

After the soldiers cleared out the condemned buildings on Pennsylvania Avenue, they marched on Camp Marks and burned it down. The bonuseers suffered seven casualties; the movement was thoroughly crushed. "Every drop of blood shed today or that may be shed in days to come as the result of today's events can be laid directly on the threshold of the White House," declared Sergeant Waters, the Bonus Army spokesman, and the American public seemed to

bonus legislation and refused to meet with Bonus Army spokesmen.

As spring turned into summer, the situation escalated. The veterans' protests became more urgent; clashes with police became more frequent, and rumors circulated that the Bonus Army was infiltrated by subversives. When two protestors were shot during a confrontation with local police, Hoover seized the opportunity to call out federal troops and drive the Bonus Army from the capital. The column of troops that bore down Constitution Avenue included a tank unit commanded by Major Dwight D.

agree. Hoover was trounced by Franklin D. Roosevelt in the 1932 presidential election.

New Deal: Roosevelt's New Deal brought some relief to Washington by creating hundreds of federal jobs. Workmen were hired to scrub the Washington Monument and to manicure parks; artists were commissioned to decorate public buildings; librarians and archivists were given work tending government documents.

But the Depression's grip on Washington didn't truly ease until the US entry into World War II. On December 7, 1941, Japan attacked the US Navy at Pearl Harbor, and

Washington was once again swept into war. Anti-aircraft guns were mounted on rooftops; guards were posted at reservoirs, bridges and railways to protect against saboteurs. A secret bunker was constructed for the president beneath the White House. Bullet-proof glass and black-out curtains were installed in the Oval Office. The city's great monuments were left unlit. There was even a plan to paint the Capitol dome black in order to protect it from air attack.

Faced with the enormous task of building and coordinating a 7-million-man military, the federal government grew faster and larger than ever before. Hundreds of "gov-

Roosevelt authorized the top-secret Manhattan Project for the rapid development of the atomic bomb.

Tragically, Roosevelt never saw the outcome of the war. After leading the country out of the Depression and into the greatest war of the century – and transforming Washington into an international center of power – Roosevelt died of a stroke. Less than a month later, Roosevelt's former vice-president, Harry S. Truman, declared victory in Europe. Truman also authorized the deployment of the world's first nuclear weapons – the first on Hiroshima on August 6, followed by another on Nagasaki three days later.

ernment girls" arrived in the capital to take up posts as secretaries and clerks. The newly built Pentagon (completed in 1943), the largest office building in the world, quickly filled with military personnel. The Office of Strategic Service, forerunner of the CIA, was formed in order to handle espionage and other covert affairs. In 1942, President Roosevelt received a letter from Albert Einstein advising him of groundbreaking experiments in atomic fission. Some time later,

Japan capitulated. World War II was over. Washington and the world had been transformed. And a far more complex and insidious conflict was already under way.

Despite peacetime demobilization, the federal government continued to grow in its new role as a world power. With fascism dismantled in Europe, the Truman administration turned its attention to the "containment" of Communism, indirectly spawning a new generation of think tanks, consulting firms, political-interest groups and bureaucrats dedicated to the pursuit (and some would say the perpetuation) of the Cold War.

Left, Extra! Extra! **Above**, these Senators got everyone's vote.

While American troops fought a bloody "police action" against Chinese-backed troops in North Korea, Senator Joseph McCarthy manipulated Communist paranoia at home in order to advance his political career. "I have here in my hand a list of 205 [people] known to the Secretary of State as being members of the Communist Party and who nevertheless are still working and shaping the policy of the State Department," McCarthy announced during one of his inflammatory speeches. Although his accusations were groundless, the mere insinuation was enough to sully reputations and ruin careers. Blacklists, red-baiting and loyalty

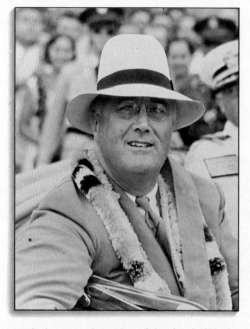

oaths became the order of the day in Washington as McCarthy targeted first the State Department and then other branches of the government and military in his hunt for "Communist sympathizers."

The election of John F. Kennedy in 1960 brought a welcome change of atmosphere to Washington. Although an ardent supporter of the Cold War, the young charismatic president forged an idealistic national agenda stressing individual activism ("ask not what your country can do for you, but what you can do for your country") and promising a "new frontier" of social re-

forms. Abroad, Kennedy escalated the American military presence in South Vietnam and played a white-knuckle game of nuclear brinkmanship with Soviet Premier Nikita Khrushchev over the placement of Soviet missile bases in Cuba. At home, Kennedy was increasingly preoccupied with the explosive issue of desegregation, and with the growing urgency of the civil rights movement and its most prominent leader, Dr Martin Luther King, Jr.

In the early 1960s, Washington itself was still very much a segregated city. District schools had been openly segregated until the Supreme Court's 1954 Brown vs Board of Education of Topeka decision. Not long before, black congressmen were barred from whites-only bathrooms on Capitol Hill. In a televised address, Kennedy informed the nation that blacks had "twice as much chance of becoming unemployed... one-third as much chance of becoming professionals... (and) about one-seventh as much chance of earning $10,000 a year" as whites. He had only to look outside the White House to see the grim reality these statistics represented.

While Kennedy was trying to push his civil rights bill through Congress in early 1963, plans were already being drawn up by Martin Luther King and other civil rights leaders for a massive March on Washington. On August 28, some 250,000 people converged on the capital to voice their support for civil rights legislation. As the nation watched, whites and blacks locked arms and marched to the Lincoln Memorial, chanting slogans, carrying placards and singing "We Shall Overcome," the unofficial theme of the civil rights movement.

Dream on: With an enormous crowd gathered around the Reflecting Pool, King delivered what is perhaps the most famous speech by a black American. "I have a dream," King sang out. "It is a dream deeply rooted in the American dream. I have a dream that one day this nation will rise up and live out the true meaning of its creed: 'We hold these truths to be self-evident, that all men are created equal.'" For many, it was the high point of the civil rights movement, an enormous upwelling of support, a symbol of interracial harmony and a confirmation of King's philosophy of nonviolent social change.

And yet, the March on Washington seemed to do little to speed Kennedy's civil rights legislation through Congress. The bill was still stalled in the House of Representatives three months later when, on November 22, 1963, the news reached Capitol Hill of President Kennedy's assassination.

Crisis of confidence: If anything, Kennedy's successor, Lyndon Baines Johnson, deepened the federal government's commitment to civil rights. He dispatched national guardsmen to Selma and Montgomery, Alabama, to protect "freedom riders" from local police. He pressured Congress to pass the

mid-1960s racial conflict was approaching the flashpoint in cities throughout the country. Riots broke out in Los Angeles, New York, Detroit, Philadelphia and elsewhere, underscoring black frustration at the slow pace of change. In the spring of 1968, Martin Luther King organized a second March on Washington to drive home the need for economic equality as well as equal rights. But King never made it to Washington. On April 4, 1968, while members of King's Poor People's Campaign awaited his arrival at Resurrection City – a small shantytown located on the Mall – Martin Luther King, Jr was assassinated in Memphis, Tennessee.

civil rights bill in 1964, and developed comprehensive social programs, including a massive "war on poverty." He also strengthened the US's involvement in the Vietnam War, increasing the number of American soldiers from 20,000 to more than 500,000 and stimulating a backlash among the already active antiwar movement.

It was a long way from Capitol Hill to the poorest neighborhoods, however, and by the

Left, Roosevelt made Washington an international power center. **Above**, King's "I have a dream" speech, 1963.

The reaction in Washington's poor black neighborhoods was immediate. As the news of King's death spread, an angry crowd began gathering at the corner of 14th and U streets, while groups of youths went to neighborhood shops demanding they close in deference to King's passing. By the following day, the crowds had turned into unruly mobs, and the scattered outbreaks of arson and looting had blossomed into a full-scale riot. Hoping to defuse unrest throughout the nation's cities, President Johnson asked Americans of all races to "reject the blind violence that has struck Dr King who lived by nonviolence." Johnson released federal workers in Washington early that afternoon, creating a massive traffic jam that served only to hamper police, firefighters and emergency medical teams.

The situation continued to spin out of control, and police were unable to slow it down, much less stop it. Entire city blocks were engulfed in flame, belching thick black smoke over Capitol Hill and the White House; shops and supermarkets were gutted by looters and set on fire; clashes between the police and rioters grew increasingly brutal. After consulting with city officials and civil rights leaders, Johnson called out the national guard and regular army – dispatching over 5,000 soldiers into the most troubled neighborhoods. Gradually, as soldiers secured the streets, the violence wound down. In 36 hours of rioting, the city had sustained 12 deaths, 1,000 injuries and some $27 million in property damage.

Political disaffection: But the Washington riots were only a symptom of a more pervasive and deep-seated political disaffection. Protestors had always come to Washington to air their grievances, but starting in the mid-1960s they seemed to come in ever-increasing numbers and with a burning sense of urgency. They staged sit-ins, tent-ins, think-ins and peace-ins. They blocked traffic, occupied federal buildings, petitioned legislators and practiced passive resistance. The more radical among them threw rocks, bottles and firebombs and purposely engaged police in combat.

Although the protestors represented all sorts of special interests – the Black Third World Task Force, the Student Mobilization Committee, gay liberation, women's liberation, Vietnam Veterans Against the War, flower children, labor unions, the American Indian Movement, and many others – the overwhelming focus of their demonstrations was the Vietnam War. The protest movement culminated during another March on Washington in which an estimated 750,000 antiwar demonstrators descended on the capital, making it one of the largest protests (if not *the* largest) in Washington's history.

Disenchantment with the "establishment" seemed to crystallize in 1972 when Vice President Spiro Agnew came under investigation for a variety of charges including tax evasion and accepting bribes. Agnew resigned in October 1973 and was later convicted of tax evasion. By that time President Richard Nixon and several key members of his staff were also being investigated for their part in the cover-up of the Watergate break-in. Nixon vehemently denied any knowledge of the attempted burglary and wiretapping of Democratic Party headquarters at the Watergate building, promising Americans that he was "not a crook."

A special prosecutor was appointed to look into Nixon's involvement in the scandal, starting a highly publicized tug-of-war over Nixon's secret Oval Office tape recordings. The president eventually surrendered the tapes, although an incriminating eight-minute silence remains a mystery. With his credibility fatally undercut, and impeachment proceedings already underway, Nixon finally admitted what the press and public already suspected: that he had stopped an FBI investigation of the Watergate break-in that would have implicated members of the White House staff. Nixon announced his resignation on August 8, 1974. He was the first president to give up his office.

Nixon's resignation set off a crisis of confidence that would take the better part of a decade to mend. The remainder of Nixon's term was assumed by President Gerald Ford, who stirred up yet another controversy by pardoning Nixon of any crimes he might have committed. Democratic president Jimmy Carter took office in 1976 promising to move beyond the malaise and disaffection of the Vietnam and Watergate years, only to be politically paralyzed by a major recession, the Mideast oil crisis, the Iranian revolution, the taking of Western hostages and a botched rescue attempt.

When Ronald Reagan took office in 1980 after a landslide victory, Washington's conservative political establishment was on the eve of a major resurgence, but Washington itself – the city beyond the marble monuments – was heading for troubled times.

Right, demonstrators from all over the US came to protest against the Vietnam War.

It's often said that Washington is really two cities. The Washington most people know is a city of diplomats and public servants, press conferences and cocktail parties. The other Washington is a city of run-down neighborhoods, intractable poverty, street crime and crack houses.

But there's a third Washington, too, less concrete than the others. As the nation's capital – the stage on which national and international politics are played – Washington occupies a certain symbolic space. What happens in Washington is emblematic of what happens in cities throughout the country. And what's happening in Washington is enough to make anybody frightened about the future of America's inner cities.

The story of violent crime is all too familiar. Drug gangs move into a neighborhood and innocent people suffer. This is a poor state of affairs to happen in any city. But to occur at such an alarming rate in Washington, DC – a monument to the nation's highest ideals of democracy, freedom and equality – is particularly chilling.

Millions of tourists visit Washington each year, but few see this side of the city – the poor, predominantly black areas "behind the marble mask" of statues, museums and government buildings.

Murder capital: The 1980s brought mixed fortune to Washington. A real-estate investor with money in a plush downtown property, or a young professional riding the crest of the Reagan revolution, probably did very well indeed. The catch-phrase of the 1980s – "greed is good!" – was as valid in the capital as it was on Wall Street. And although a few wheeler-dealers ended up on the business end of a subpoena, there were always more winners than losers, especially among the big-time players.

For Washington's lower classes, however, things didn't go well. Ronald Reagan's much-touted trickle-down theory – which stated that wealth at the top of the economic scale flows naturally to the bottom – apparently did not take into account the many ways cash is diverted on its downward journey. People on the lower rungs of the economic ladder were slipping through the cracks and the fallout was painfully obvious. Between 1980 and 1989, homelessness shot up perceptibly. In 1990, there were an estimated 6,000 to

10,000 homeless people in Washington, many camped out on ventilator grates, in doorways, overcrowded shelters and welfare hotels. Despite the metropolitan area's considerable wealth (an average per capita income of $23,491 in 1989, well over other cities), a full 17 percent of Washington residents lived below the US poverty line, and most of them were black. The average income of black households was 54 percent of white households. Infant mortality was nearly double the national average and continues to be at or near the highest in the country. In schools, drop-out rates were among the worst in the

Preceding pages: poverty and picture-taking. Left, Congressmen on Capitol Hill. Right, by 1988 DC had the highest per capita murder rate in the United States.

country. And so far improvement has been pretty minimal.

By the late 1980s, Washington was also suffering from a drug problem of epidemic proportions. And with drugs came violence. Between 1985 – the year crack cocaine was introduced – and 1988, the number of yearly homicides in Washington jumped from 148 to 372, giving Washington the highest per capita murder rate in the country (60 per 100,000) and an undisputed claim to being the murder capital of the nation. In 1990, the number leapt again, to far more than one murder every day.

As one journalist remarked around that

federal officials and city police, education programs, additional prisons and rehabilitation facilities. Bennett resigned his post several months later, claiming that "What we promised to deliver, we delivered." But the evidence seemed to indicate otherwise. The murder rate had increased yet again; prisons were still dangerously overcrowded; waiting lists for drug programs were longer than ever; and there was no discernible decrease in the availability of drugs.

Throughout the crisis, municipal and federal officials seemed more interested in passing the buck than in solving the problem. Three-term mayor Marion Barry, an out-

time, the US capital was "statistically more dangerous than Belfast or the West Bank," outdoing both the Israeli-occupied territories and the whole of Northern Ireland in the number of violent deaths. The majority of victims and perpetrators, he continued, were young black men. "Homicide is… by far the most common cause of death among black males between 15 and 34 in Washington."

In April 1989, the newly appointed federal drug czar William Bennett, declared Washington a "test case" in the national war on drugs. Bennett's battle plan stressed beefed-up law enforcement, cooperation between

spoken veteran of the civil rights movement, complained about the lack of federal dollars and Bennett's bull-in-a-china-shop tactics. Federal officials responded by huffing and puffing over municipal foot-dragging and the growing evidence of corruption in DC government, a charge that was amply substantiated by the subsequent conviction of 12 city officials. All the while, rumors were swirling around the city that Barry himself was abusing cocaine, an allegation he repeatedly denied. Although Barry was never charged with any criminal wrongdoing, the story put an enormous crack in the mayor's credibility and provided grounds for a full-fledged federal investigation. Suspicions were confirmed about two years later when the FBI lured Barry to a hotel rendezvous with one of his former mistresses, a striking ex-model, and then videotaped the mayor buying and smoking crack cocaine. Diehard Barry supporters immediately cried "entrapment," claiming the FBI sting was part of "The Plan," a conspiracy to oust Barry, discredit black leaders and take over the city.

In the end, he was convicted on only one misdemeanor count of cocaine possession (out of 11 drug counts and three perjury counts), and was knocked out of city politics

ton has long been considered a center of black political leadership – a fact that has vexed the perennial battle over District home rule and possible statehood. As far back as 1865 – when DC citizens didn't even have the right to vote in federal elections – it was generally accepted that home rule meant some degree of black rule, a situation that ignited bitter debate in Congress over black suffrage in Washington.

Today, of course, the situation is quite different. Washington residents vote in local and federal elections; the mayor and city council initiate local legislation. But District government is still not autonomous. Under

only temporarily. Sentenced to six months in jail, Barry again ran for mayor in 1994. Shunned by both the black and the white middle class, he was re-elected nevertheless, finding favor (and votes) with the city's mainly black underclass, the people he calls "the least, the last and the lost."

Home rule: The ordeal of the Barry scandal put issues of race and racism into high relief. With a 70 percent black majority, Washing-

Left and **above**, Washington, home to lobbyists and protests, is currently divided over the issue of home rule.

the Home Rule Act of 1974, the US Congress has the power to review and amend District legislation, including the budget. Supporters of limited home rule cite Washington's history as a federal district and Congress's obvious interest in the management of the capital. The charge is still being made, however, that influential factions in Congress and in the city are simply unwilling to hand over the reins of power to black leaders.

The irony of the District's political status is difficult to miss. The District of Columbia is not only the capital of the US, it is purported to be the capital of the free world. So why is it that DC has no representatives in the US Senate and only one non-voting delegate in the US House of Representatives?

The answer is simple: because the District of Columbia is not a state. It has enough people to be a state (the District's population is higher than that of Vermont's, Alaska's or Wyoming's), and District residents certainly pay enough federal taxes. But as supporters of statehood often point out, a new state of Columbia would be entitled to two seats in the Senate and one voting seat in the House of Representatives. And considering the District's demography, those seats would most likely be filled by black Democrats.

As Senator Edward Kennedy, a longtime supporter of DC statehood, put it, Washington suffers from the "four toos": "The District of Columbia and its residents are too urban, too liberal, too Democratic and too black." Columnist Carl Rowan makes the point even more strongly: "It is obvious that racism and political bigotry are what really block the way to statehood for the District of Columbia… When Hawaii was up for statehood, the opponents mostly whispered that there ought not be a state run mostly by Asians. Now the bigots are saying openly that statehood for the District of Columbia would produce the 'disaster' of two black members of the US Senate."

Whether any government officials have actually entered this type of bigoted statement into the congressional record is doubtful, but the frankness of Rowan's remarks are indicative of just how inflammatory and polarized the issue of race has become. Washington, the US government's monument to itself, has become a national proving ground for the limits of black political power. And when the question of District autonomy is dragged out again (and it surely will be) – whether that autonomy takes the form of full home rule or statehood – the debate will not only reveal thinking about good government, but act as a measure of the relative tensions surrounding race relations in the wake of the civil rights movement.

What the future holds for Washington is anybody's guess. A quick look at the city's problems is enough to convince anyone that the prospects are daunting. The District's substantial black middle class, frightened by urban violence, has fled to the suburbs, taking their substantial tax dollars with them. The city itself is almost bankrupt. Putting Washington back on an even keel, and managing the historic tug of war between City Hall and Capitol Hill, is an uphill challenge.

Washington is the nation's capital, the place where America and other parts of the world look for direction. It's also a black-majority city and a flagship of black political leadership. Although its problems are considerable, few cities can draw on the pool of talent and resources available to the national capital. Optimists say that Washington has already got a hold of its bootstraps and that it's only a matter of time before it pulls itself up; one indication might be the opening of a Metro station in Anacostia, and the hope of much-needed revitalization to this depressed area. Optimistic signs are needed, because Washington doesn't just belong to Washingtonians, it belongs to everyone.

For a guide to how the American government works, see the "Travel Tips" section.

Left, despite urban problems, many are still optimistic. **Right**, suburban values still apply.

Washington, according to John F. Kennedy's jibe, is one of those cities that mixes "Southern efficiency with Northern charm." Times have changed since that remark, but this almost laughably small place – a diamond-shaped area of modest residential streets – is one of the most contradictory capitals in the developed world.

For a start, it is described as a town – and, despite the glittering presidency of John Kennedy, a pretty provincial one at that. The foremost argument that engaged residents and visitors at that time was whether it was a Southern town or a Yankee one. Now the question of tourists who stroll along the Mall marveling at some of the world's finest museums is more likely to be: does anyone, apart from that man in the White House, actually live here? The city appears devoted to official buildings, official business and people who visit. It seems detached from the nation it governs. But to its inhabitants it is very much an established city – in fact, it would be more true to say that it is four cities.

The four faces: There is the Washington that is most generally conjured up by the name – the administrative city that governs the vast military and bureaucratic machine that Washington has become. This is the city defined by the White House, the Pentagon and the Capitol, and the legions of local inhabitants who make the machine work.

Then there is social Washington, hovering not so discreetly behind the closed doors (to anyone who does not clutch an engraved invitation) of the exclusive salons of Georgetown, Kalorama and Embassy Row. Its purpose is to woo, soothe, encourage, coerce and promote useful relationships among the politically influential. For this is not a city like New York or San Francisco that has grown up around the more usual physical and cultural needs of a socially

integrated community. Its crème de la crème are not drawn together by vibrant local theater, innovative restaurants, imaginative grocery stores, fashionable, witty or daring style. The thing that counts most is power. It was at the exclusive Georgetown salon of Pamela Harriman, later made US Ambassador to France, that Bill Clinton was first veted then promoted to run for president.

The third Washington is the city referred to by both its white and its African American

residents as "Chocolate City" – the 70 percent black Washington known as the crack and murder capital of the world.

These are the Washingtons that make up the nation's capital, familiar even to those who know it only from photographs. But there is a fourth Washington, and it is this Washington that is finally forcing the capital into becoming a coherent, normal place to live, functioning beyond the shadow of the Capitol. It is the Washington that lies outside the District of Columbia line.

In Chevy Chase, Bethesda, Arlington and the nearby environs of Maryland's Mont-

Preceding pages: singing the national anthem at a Redskins football game; Vietnamese wedding guests; USA today; a capital service. **Left,** satirist/columnist Art Buchwald. **Right,** talk-show king Larry King.

gomery County – the second wealthiest county in the nation – plus Virginia's Fairfax and Prince George's counties, are the suburbs where these days you will find burgeoning business and residential Washington. While demolition teams scrape away downtown DC to erase the old ghettos still clinging to the skirts of Capitol Hill, out beyond the DC line a vibrant new Washington has been growing.

The face of the future: DC, kept deliberately unattached to either of its neighboring states in order not to show favoritism, is probably the last American city under renovation and construction in the classical quasi-European

Society. This dream for a nation in which citizens would have the best in education, medical and social care provoked a government drive to increase manpower in these professions. The result was a surge in staff levels at the departments responsible for overseeing them.

Unable to adequately accommodate these new bureaucrats in the old federal buildings and state departments in town, some government offices made the move into the suburbs. Major international banking and communications institutions followed, spreading outwards in Virginia in the direction of Dulles International Airport and making the

style. Yet while old columned buildings receive face lifts and once-problem areas become gentrified, what is now recognized as the standard modern American city mushrooms on the other side of the District line. Pushing outwards beyond the Beltway (the 10-lane traffic nightmare of a highway that girdles the city) are the high-rise office buildings, the shopping malls, the freeway strips that signify the city of the future anywhere in America.

This new Washington is the city that has grown out of President Lyndon Johnson's grandiose program in the 1960s for the Great

suburb of Reston a burgeoning city. The effect is almost a reversing of the power process, with the activity of the arteries in the suburbs helping the central body function. Increasingly, what takes place on the outskirts of town supports, justifies and shores up the activities and continued existence of the business of the center.

What pushed, with explosive suddenness, the process of transforming Washington from a sleepy Southern town into a forceful power city were the race riots of 1968 that followed the assassination of Dr Martin Luther King. What these fires began, the demolition teams continued, and the political process took over. In 1970 the redevelopment of Washington began, including the idea of pulling it down and rebuilding it afresh. Requests for building and development permits were made and fulfilled, and the process of cleaning up the city was underway with a vengeance.

Marion Barry, who took office as mayor in 1978, used his powers to push the construction program forward with even greater fervor. Whole areas were razed while others were restored. To see the contrast between old and new, stand on Dupont Circle, where Massachusetts Avenue crosses Connecticut Avenue. The Connecticut Avenue to your

things, that this would discourage politicians from spending too much time here gathering power. While the backbone of government bureaucracy is necessarily run by a permanent staff, people in high political office have traditionally committed themselves to Washington only for the duration of the President who appointed them.

PR politicians: These days politicians who once would have returned home after the end of their term of office now choose, in increasing numbers, to stay on to become PR men, lobbyists or consultants in the mushrooming think-tanks. You can understand their desire to stay put. Washington is an

south is new and high-rise. The block of Connecticut to your north is jumbled, low-rise and on a more human scale.

With this transformation, Washington began to attract people with firm commitments to putting down roots. This was unlike the intentions of the original founding fathers, who sited the capital on an uncongenial swamp because they hoped, among other

Left, director and Degas: J. Carter Brown, former head of the National Gallery. Above, power and the press: Mrs Katherine Graham of *Washington Post* fame.

attractive and lucrative city in which to play power games.

These are not the only group of people who now make a point of establishing at least one of their homes in Washington. The growth in government, banking and institutions has drawn to the city a positive plethora of lawyers, to the point where they have become the butt of caustic jokes. There are over 55,000 of them working in practices large and small, but over 100,000 people in Washington actually have law qualifications. This is more than the number of doctors in the city, despite the fact that in the Maryland suburb of Bethesda sits the vast compound of the National Institute of Health, the prestigious research center set up by President Nixon's government to find a cure for cancer. But government needs lawyers to construct and implement the law and to protect itself, and businesses need lawyers to confront the government. Now litigation appears to have become a way of life among the residents, too.

Shrink city: Washington has also become a major employer of specialists in emotional problems, with more therapists, counselors and psychiatrists per capita than any other American city. Perhaps the pressures of power

bracket. There are good theater companies, much relished by indigenous Washingtonians, but outside of the Kennedy Center few consistently glittering theatrical events.

While there is a constant carousel of nightclubs and music cellars for students and the yuppie community, there is no glitzy night life for the power people. This is part cultural: Washingtonians have to get up far too early to party all night long.

Political Washington is a city that closes down early. Wilbur Mills, the all-powerful chairman of the Congressional Ways and Means Committee who leaped into the fountains in some disarray with fan dancer

are just too great for some. Despite this growth, however, Washington is still a comparatively slow-paced, provincial city, although its polish increases daily. While its New York neighbors may find it, as Barbra Streisand did, "a stuffy city," it is no longer the backwoods hick town of two decades ago. It just has a way to go.

There are over 5,000 restaurants in the city, where Washingtonians can dine on the national cuisine of practically any country in the world. Yet without an expense account there are few gourmet establishments in the "international cuisine" or "fine dining"

Fanne Foxe, would agree that it doesn't pay to be seen in enthusiastic party mode, unless the spectators are part of the party. Politics dictate Washington's night life. Fund-raising dinners are more valued than gourmet occasions, and these days most events are run by PR consultants on behalf of lobbyists.

Although Mrs Pamela Harriman, widow of Ambassador Avril Harriman and herself an ambassador to France, will always be cited as one of Washington's most prominent hostesses, the days of a coterie of influential women who could make or break a political career have passed.

Nevertheless, old money, new habits and/or general behavior moves in and out of fashion and depends entirely on who's in the White House. A case in point is the Clinton administration, when social Washington lost a good deal of glamour and pizzazz. Clinton's "teenage" advisors (as they were disparagingly, sometimes enviously referred to), were rarely seen behaving with the kind of flamboyance usually expected of their age group. There were also serious clashes with the people who fondly remembered the neat, organized George Bush years. In his book *Unlimited Access*, FBI agent Gary W. Alrich wrote of his unease at seeing "oddly dressed

Gazing up and down the Mall, this would seem to be the most civilized of cities. Yet it also has one of the highest murder rates in the world. Almost 100 percent of these crimes occur in the North East and South East, areas that are predominantly African American and Hispanic. American apartheid may legally have ended in 1964, but Washington is an apartheid city, with middle-class whites living west of the 16th Street line that divides the city from the north down to the White House. Unemployment and violence are part of the daily lives of those who live in the east.

The motives for this state of urban warfare in the east part of Washington have vexed

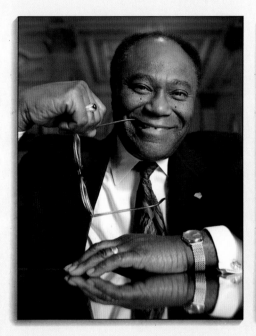

new personnel" in the White House, dressed in "jeans, T-shirts and sweat shirts." Each president brings his own personality to DC, and what is acceptable behavior this administration will no doubt be out of favor next.

Boulevards and fire bombs: Washington is a handsome city. Any architectural appetite can be satisfied here, from Egyptian and Greek to Victorian and the post-Modern.

<u>Left and right</u>, Washingtonians to watch: socialite Polly Fritchey; commentator David Brinkley; black think-tank leader Eddie T. Williams; society hostess and diplomat Pamela Harriman.

and perplexed sociology departments in learning institutions throughout the nation.

Because the place still in flux and development, it is difficult to define. Its crime and welfare problems call for real and sweeping efforts in order to resolve them. But this focus on one part of Washington should not obscure the others. This is, after all, four cities. Desperate, magnificent, stylish and provincial, Washington is also a town which possesses a rare, distinctive quality. It's a place where, in the words of Ralph Waldo Emerson, "an insignificant individual may trespass on a nation's time."

Washington, DC was named Chocolate City by the black youth magazine *YSB* (the initials stand for Young Sisters and Brothers). They should know. The magazine based its editorial offices in the capital, part of the Washington-based Black Entertainment TV empire. The growing black role in media ownership, much of it centered around Washington, is just one example of a confident black professional class. This is an aspect of Washington that the headlines rarely mention, amid the crime and murder statistics that give the capital its international notoriety.

High-ranking supremos: Black Washington is more than just the figure of Marion Barry, whose behavior when mayor garnered him many national headlines. In recent years there have been a number of high-ranking supremos, from General Colin Powell, who as chairman of the Joint Chiefs of Staff, obtained the highest rank ever reached by a black soldier, to Sharon Pratt Kelly, the first black woman mayor of a major US city.

But within just a few blocks of the White House and the Capitol are the weed-strewn lots and crack houses that cluster just north of Massachusetts Avenue around 14th Street. Open-air drug markets flourish where Quincy and Newton cross 14th Street, spilling over to the basement areas where addicted prostitutes offer sex for $5 and less, the price of a vial of crack.

These are the mean streets which have established the city's crime-ridden reputation, with one murder for every 120 inhabitants. The arrest of Mayor Marion Barry in 1990 on drug charges (most were subsequently dropped) confirmed the international image of the city as one vast ghetto surrounding a besieged core of public buildings and government offices which a largely white bureaucracy visited nervously by day, fleeing home at night to the suburbs.

And yet Washington is also the home of a prominent black middle class, although it,

too, is fleeing to the suburbs in ever increasing numbers. In the 1980s the city had an average 14 percent of its population on welfare – one of the highest proportions in the country – yet it enjoyed the second-highest per capita income (after the state of Alaska). The federal government's laws against racial discrimination in employment created job opportunities in an ever-growing federal bureaucracy. This was good news for awhile, but a series of strict cut-backs has meant fewer and fewer jobs all around.

DC's Dunbar High, on the corner of 1st and N streets NW, was the first black high school in the country, and it produced generations of black leaders, like Benjamin David, the first black general, Charles Drew, the medical scientist who discovered blood plasma, and Edward Brooke, the first black senator of the 20th century. The relatively new University of DC and the long-established Howard University, often called "the black Harvard" with its 18 schools, 12,000 students, 8,000 employees and $500 million annual budget, have created a strong intellectual foundation.

Preceding pages: Sunday in Shiloh church. **Left** and **right**, Young Sisters in the city.

Along Upper 16th Street, known locally as the Gold Coast, is a suburb of expensive homes for the city's black elite. On Sunday mornings, the streets around the fashionable black churches of the Gold Coast and Shepherd Park are thronged with luxury cars and well-dressed families. But this prosperous and growing middle class tends increasingly to behave like its white counterparts, and flee the problems of the inner city. Head northeast of the DC boundary and you reach Prince George's County, which in 1990 became the first suburban county in the country to boast a black majority population.

The roots of Washington's black community go back to the founding of the city in the

design plan by a free black surveyor called Benjamin Banneker. On the eve of the US Civil War in 1860, there were some 11,000 free blacks in the city, and over 3,000 slaves. After the Civil War and the abolition of slavery, the Freedmen's Bureau launched the great institutions like Freedmen's Hospital and Howard University which would become the pioneers of black progress.

An interesting reminder of these hopeful days after the emancipation of the slaves is the Frederick Douglass Memorial Home and Museum, at 1411 W Street SE, in the heart of what is now the ghetto of Anacostia. The first black abolitionist, Douglass might be down-

nity go back to the founding of the city in the established white South. Located south of the Mason-Dixon line, the old boundary between the slave and the free states, the nation's capital was born in the curious contradiction between slavery and black genius. In plush Georgetown, which was a black community until the 1940s, there is a street called Volta Place, one of the streets where slaves from West Africa's Volta river were bought and sold.

And yet when the city's architect Pierre L'Enfant died penniless, his initial sketches were reconstructed and made into a viable

cast by the levels of crime around his old home. But as an escaped slave he would relish the fact that the city government of Washington is now run by the great-grand-children of slavery.

It has, however, proved a bitterly slow and uneven process. In 1922, when the Lincoln Memorial was dedicated to the Great Emancipator, a separate stand was erected for black dignitaries, a symbol of the segregation which still governed the city's schools, restaurants and theaters. Only the trolleys, the buses and the stands of Griffith Stadium were integrated, but not the baseball field itself. The 1920s saw the black population of Washington fall to its lowest ebb, no more than 25 percent, and the demographic tide which now makes the city two-thirds black began to flow only with Roosevelt's New Deal and the government's explosive growth during World War II.

But the black character of modern Washington was shaped by two crucial events. The first was the Supreme Court's order to desegregate the school systems in 1954, which dramatically accelerated the white flight to the suburbs. And, 14 years later, the assassination of Martin Luther King sparked off the racial riots and the looting and burn-

century as a fief of Congress, the city was able to vote for its own school board in 1968, and for its own (non-voting) delegate to Congress in 1971. In 1974, the city finally won the right to elect its own mayor and largely black city council. This helped spur the growth of the black middle class, as they appointed sympathetic police chiefs and blacks rose in the civic bureaucracy.

The destruction of so much of the city center created a golden opportunity for property development, new office buildings to house the growing federal bureaucracy and the lawyers and lobbyists and consultants and corporate offices that began to grow

ing which reached within four blocks of the White House. The white flight was followed by the steady drift of shops and service industries and jobs to the suburbs, and created the social condition which became known as the inner city. The 1968 riots and the fires created the conditions for a rebirth.

The riots reinforced the case for giving the national capital enough democracy to elect its own form of civic government. After a

Left, weighing in at Union Station. **Above**, Colin Powell became chairman of the Joint Chiefs of Staff, the nation's highest-ranking black soldier.

around it. The buildings meant construction jobs, service jobs and property taxes.

By 1990, there were over 49,000 civic employees in this city of 554,000 people, the highest proportion in the country. Mayor Barry created a political machine, a vast patronage system which mobilized an electorate already solidly loyal for the Democrats. It was the only electoral community in the entire US to vote against the national landslides for the successive Republican presidents, Richard Nixon, Ronald Reagan and George Bush.

America had seen this kind of ethnic machine politics before, with the 19th-century Irish in Boston, or the Italians in New York in the 1930s. What helped turn Washington so sour was crack cocaine. From a peak of just over 200 murders in 1981, the murder rate dropped steadily until 1985's low of 153. Then came crack, and the killings soared annually to over 500 murders a year after 1990, with the fastest growth among young black males. The District's substantial black middle class fled to the suburbs. A survey conducted in the early 1990s found that around 42 percent of young black urban Washingtonians were either in prison, on probation, on parole, awaiting trial or being sought by the police. Three out of four people in District jails are inside for drug-related offences. Their share of the prison population has tripled in the past 10 years. Their recidivism rate averages 70 percent.

Emergency: This is the bad news of the city. And a few blocks south from the R. F. Kennedy stadium, home of the Redskins football team, it is on display at the vast emergency center at DC General Hospital on a weekend night, when the ambulances line up to deliver the latest crop of shooting and stabbing victims and drug overdoses.

The good news about this highest profile of America's black-run city can come in odd ways, like the springtime riots of 1991, when DC's Hispanic population in Mount Pleasant spent three nights burning and looting in protest against police "racism" – black police, that is, which makes an intriguing change from the black attacks on racist white police in the 1968 riots. And in the District Courts on Indiana Avenue, for all the depressing parade of black defendants in the dock, the black lawyers and black judges and black reporters on the press benches suggest a more hopeful society emerging.

Marion Barry, who many thought would never enter politics again after serving six months in jail for drug offenses, re-turned to the mayor's office four years later. This comeback shows what can be achieved, and perhaps this spirit of resurgence will filter through to black Washington as a whole.

Right, life can be hard for an unemployed black man in the nation's capital.

A popular reinterpretation of the CIA's initials among savvy Washingtonians is "the Culinary Institute of America." This is a dig at the extraordinary coincidence of the sudden surge in new ethnic restaurants that comes with the ebb and flow of political events around the globe. Democratic American voters – and Republicans, too – may object to some of the meddling in the internal affairs of small and distant countries, but they can always look forward to something new to eat at the end of the revolution.

Country cooking: After the fall of Saigon Washington was suddenly introduced to the delights of Vietnamese cooking. And not just with one single restaurant. The whole extended family fled too; uncles, aunts, cousins, in-laws established Vietnamese eating places all over town. Wilson Boulevard in Arlington, Virginia, on the other side of the Potomac, is fondly know as the Ho Chi Minh Trail. In the early 1980s, Ethiopian cooking, no less, became popular. And with the Soviet invasion of Kabul, an assortment of Afghani restaurants sprang up.

Inevitably these refugees are go-ahead and determined individuals with all the drive to make things work in their new life. Their bent for enterprise and sense of initiative is generally high; after all, the CIA is unlikely to give much support to incompetents.

The United States has been the first home of political or religious refugees ever since it was born. Indeed, that is why the nation was born. So it can be no surprise that for today's survivors of domestic revolt, America should still appear as the welcoming new motherland, willing to offer comfort and succor to all in need – or a goodly portion of them, at any rate.

Every nation has its own immigrant influx, but while West Indians and Asians gravitate towards Britain, Algerians towards France and Turks towards Germany, every-

one gravitates towards the United States. The original "melting pot" that America held itself to be was based on a mix of European races. These days, as America's political influence stretches throughout the entire world, immigrants come from every nation. Though it has remarkably stringent immigration laws, it does turn a relatively kind eye on political refugees, particularly those from a nation in which the United States has been overtly or covertly involved. It would be

hard not to look favorably upon the immigrant applications of that country's people, particularly when so many of them used to run the pro-American faction back home.

Once here, the new Americans tend to gravitate towards the areas of the city in which their fellow countrymen are already established and to the jobs their fellow countrymen already hold. So that a large number of Washington's cab drivers are Iranian and Ethiopian. Filipino women become housekeepers and cleaners, while the Chinese congregate in Chinatown on H Street NW and join the catering trade. With their flamboy-

Preceding pages: Washington's cherry blossom trees originally came from Japan. **Left**, flower of the Orient. **Right**, fish, wings and tings.

ant shop signs, street names in Chinese, touches of Chinese influence in the architecture, and stores packed full of products and goods identifiable only to the aficionado, they have succeeded in turning a small tract of central Washington into a country within a country.

There is also a large Russian community that reflects several generations of its own nation's turbulent history, from the elder generation of titled White Russians who came to Washington to escape the revolution, through the influx that fled the horrors of Stalin's purges, to the newest arrivals of political and Jewish dissidents. Their focus

is the Russian Orthodox churches, St John the Baptist on 17th Street NW, and St Nicholas on Massachusetts Avenue NW. For the Russian Orthodox Christmas on January 7 they offer a midnight mass with marvelous music, and a wonderful celebration on Easter Sunday as they emerge from church rejoicing "*Kristos Voskreseniye*" – Christ is Risen.

Some of these new Americans become skilful small-time entrepreneurs, making the most of their contacts with their original homelands by organizing sales in hotel rooms, advertised on local radio, of leather goods, jewelry or fabrics brought in by visiting family. Others stand at tables along the streets of Georgetown selling the hats of Afghani freedom fighters or jewelry made by Asian, Indian or Oriental village women.

The enlarged migration to Washington began after World War II, when America turned itself into a superpower. Washington suddenly became deluged by an influx of foreigners accompanying the tangible expressions of the rest of the world's concern or excitement – depending upon the government back home – at the United States's new political powers.

This was certainly the capital in which to have a footing. Embassies opened, Washington became home to the World Bank, the International Monetary Fund and countless other international financial corporations and political institutions. The foreigners made plans for long-term postings. All this was new to a capital that had deliberately isolated itself on an unwelcome swamp.

But with the Golden Years of the 1950s, everyone wanted to stay on. The "other superpower," after all, was a less congenial posting. So the infrastructure began to grow to support the tastes and requirements of all these foreigners. With citizenship more easily acquired then, staff attached to foreign businesses became American and opened shops to supply their ex-countrymen with the specialist foodstuffs, clothing and reading matter which they desired. Washington's foreign community established itself.

By and large, each community of new Americans gets on fine with each other because most of the communities are equally balanced and relatively small. Besides, they recognize that they are still the newcomers. They are here committed to making a success of their new status that will benefit their children for generations to come. One does not abuse one's host. The situation changes when it comes to single ethnic groups who are themselves American but forced economically to settle in one part of town, or when a single ethnic group expands greatly beyond the rest.

Then the potential for mass disaffection, rioting and protest arise; witness the race riots of 1961 and the black vs Hispanic uprising during the spring of 1991. Apart from the disturbing suspicion and rivalry which is currently building between the growing Hispanic community and the African-American community, the dividing line in Washington is less between the individual ethnic communities, than between white Americans and everyone else.

Of all the murders that take place regularly in the capital, almost all occur in the non-white sections of Washington, particularly the east. In 1991, more murders took place within a stone's throw of Georgia Avenue than in the entire British Isles. There is hope, however, in combating the spiraling crime

Plans and schemes for Anacostia are ambitious. The grandest is the Anacostia Cultural Complex, a $200 million dollar theme park on the waterfront. Only time will tell if these plans will work, however, for money has been pumped into Anacostia before, and it still remains a place of great unquiet.

But, Washington's ethnic mix has made for a city that has lost its provincial edges. Any day of the week you can hear on the streets of downtown four or five different languages. There is almost no culinary speciality that is impossible to find. No longer do Washington's cinemas only screen Hollywood's output. There are movie houses

rate and racial unrest. Much of this optimism lies with the opening of a Metro stop in deprived, strife-ridden Anacostia. The station's 1,300-car parking lot just off a major interstate should draw commuters from prosperous Prince George's County, and real estate investors are already moving in. Commercially zoned land not far from the station has risen to a value 10 times its price less than a decade ago, and the Metro stop area has been billed as a "regional center for economic development."

Left, tri-colored bicep. Above, land of the free.

that show nothing but films in foreign languages – from the Kung Fu cult films of the East to the art films of Central Europe and the former Soviet Union. Local art galleries regularly mount shows these days from countries whose work previously remained at home.

Though the ethnic communities have made a commitment to America, they have created by their presence a valuable and rewarding opportunity for themselves, their children, and the rest of Washington's residents and visitors to appreciate what their culture has to offer the rest of the world.

POLITICS AND OTHER POWERS

Washington is the most political of cities, designed and built to be the capital of what has become the last superpower. But while the stone and marble structures which house and embody government power are plain to see, the reality of power remains elusive. An American president may find it easy to despatch aircraft carriers and troops around the globe, but he can have trouble getting his budget, or his nominee to run a major department, through Congress. Congress may pass a law, only to find the White House defies it, or the Supreme Court redefines it.

The power and the story: For the visitor, therefore, the power structure of Washington which is on show in the tours of Congress and the White House and FBI can be deeply misleading; it is part of the reality of power, but only a part. There are two maps of the power process to bear in mind. One is public, and made up of the great and imposing buildings from which power is exercised. The other is private, secret and composed of a series of subtle and personal links through which power is wielded and enjoyed.

The public face of power is etched in a series of straight lines, running as true and potent as the legendary ley-lines of ancient Britain. One axis of power runs along Pennsylvania Avenue, from the White House to the US Capitol and the Supreme Court just behind. To the south of this great artery is the Federal Triangle, housing the great departments of government from Justice to Agriculture to the National Archives, and the Federal Trade Commission and the Internal Revenue Service. Another axis runs to the Pentagon, just across the river. A third heads out to the Virginia suburbs in Maclean, where the CIA has its vast headquarters.

Each of these power centers has its own suburb. The Pentagon has spawned its own bureaucratic military-industrial complex. And the US Congress has become a veritable city in its own right, with it own subway

system to ferry the senators and representatives and their staffs around the complex of office buildings which surrounds the Capitol. To the north are the Dirksen and Hart and Russell buildings, each named after a powerful senator, and each containing the vast and formal committee rooms where so many public hearings and so much history has taken place. Joe McCarthy's witch-hunts for Communist sympathizers in government, Fulbright's Foreign Relations Committee hearings against the Vietnam War, Sam Ervin's probes into Richard Nixon's complicity in Watergate – these marble halls witnessed all these dramas.

Less well-known are the grandiose office suites where each of the 100 senators have over 30 staff members whose salaries are paid by the taxpayer. Much of their time is taken up processing the 25 million letters a year Congress receives from the voters.

On the House: To the south of the Capitol stand the Cannon, the Longworth, the Rayburn, O'Neill and Ford buildings where the 435 members of the House of Representatives reside in slightly more modest splendor. House members average about 14 staff members, but their committee rooms defer not at all to the Senate's self-importance. The basement of the Rayburn building contains the House gym, one of the few places where the legislators can get away from voters, journalists and lobbyists and hang around with each other. Celebrities can be squeezed in, but only to be useful, like the way Arnold Schwarzenegger was recruited to give advanced tuition in weight-lifting.

The B-2 Stealth bomber was almost killed in this gym, for it was here that the liberal Congressman Ron Dellums and the conservative Republican John Kasich struck up the weight-lifting friendship which let them realize they both had good reasons to oppose the expensive warplane. If you want to watch the House in action, don't bother going into the public gallery around 4pm. That is the time of the daily basketball game in the gym.

It is by no means a luxurious place. The

swimming pool is a modest 60 feet long, and it contains a basketball and paddle ball court, weights, stationary bicycles, two treadmills and a stairmaster. The Helene Curtis company provides free soap, and there are constant complaints that the towels are too small. The attraction is the company. George Bush stopped by to play paddle ball, and the vice president was a popular attender at the basketball game, being one of the few politicians generous enough to pass the ball to other players. "No politician feels he cannot score from any given point on the court once he has his hands on the ball," confides Congressman Byron Dorgan, a North Dakota Democrat. "There is virtually no passing."

Because of the cramped locker room, it is a single-sex gym. A smaller women's gym has been opened upstairs. But the House gym is getting too crowded for serious workouts; when a noted Speaker of the House decided to lose 100 pounds, he went to the gym of the University Club on 16th Street instead.

Executive suburb: One of the fastest-growing suburbs is the White House itself. The Treasury huddles close alongside to the east, but beyond the western wing, which Richard Nixon transformed from a swimming pool into a press room, stands the evidence of the growth industry of the presidency: a large 19th-century building of gray stone and pillars, the Executive Office Building.

It used to be sufficient to house the entire civil service, the Navy and Commerce and the State Department. These days, it cannot even house the White House staff, whose more than 2,300 members have spilled over into a red-brick New Executive Office Building on the far side of Pennsylvania Avenue. It is more luxurious than it looks – $350,000 was spent just to redecorate the gym. The EOB has the best vending machines and automats in town. At 3am, White House workaholics can get cash, pay their bills, shuffle their bank accounts, buy stamps, send off a last-minute anniversary present to the spouse they never see via Federal Express, and get hot macaroni and cheese or cold baloney sandwiches along with a health drink. They can do all this without ever seeing another human being.

The bowels of the White House are the center of the discreet power structure which really runs the political side of the city. The White House mess is one of the most exclusive places in town – like the White House tennis court, even presidential assistants have to go on a waiting list. Most of them settle for the spartan cafeteria in the EOB, where staffers openly wonder how much of the $2.4 million that the taxpayer spends each year on subsidizing the 22 exclusive dining rooms in the Capitol and Pentagon and White House ever filters down to their plates. (The hospitality prize goes to the Pentagon, which averages $100,000 in revenues for every $450,000 in subsidies).

House arrest: In the early 1980s, you could tell the White House staff by the tiny chains around their necks, carrying the computerized ID card which gets you past the guards and the world's highest-tech gate. The gate cost $1.3 million to erect and to stop assaults by suicide bomb trucks its stanchions are sunk 22 feet deep into the ground.

These days many people possess White House ID cards, even journalists (who go through a prolonged security check before getting White House accreditation). The cards are about a quarter-inch thick, and are said to spit out details of your grandmother's bank account and your sexual preferences when stuffed into the appropriate computer. They remain the quintessential Washington fashion statement.

Such is the prestige of the White House pass that it will get you into the Pentagon, the State Department and other great buildings of government. But there is another structure of power for which they are completely useless. Most of this is private, like the Cosmos Club on Massachusetts Avenue (Anglophile-diplomatic) or the Metropolitan Club on H Street (lots of lawyers, best crabcakes in town). There are power salons, too, like those run along the lines of Pamela Harriman, uncrowned queen of the Democrats. A British aristocrat who was married to a son of Winston Churchill, she then married Averell Harriman, former ambassador to Moscow and governor of New York before becoming an ambassador to France herself. Until she laid down the reins as publisher of the *Washington Post*, the home of Mrs Katherine Graham carried a similar weight. And in circles of this wealth, "home" is not only Washington, as Mrs Nancy Reagan discovered to her pleasure when invited to spend a weekend at the Graham country cottage on Martha's Vineyard.

Breakfast of champions: The serious political sessions, when the fund-raisers confer with the Congressmen, take place in private dining rooms in the big hotels, or in the corporate suites and the think-tanks. Powerful people have to eat, and on any given day, they will be breakfasting and lunching and having drinks in a series of discreet places.

nar suppers on Soviet affairs, and domestic policy-makers meet the Brookings economists over no-alcohol lunches.

This personalized power structure has an occasional public face, seen at a handful of restaurants. The fashions change all the time. In the Kissinger years, Sans Souci (now gone) and Maison Blanche (1725 F Street) were the fashionable places. In the 1980s, Nancy Reagan made the reputation of the Jockey Club (2100 Massachusetts Avenue), currently enjoying yet another revival. Though his detractors joke that President Clinton's favorite watering-hole is Wendy's the hamburger chain, his taste in food

There are the private rooms of the National Press Club, the top floor of the arms controllers' think tank on Dupont Circle, or the Heritage Foundation on Massachusetts Avenue NE. The stretch of Massachusetts Avenue between 17th Street and Dupont Circle offers the private rooms of the Brookings Institute and the seventh floor of the School of Advanced International Studies of Johns Hopkins. CIA and State Department experts, academics and the occasional journalist gather here for utterly off-the-record seminars.

Above, the Republican Whip office.

spreads from the elegant Bombay Club at 815 Connecticut Avenue to the Italian Ciao Baby Cucina, which replaced Twenty One Federal (1736 K Street), Bice (601 Pennsylvania Avenue) and Obelisk (2029 P Street). Then there are the Capitol Hill restaurants like the Monocle and La Colline, where senators go when they get tired of the famous pea soup in the Senate dining room.

Just up Connecticut Avenue is the basement restaurant called Joe and Mo's, where George Bush made one of his first social calls as president. It was at a back-room party thrown by the conservative guru William

Buckley. Joe and Mo's is one of the last bastions of the three-martini lunch. The more health-conscious diners, a diet made popular by members of the Clinton crew, head along to any number of restaurants where the organically minded can eat pasta and drink mineral water.

Apart from food, the other two commodities that bind the Washington power structure together are gossip and money. The best insight into the process always came from two eminent *New York Times* reporters. Political correspondent R. W. "Johnny" Apple caught the heady flavor of power in an article about the Washington mood on the eve of the

Persian Gulf war: "In news bureaus and Pentagon offices, dining rooms and lobbyists' hangouts, the fever is back – the heavy speculation, the avid gossip, the gung-ho here's-where-it's-happening spirit that marks the city when it grapples with great events." What Apple did not say was that his own home in Georgetown, like the houses of the diplomats and senior bureaucrats which cram this elegant inner suburb of townhouses, was one of the places where the gossip was taking place.

The media is the custodian of political gossip, just as the TV programs and the Op-

Ed pages make up the playing field where the power-brokers conduct their negotiations in public. The heavyweight journalists on the heavyweight papers are part of the process. Witness this second quotation from Johnny Apple's *New York Times* colleague, Hedrick Smith: "I remember a small private dinner at the White House with President Carter in 1978. Eighteen of us were gathered around the table in the family quarters.

Over coffee, President Carter talked about policy. I have a vivid memory of his acute frustration over the entangling ways of Congress. His top priority, his energy legislation, he told us, had to pass through 22 different congressional committees and subcommittees. The process had become an impossible legislative steeplechase. Viewing the new power game from a different angle, Tommy Boggs, a highly successful lobbyist, grinned and said to me 'The Washington establishment has been blown wide open'."

Hedrick Smith crammed a great deal of information into that paragraph; about the way media folk mingle with the mighty; about the tangled and complex web of the political process; how the profusion of Congressional committees can slow and change that process; and the way the lobbyists relish the opportunities this presents to them. Twenty-two Congressional committees means 22 groups of politicians who are vulnerable to their voters and to the big industrialists who employ these voters.

Fund capital of the world: Then, of course, there are fund-raisers, people who are keen to understand the problems a politician faces in affording the TV time he needs to get elected. Washington is the fund-raising capital of the world. A Senate race in California costs $20 million these days. A hard-fought Congressional race in New York can cost a million dollars.

The PACs, the Political Action Committees which provide the main conduit that takes money from interested citizens and transfers it to political candidates, raised and spent more than $350 million in one recent non-presidential election year. So another way to view the Washington power structure is to look at the skilful money-raisers among the PACs.

The top PACs' contributions to individual candidates were:

Teamsters trade union, $2.9 million
American Medical Association, $2.9 million
National Association of Realtors, $2.9 million
National Education Asssociation (the teachers' union), $2.3 million
United Auto Workers, $2.2 million
American Federation of State, County and Municipal Employees, $1.9 million
Association of Trial Lawyers of America, $2.3 million
National Rifle Association, $1.7 million.

If any official of these organizations telephones a Congressman, he is unlikely to be put on hold. And a journalist from the big papers, the *New York* or *Los Angeles Times*, the *Wall Street Journal* or the *Washington Post* or *USA Today*, will also be put straight through. The same applies to the main TV networks and CNN, and to the top diplomats of the main allies. So the main media offices and embassies, and the Georgetown and Cleveland Park homes of the top diplomats

and journalists, are also part of the secret map of political Washington.

There are a handful of occasions when all the elite of Washington congregate in a single place, and the politicians, the fund-raisers, the diplomats and media come together as one great herd. An example is the annual ball for the Washington Opera, usually thrown by the French ambassador. The summer garden party held in honor of the Queen's birthday by the British Embassy is another; the guest list of 2,600 people put together for the Queen's recent visit was a definitive round-up of Washington's top people. Such occasions have one thing in

common apart from the guests; the DC police force calls them "limo-locks," from the traffic jams of the sleek, long limousines.

There is only one event which needs so many limos that reinforcements have to be driven down the I-95 freeway from New York. This takes place every four years in January, on a president's inauguration day. The weather is often very cold. When John Kennedy took the oath in 1961, the temperature was below freezing. In 1985 it was so cold they held the event indoors. But whatever the weather, the limo-lock grips the streets just behind Pennsylvania Avenue,

Left, a bearded embrace. **Above**, TV supremo Barbara Walters (center) at a politically useful Washington function.

which give access to the windows and the rooftops from which the fortunate nibble their canapés and sip champagne as the president and his wife wave their way back from the swearing-in on the Capitol steps on their triumphant parade to the White House.

The limos lock again in the evening, for the inaugural balls. These now take place all across the city, in the vast and echoing Armoury, in the marbled hall of Union Station, and at the big hotel ballrooms. The political power-brokers of all 50 US states, the fund-raisers and the donors, the far-flung members of the new White House family and the new Cabinet all gather for a glimpse of the

president and his spouse as they take the floor for a token waltz, and then glad-hand their way out of the door to the next ball.

If this does not sound like much fun, that is because the real pleasure of Washington is not in the lavish and sleek way this city entertains itself, but in the erotic grip of power. Henry Kissinger was never a handsome man, but his power was aphrodisiac enough for his escorts to be some of the most beautiful women in the country. But sex is dangerous in Washington – for proof, see the next chapter, "Political Stings and Scandals". The climate may be changing, how-

ever. Massachusetts Congressman Barney Frank survived a bruising scandal in which a gay prostitute who had lived in his Capitol Hill house was discovered entertaining clients when Mr Frank was helping run the country in Congress. And the attempts by radical gays to "out" (publicize) the homosexuality of a senior Pentagon official during a recent administration did not create the anticipated public furor.

Some of the greatest sexual events of the city's history deserve to be on the tourist trail, however. There was the Congressman's divorced wife who claimed to have enjoyed late-night sex on the steps of the Capitol. The particular step is unknown, but none of them looks comfortable. There is the private room of the Monocle restaurant where a famous Massachusetts senator was found "in the passionate embrace of his public affairs," as the French newspaper *Le Figaro* delicately put it. And although it is not part of the public rooms, there is the famous broom cupboard in the White House where President Warren Harding is reported to have hidden with his mistress while his enraged wife stalked the hall.

Gore Vidal, the novelist of Washington and its ways, once observed that Washington had become the modern Rome, and it was therefore to be expected that it would develop its own scandals to rival those of the Caesars. The difference is that the power of Rome's emperors came to overwhelm the Roman republic and the institutions of law and senate which had built its greatness. And in spite of that vogue phrase "the Imperial Presidency," the democratic institutions of the United States have proved to be of sterner stuff, and the concept of the American empire is more metaphor than reality. The secret of political Washington is the way the private and the public maps of power interact to diffuse that power and spread it through the Congressmen and corporations and media to let it flow back to the 50 states which find their focus in this modern Rome.

Left, reporter "Johnny" Apple with the former British ambassador Robin Renwick and wife. **Right**, lobbyists in the lobby of the Willard Hotel, where the term is thought to have originated.

POLITICAL STINGS AND SCANDALS

Scandals are system-specific; they reveal a lot about the nature of the society in which they take place. Britain tends to like sex scandals, the French go for financial scams, but Washington is obsessed with power and its abuses.

Occasionally sex alone can make a Washington scandal, like the oddly innocent occasion when chairman of the House Ways and Means Committee Wilbur Mills was found frolicking in the Washington fountains in the smoking crack cocaine with a former mistress (*see pages 54–55*). Everything was captured on film, including the Mayor's half-hearted and unsuccessful attempt at seduction. During the trial that followed, sympathetic Washington blacks sported T-shirts that read "I saw the tape – Bitch set him up."

Power generates more dramatic scandals than sex and drugs because of the US political system which tries to divide power between the executive, the legislature and the

early hours with his stripper mistress Fanne Foxe. And US Senator Gary Hart lost his bid for the 1988 Presidential race when he challenged the press to follow him to verify that he was not being unfaithful to his wife. The *Miami Herald* watched his back door, and proved him to be a liar and a fool. Bill Clinton, both as candidate and as president, fared somewhat better when his name was linked with a number of young women.

A sex scandal becomes even sexier when it is linked to drugs. Witness the celebrated "Sting" operation of 1990, when Mayor Marion Barry was arrested in a hotel room judiciary branches of the government. Inevitably, they fight for the spoils. But the post-war prominence of Washington as a super-power capital has raised the stakes of the power struggles, and added the juicy new ingredients of spy wars. It's a poor scandal these days that does not include the CIA.

The FBI tries its best, however. The legendary first FBI director J. Edgar Hoover is said to have kept his job for so long because of the secret files and tape recordings he kept on everyone else in the power game. Hoover's excuse was the FBI's charter to run counter-espionage inside the US, while the

CIA was restricted to operations overseas. Looking for elusive evidence of King's Communist Party links, the FBI instead collected tapes of Martin Luther King's bedroom activities.

Hoover's snoopers: Hoover's collection of evidence about the sex life of President John F. Kennedy and Attorney-General Robert F. Kennedy, including their affairs with Marilyn Monroe and the President's dalliance with Mafia molls, ensured that the FBI

end of financial fraud, like the Clinton's Whitewater property scandal in Arkansas, or the Arabscam operation in which FBI agents pretended to be Arab sheikhs and videotaped Congressmen taking bribes. This latter event recalled some of the historic Washington scandals like the Teapot Dome, back in 1923, during the presidency of Warren Harding. Albert Fall, the Secretary of the Interior, persuaded the Navy Secretary to transfer government oil reserves to the con-

director was unsackable. President Lyndon Johnson put it succinctly: "I'd rather have him inside the tent pissing out than outside pissing in." After Hoover died in office, the FBI scandals began to leak out, including the largely illegal COINTEL Progamme, in which the FBI organized and authorized break-ins and burglaries against Black Panthers and activists protesting the Vietnam War.

Recent scandals have been at the boring

trol of the Department of the Interior, which then leased drilling rights to private investors. Fall earned $100,000 from the Doheny oil corporation, and $300,000 from the Sinclair oil company for leasing the vast Teapot Dome oilfield. When found out, Fall resigned, and went to work for Sinclair. He was later convicted of taking bribes worth, in modern terms, at least $10 million.

This was peanuts compared to the sums involved in the greatest Washington scandal of the 19th century, the $4 million in 1870s money siphoned off from the Internal Revenue Service by the Whiskey Ring. This was

Left, Richard Nixon accepts responsibility on nationwide television in 1973 for the Watergate break-in. **Above**, the Watergate complex.

a group of distillers in St Louis who were closely involved with Colonel Orville Babcock, the chief aide to President Ulysses S. Grant. They provided him with a beautiful blonde courtesan known as The Sylph, whose red underwear became legendary, and cigars wrapped in $1,000 bills. Babcock was twice acquitted of wrongdoing, after President Grant gave evidence to the court on his behalf. Babcock, who had been General Grant's military aide in the Civil War, almost managed to win the island of Santo Domingo for the US flag through bribing its President, Buenaventura Baez, but the Senate refused to ratify the deal. The feats of

reminder of the 1972 Watergate scandal in a book called *Silent Coup*. The book claimed that the real Watergate conspiracy had been hatched deep inside the Pentagon in order to discredit Nixon for his detente policies towards the Kremlin.

Watergate remains the classic scandal because it led to the fall of a president. It all began in the election year of 1972, when a team of dirty tricksters attached to the Nixon re-election campaign were accidentally caught red-handed when they tried to bug the headquarters of the opposition. The offices of the Democratic National Coalition were in Washington's prestigious Watergate

"Orville the Incredible" had everything – sex, bribes, tax evasion and secret international deals by a military hero working inside the White House. He provided the first of the classic Washington scandals, and even got away with it.

Washington's best scandals never die, but rumble endlessly on through the courts and media, and then through books and the yellowing copies of old newspaper files, until they finally pass into legend and develop a new kind of life as footnotes to history. Ex-president Richard Nixon, for instance, found the 1990s opening with a best-selling

building (then owned by the Vatican). Bob Woodward and Carl Bernstein, two cub reporters on the *Washington Post*, were in the police court when the bugging team came up for trial – and a White House phone number was found in their possession. So began the long and tangled trail which finally connected Richard Nixon to the former CIA agents in the bugging team. Two years after the Watergate break-in, Nixon was finally forced to resign.

But the theories of what really lay behind Watergate continued long after Nixon's disgrace. There was a theory that the CIA deliberately discredited Nixon to avoid an inquiry into its own (illegal) covert operations in dealing with protesters against the Vietnam War. The Soviet newspaper *Pravda* claimed all along that "forces of imperialism and the military-industrial complex conspired against a peace-loving President who had reached new understandings with the Soviet Union." The Chinese suggested that the KGB had helped topple Nixon because he had become too friendly to Beijing. *Silent Coup* was one of many conspiracy theories. One of the villains in this revamped version of the ultimate Washington scandal was Bob Woodward, the *Washington Post* reporter

Even while *Silent Coup* made the best-seller lists, Washington was awash with other reverberations of the scandals of the previous decade. A crack in the CIA's wall of silence over the long-dormant Irangate scandal (in which the Reagan administration covertly backed the right-wing Contras in Nicaragua) widened into a breach which brought a new round of criminal charges in the affair which simply refused to pass into history. Five senior CIA officials were formally placed under scrutiny by the Irangate Special Prosecutor, after Alan Fiers, the Agency's head of operations in Central America from 1984 to 1986, turned state's

who helped break the original Watergate story. Before getting into journalism, Woodward had been in Naval Intelligence (true) where he had briefed senior Pentagon staff including the future White House aide General Alexander Haig (unproven). Haig later became the *Washington Post*'s Deep Throat (unproven), the inside source whose leaks to Woodward from the White House sank the Nixon Presidency (true).

Left, Hollygate: *All the President's Men*. **Above**, J. Edgar Hoover kept files on both John and Robert Kennedy.

evidence in order to avoid further charges.

This revival of the Irangate affair, and the return of the time of troubles for the CIA, gave an eerie new life to issues that seemed long buried, from the Irangate scandal, to the October Surprise, to the trial of Panama's Manuel Noriega which explored the CIA's readiness to wink at drug trafficking by its sources. What they all had in common, including the way that the BCCI international banking scandals threw up links to the CIA, was the way the Reagan presidency gave its spies and covert operators a free-wheeling license to operate, with scant regard for law and morality, in the name of national security. The single name which linked all the cases together was President Reagan's own spymaster and Director of Central Intelligence, the late William Casey.

The most dramatic of these cases is the "October Surprise," the allegation that the Reagan campaign conspired with Iran in 1980 to prevent the release of the hostages from the US Embassy in Tehran before Reagan challenged Jimmy Carter for the presidency. William Casey, a member of the Reagan campaign team, is said to have held secret negotiations with Iranian officials in Paris and Madrid in 1980, designed in effect

got around this by using proceeds from the covert sale of arms to Iran, a ploy which Casey claimed to have inspired in a bizarre deathbed confession to the *Washington Post* journalist Bob Woodward (there's that name again). But Irangate contained all the crucial ingredients of a really juicy Washington scandal. First, Congress could get its own investigating committees involved, and second, the law had been broken so there was a court process with leaks from lawyers and from the grand jury. Third, there was some bizarre black humor which helped fix the scandal in the public mind.

The tabloid media which helps fix the

to help Ronald Reagan steal the election.

Mr Casey was also a shadowy presence in court in the trial of Manuel Noriega in Miami, where the defense called into evidence bank statements which showed that Noriega was on the payroll of Casey's CIA as a regular informant, and that his dealings with Cuba and with Colombian drug-runners were at the CIA's behest.

In the Irangate affair Casey was again a central figure. Congress was appalled by Irangate because it had legally banned the US government from financing the Nicaraguan Contras. The Reagan administration

image of any scandal likes an oddity. Take the Pumpkin Papers, at the heart of the scandal which gave us the word McCarthyism. Whittaker Chambers, an ex-Communist who began testifying in the late 1940s about Communist sympathizers in government before the hearings of the then Congressman Richard Nixon and Senator Joe McCarthy, owned a farm in Maryland. It included a pumpkin patch. One of the highlights of his testimony against the State Department official Alger Hiss was that some secret papers had been hidden in one of his pumpkins.

The Irangate affair also began bizarrely,

when White House aides took a cake and a Bible to the Ayatollahs in Tehran, to start the relationship which led to the transfer of $150 million in US arms and spare parts from Israel to Iran. Irangate became special when the villain of the case became a hero. Marine Colonel Oliver North, a zealous military aide in the National Security Council of the White House, stood before the US Congress in his uniform and his medals and announced that his only crime was patriotism. Finally, there was a beautiful woman in the case, Oliver North's secretary Fawn Hall, who smuggled some of the crucial documents out of the White House in her underwear.

TV. But Irangate returned to the headlines when the Special Prosecutor began probing into the work of the CIA in central America when the Irangate funds were steered to the Nicaraguan Contras. (Oliver North, in the meantime, became a high-profile DC politician.) This focus on the CIA's role not only placed the late William Casey in the spotlight, it also turned up the heat on Casey's deputy director, Robert Gates, President Bush's choice to be the new director of Central Intelligence. Mr Bush had other reasons for disquiet at the way the ghosts of the scandals were crawling from their graves. As the vice-presidential candidate in 1980,

North was later convicted of obstructing the course of justice by shredding White House documents before the investigators came to collect evidence. The popular President Reagan rode out the scandal by suggesting that he had not been paying attention at the time. This claim was widely believed after the White House admitted that by 6pm on an average day he was usually in pyjamas for a quiet evening dozing in the front of the

Heirs and disgraces: left, Lt-Col. Oliver North; General Manuel Noriega. Above, Marion Barry, the mayor who came in from the cold.

and named by some witnesses as a possible participant in the October Surprise meetings in that year, the President had a personal interest in the matter. As a former director of the CIA at the time when General Noriega was apparently recruited as a CIA agent, George Bush had a professional interest in that case too. But he probably never got to know him well enough to investigate Noriega's red underpants, worn to fend off the voodoo spells of his enemies. The legendary Sylph of President Grant's scandalous years doubtless had other, more wholesome, motives for her choice of scarlet underwear.

"My dear," the State Department's legendary Chief of Protocol, Ambassador Joseph Read was once overheard to announce at an embassy party, "you've no idea how many diplomats I have to expel each day! When I started this job I told them to ring me at any time day or night if they had a problem. These days, I only answer the phone for homicide or pillage."

Overseeing the manners of Washington's foreign embassy community is a taxing job, if the behavior of its other foreigners is anything to go by. There is a temptation among those representing their businesses *en poste* to a little informal delinquency – be it only in ignoring the parking rules, in chauvinistic comment, or in a somewhat aggressive response to the nation's speed limit. Diplomatic behavior, too, tends to get a little out of hand. After all, there is nothing so pleasant as pushing against the fences when one is an almost-protected species.

Diplomatic impunity: Protected these diplomats certainly are, with their traffic-snarling motorcades, their exclusive "S" license plates that exempt them from paying fines for parking anywhere they please or for blocking the narrow side streets of Georgetown with rows of limousines as they are delivered to and from their parties.

These pivotal events where policies, not recipes, are discussed and proposed, are generally held in the residences of the ambassadors. The formal bureaucratic work is done in the less glamorous chanceries. Washington's embassies are for the most part wonderfully pompous or exotic edifices, with columns, turrets, gargoyles, stucco and fluting and – considering their central situations – set in astonishingly large gardens. Most of the embassies line Massachusetts Avenue and 16th Street.

The fact that the embassies, though well

protected, are accessible to the public, being placed as they are so directly on the street, makes them vulnerable to protesters and pickets. This is not necessarily a bad thing. Though a law banning demonstrations within 500 feet of embassies was in force at the time, picketers during the mid-1980s at the South African Embassy, opposite the British Embassy, nevertheless got their anti-apartheid message across. The effect that their regular shouts, placards and arrests had

on the traffic on busy Massachussetts Avenue helped to dramatize and change the way Americans looked at South Africa and the plight of black South Africans.

Of course, having an embassy doesn't guarantee keeping one. When an ambassador's government falls back home, the ambassador often falls too, particularly if his demise has been caused by a coup or revolution that has ousted his entire party of support. Some diplomats squat defiantly in place: the Panamanian Embassy sided with their American hosts and refused to recognize General Manuel Noriega, accused of

Preceding pages: the ambassador of Myanmar (Burma) with family. **Left,** lunchtime at the official French residence. **Right,** maid takes a break from duties in the Spanish Embassy.

drug-running and other wrong doings. From one day to the next, an ambassador may be required to pack up the champagne and wait until his flight back home leaves.

The embassies themselves generally survive, but not in the case of the Iranian Embassy of the 1970s, once the neighbor of the South African Embassy. During that decade, this was where some of Washington's most lavish parties were held. "The youngest champagne we serve is Dom Perignon '69," was the house motto. Journalists writing social columns could not be chastised for using that over-worked word "glittering." The guests were as exclusive and flowing as

Anglophiles relish, though other Americans, less patriotic, may giggle.

It is important, as social occasions tend to follow a regular pattern, to be able to offer an angle that captures the interest of Washington society. It can be something as simple as where one comes from: the embassies of Eastern Europe, so much in the news for awhile, enjoyed a sudden, though passing, vogue. Later on, the Hungarian Embassy was the focus of Washington gossip with the arrival of a charming ambassador who had no previous diplomatic experience at all. *Le tout* Washington waited agog as rumors circulated of Hungary's displeasure at its am-

the champagne. But when the Shah was toppled, so was his ambassador in Washington. The Embassy was seized in 1980 by the United States and converted into offices for the State Department.

Diplomatic life appears from the outside a pleasant, if repetitive affair. There are the stylish parties, the useful luncheons, the important dinners, the drinks parties, the cultural events and National Day celebrations. At the British Embassy, a traditional brick manor house design by Edwardian architect Sir Edwin Lutyens, dinner guests raise their glasses to the health of the Queen, which

bassador's social success – too politically incorrect for them, perhaps, though Washington loved the dogs, the parrot and the mynah bird that came with the household. He was recalled at exceptionally short notice back to the motherland.

Social success is a fragile thing. The Canadian Embassy, with its glamorous youngish ambassador and his wife, were the center of attraction for some time, until the wife, furious that a much-courted White House aide was not about to grace her party, slapped her social secretary in front of Canadian journalists, an unfortunate audience. Despite her success creating a desirable social salon of opinion makers, power brokers, respected politicians and journalists, that slap swept it all into thin air and public disgrace.

Though the ambassadors of those nations playing a central role in world politics have a serious and influential job to do, for many lesser nations and their senior diplomatic staff, the posting is a gentle passage in which to enjoy being part of a civilized city with a ready-and-waiting social scene. But those at the less prestigious end of the embassy lists are not as likely to be invited to participate quite so frequently; ambassadors whose pay checks seem so often delayed are reduced to

young audiences on the edge of their seats.

No sneakers: But if nothing else needs to be borne in mind to keep one's social head above water, the absolutely crucial thing to understand on the dime-thick invitation cards is the dress distinction between "Informal" and "Casual." There is never a call for blue jeans and sneakers in the latter category. And a scribbled "P.M." in the lower corner does not stand for after lunchtime, but for *Pour Memoire* – "to remind you."

These wives' spouses may arrange small informal lunches to lobby mid-level Capitol Hill bureaucrats, or an off-the-record meeting ("but read my lips") with local journalists

living on the canapés and snacks of the cocktail circuit.

For the diplomatic wives who do not work there are charities and fund-raising committees to join, art gallery lectures to attend, instructive courses to take and the amateur theatrical to give one's all to. The Adventure Theater at Glen Echo for children is a popular repository of diplomatic talent, with embassy wives throwing themselves into dramatizations of fairytales that keep their

Left, fruits of the job: shopping at Safeway's.
Above, African ambassadors at a UN reception.

and foreign correspondents, while their ambassadors tackle the serious negotiations with Congressional heavyweights and State Department officials. Though these meetings may appear relaxed occasions, the ambassadors are unlikely to be discussing the latest exhibition at the National Gallery of Art. They will be using this and any other opportunity to broach policy issues – their own and those of the United States.

Among the embassy community, as on Capitol Hill, working breakfasts are popular. Not only is this a useful time of day for a visiting politician to meet his own press for in-depth briefings, but in some cases the restricted size of these events makes them admirable occasions for dropping "exclusive" information. The need for embassy officials to create opportunity to make their nation's views understood has become such a competitive race in a tight but filled social year that public relations firms in Washington have been booming.

These experts in the arts of subtlety and the profitable use of hospitality devise all manner of social events in order to draw to their receptions for visiting musicians, traveling art collections or conservation activists, those American officials who can exert some

everyone on the scent of the story of what is really going on.

There are over 1,000 foreign correspondents, including film cameramen, filing millions of words for newspapers, journals, radio and television stations. There is hardly a recognized nation, however small, however impoverished, that does not have at least one press representative in Washington.

Many use the facilities of the National Press Building on 14th and F streets, NW. Unlike the senior diplomats with their established run-of-staff residences, the correspondents live where they choose, throughout the city and its suburbs. While in general a

real influence over their clients' particular foreign nation.

Taking note of all this in the hope of making sense of it for the readers back home and, more importantly, reporting what is taking place on the Hill and in the White House are the foreign correspondents. Correspondents, too, need to build their contacts, in order to have to hand interpreters of the political scene prepared to be quoted in the foreign press. So they join in the round of the breakfast briefings, the lunches, the dinners at embassies, in diplomatic households and the homes of other news media hounds;

diplomatic tour in Washington lasts for three years in the larger embassies (though of any length greater for smaller nations), journalists are usually in town for the full span of a presidential term.

They come in, if they can, with the election campaign or the inauguration of a new president. There is a practical side to this timing. Congressmen and senators, state officials and bureaucrats weighed down by their own work, may not find the time, once they have their feet firmly under their Capitol desks, for a correspondent newly arrived in the middle of a presidential term, particularly one from a country that may not have much significance for them. It is easier to make and develop those crucial contacts when all parties are "new and eager boys" together. The optimum time to make contacts with the administration is during the election campaigns, when staff members enthusiastically make themselves available to members of the press from anywhere. They all use the same campaign planes, stay at the same hotels, and drink at the same bars.

Career opportunities: The foreign community also includes vast numbers of employees of foreign businesses, large and small, who can be posted for whatever stretch of

taking place on the Hill, in the Pentagon budget, at the World Bank or the International Monetary Fund. Hence a watchful eye is necessary.

A quick read through the yellow pages of Washington's telephone directory gives a glimpse of what may be happening politically, economically and socially in the rest of the world. As the lists of Vietnamese restaurants stand as a reminder of America's involvement in that South East Asian war, the high presence of Japanese firms confirms the growth of Japanese investment in the United States. The biggest investors of all, however, are the British. This creates very little stir, as

time the home company thinks necessary for the benefit of the firm. Like the journalists and many of the diplomats, they come with their children, settle into local neighborhoods, enroll their children in local schools and sign them up for baseball and soccer teams. As political decisions back home may be taken on the basis of a newspaperman's editorial or an embassy's briefing, the profits of many of the larger conglomerates depend on the Washington office analysis of what is

Left, *les enfants du France, avec pumpkins.*
Above, diplomats enjoy numerous privileges.

their names hardly show up as foreign.

Much of what can be gained in a posting abroad is in the relationships formed with the locals. A posting to Washington may be wonderfully glamorous, but the focus upon American and world affairs takes up so much time and energy that some members of the foreign community have been known to leave the capital without ever having bothered to know any Americans who didn't have a desk on the Hill. This is a pity, both for America and for the people who come here, for cultural exchange is one of the most interesting facets of life in Washington.

CULTURE AND CHERRY BLOSSOMS

Washington takes its time out seriously. Among the people who run the city and for whom the city is predominantly run, culture comes with a capital C. Dress is often black tie and the most sought-after invitations are for strictly formal events. But though the diplomats and the power brokers may set their chins for the fund-raising dinners or the theatrical season, there are nonetheless a couple of sectors of Washington that enjoy themselves in a more lighthearted way. The young residents of Adams Morgan, the African-American, Hispanic, Asian and student neighborhoods have a range of cultural activities which might well remind any junior embassy official of the exoticism of home.

While mainstream Washington makes a point of leaving its dinner parties promptly at 11pm (lights in suburban homes are out by 10.30), in Adams Morgan, or downtown on Connecticut Avenue, or along southwest Washington's waterfront and up Georgia Avenue, the beat goes on. Bars and nightclubs line the streets.

Concrete egg box: Power Washington is happy to focus its cultural life on the Kennedy Center, with its six theaters housed in a rectangular concrete egg box that overhangs the Rock Creek Parkway along the banks of the Potomac. The Opera House and the Concert Hall, home of the National Symphony Orchestra, are the sites of the most glittering of Washington's cultural events, drawing international stars and companies. Washington's opera season is always a magnet to the city's social elite. Imaginative and sometimes daring productions – from its celebrated production of Maria Ewing singing Strauss's *Salome* and writhing through the dance of the seven veils completely naked, to the very esoteric and rarely heard *King Arthur* by the 17th-century English composer Henry Purcell – draws a packed

audience ready-dressed in its cocktail best.

Culture does not have to come all dressed up, however. One lovely concert hall which is accessible to the general public is the Wolf Trap Farm Park's Filene Center, off the Dulles Toll Road in Vienna, Virginia. Although it's necessary to get there by car, this open-air auditorium has sweeping lawns in front, on which you can picnic before a performance. The repertoire includes music, ballet, jazz and pop. In Washington itself,

there are several smaller stages where a black tie would be positively out of place.

Foremost among these are the Arena Stage, the Studio Theatre, the Woolly Mammoth Theatre Company and Ford's Theatre, where Abraham Lincoln was shot. Their drawback is that they are not always well served by the capital's theater critics, who in over-praising less worthy productions do not force the companies to strive for the kind of standard one would expect from theater in a key capital city.

The exception to this is the Shakespeare Theatre at the Folger, on East Capitol Street,

Preceding pages: Cuban singer and friend on Adams Morgan Day. <u>Left</u>, the District's Charlie Byrd is well known at local club Blues Alley. <u>Right</u>, ex-Congressman's wife-cum-singer.

SE which stages Shakespeare's plays inside an intimate reproduction of the original Globe Theatre of Elizabethan London. Under the direction of Michael Hands, the company tackles Shakespeare with originality, often presenting leading actors from the film world in key roles. Stacey Keach, who became famous as TV's tough private eye Mike Hammer, impressed audiences with his intimately evil Richard III.

The National Symphony Orchestra is probably the greatest pivot for the melding of Washington's cultural with its social life. Though supported by the National Endowment for the Arts, the orchestra needs mil-

racy of its own, every bit as exclusive and powerful as the titled salons of old Europe. Every day of "the season" (September until June) these people's social calendars are filled with appointments to dine at meals that they will have paid for themselves. The meals don't come cheap and if they do come free, beware – they don't always come sponsored by the pure in heart. The private dining rooms of Washington hotels have been the scenes of breakfasts hosted by shady Savings and Loans officials eager to soften the hearts of congressmen and senators, or luncheons thrown by banks that have set the world money markets reeling with horror.

lions of dollars more each year to keep going and a doughty team of Washington's social crème de la crème see that this is earned through fund-raising. Washington's most respected public figures, hostesses and senior members of its diplomatic community spend a good deal of their social lives at fund-raising events that are dedicated to keeping the symphony orchestra and the opera offering up-market entertainment for yet another season.

In fact, fund-raising itself is a prime source of entertainment for Washington's power elite. Fund-raising has produced an aristoc-

Favors are floated, temptations subtly intimated, power increased, territory acquired, briefings given, at generous meals in hotels such as the Hays-Adams, the Ritz-Carlton, the Mayflower, and the Hotel Washington. Dinners follow a similar vein, whether actual funds are involved or not. While venerable Washingtonians congregate at four-figure-dollar plate dinners for their favorite causes, foreign diplomats along Embassy Row and in Georgetown bring together influential political figures over private dinners to express among the chink of champagne flutes the kinder, more humane version of their nation's political viewpoints.

Apart from the private dinners for the glitterati that take place in Georgetown, that area of the capital has diminished as a center for night-time fun and games. Some night clubs remain, like the Bayou, where you can hear up-and-coming bands in a concrete hall that holds around 500 people. But the commercial heart of Georgetown today is two main thoroughfares lined with overpriced boutiques and overstretched restaurants. To maximize the enjoyment potential, one should preferably be under 30 years of age, over 30 Gs in salary, and have a strong shouting voice. These are *noisy* restaurants.

Avenue NW, at clubs like the Chaconia Lounge, Eugertha's and Ibex.

Adams Morgan, a "gentrified" neighborhood of South American and Third World restaurants and clubs, is the place to go for exotic entertainment. In fact, you will probably eat as well in Adams Morgan as you will anywhere in Washington, where so often the menu reads better than the food tastes.

Honest cooking: Neither the restaurants in Adams Morgan nor those in Arlington, Virginia, just the other side of the Potomac, suffer from that Washington dining disease of pretentiousness, because their cuisine is genuinely ethnic – in Arlington predomi-

The young bloods of town love a good shout at the end of a hard day's work.

What Georgetown does have is Blues Alley, located in an alley off Wisconsin Avenue behind M Street. Blues Alley is where top-name entertainers perform, attracting to its dim and smoky room people like Nancy Wilson, Quincy Jones and Thelonius Monk. Otherwise, there is little left of the Washington jazz boom of the 1940s and '50s. What survives can mostly be found along Georgia

Left and **above**, Cherry Blossom Festival beauty contestants.

nantly Vietnamese and South East Asian – and produced by chefs who would not have been tolerated back home for anything other than honest cooking.

Washington likes to think of itself as a culinary outpost in the civilized Western world. Pampered European gourmets may sneer that it still has a long way to go, particularly if you do not have the luxury of an expense account. The problem seems to be that restaurants often try too hard, or fall into believing that quantity is the same thing as quality. Power Washington is admirably served by a range of top-line restaurants presenting excellent French, Italian and European food. The disappointing experiences come in that gap somewhere between the fast food emporia and the $50-a-head meal.

This is where the ethnic food restaurants come into their own. Most are reasonably priced and the dishes are accurately presented because of the abundance of Third World spices, pulses and vegetables found in shops along Columbia Road and in Arlington. Restaurants striving to serve modestly priced European fare are less fortunate in their supplies, being bound by laws that restrict the import of dairy and meat products essential in provincial European dishes.

Adams Morgan Day, traditionally held in September, when the streets are packed with enthusiastic Washingtonians.

Imperial blossoms: One of Washington's most public events is the annual Cherry Blossom Parade, which attracts up to 200,000 visitors. These decorative trees along the banks of the Potomac came about because of a symbolic blossoming of US–Japanese relations some 80 years ago.

It began with a remarkable American botanist, David Fairchild, founder of the Foreign Plant Introduction office at the Department of Agriculture, who is credited with introducing some 75,000 new varieties

Washington's Hispanic, Asian and African-American communities see to their own entertainment well. Along with a generous supply of specialty restaurants, one community or another appears to organize a street party or a festival practically every weekend. Usually announced ahead of time in the weekend pages of the Washington newspapers, these are exuberant events, with their beauty queens, their calypso, reggae, mariachi bands, single-stringed instruments, tin bells, cymbals and drums, decorated floats, vivid dancers and booths of strange and exotic foods. The most colorful is

into North America. His name is now accursed by many farmers and private gardeners because Fairchild brought in the *kudzu* vine from the Orient as a livestock food and as an excellent soil restorative during crop rotation. But the vine spreads so rapidly and has proved so tenacious that it has become known as the killer weed.

In his travels in the East, Fairchild fell in love with the Japanese cherry blossoms, and brought back some seedlings which he grew successfully at his private estate in Chevy Chase, just outside Washington. He sent his children strolling down Connecticut Avenue into the city, dropping cherry tree seedlings as they went. These attracted the attention of Helen Taft, who in 1910 was wife of the current president and thought Japanese cherry trees would be just the thing to cover a local eyesore by the Potomac river.

A thoughtful Japanese Ambassador cabled back to Tokyo that US–Japanese relations could be happily cemented with a gift of 2,000 young trees, which were then shipped across the world at considerable expense. The trees would last at least 30 years, said the flowery note from the Japanese emperor, which would symbolize the enduring friendship between the two coun-

In 1935, the city fathers inaugurated the annual Cherry Blossom Festival as a way to attract tourist trade. It has continued with only one interruption, from 1942 to 1951, the result of anti-Japanese sentiment. These days there is a three-hour Cherry Blossom parade, with bands and floats and a Miss Cherry Blossom contest. The date shifts with the weather and the peak time of blossoming, but is usually in the first two weeks of April. Only a few dozen of the original 1912 trees still remain, most of the rest having succumbed to old age, but the stocks are constantly renewed through exchanges with the city of Tokyo, which continue to this day.

tries. (He was not far wrong. The friendship ended when war broke out after the Japanese attacked Pearl Harbor, exactly 31 years later.) This first shipment of 2,000 trees were burned soon after their arrival when US Customs found they were diseased. Undeterred, the Japanese tried again, and in the spring of 1912 a new consignment of 3,000 healthy trees had been planted along the banks of the Potomac river and have become a pride and fixture of the city ever since.

Left, *A Wonderful Life* **at the Arena Stage. <u>Above</u>, performer at the Kennedy Center.**

For those who find parades and street festivals not cerebral enough for their amusement, there is Filmfest DC, usually held the first two weeks of May. Over the years this has developed into a showcase for premiering dozens of American and international films. With first-time screenings in cinemas across the city, exhibitions, and much publicized celebrity receptions, Washington's film festival has become one of the top film markets in the country.

All this makes for a city where it is very easy to let your hair down – or pin it scrupulously up – and enjoy yourself.

There are three kinds of sport in Washington. The first is the most visible, the informal fun that takes place on the volleyball courts near the Lincoln Memorial alongside the Potomac river, the softball and frisbee tournaments around the Washington Monument, and the impromptu basketball games played on street corners throughout the inner city on hot summer nights.

Then there are the spectator sports, the Redskins football team at the R.F. Kennedy court was opened by President Teddy Roosevelt long before World War I. It has seen tragedy, when the son of President Calvin Coolidge died from blood poisoning after carelessly lancing some blisters acquired after a hard-fought set. It has seen comedy, when Vice-President Spiro Agnew served so erratically that his doubles partners used to take cover.

President Bush's game was formidable to all who had the dubious good fortune to face

stadium and the Capitals ice hockey team and the Washington Bullets basketball team. But even though tickets for the Redskins are part of the hard currency which buys influence among lobbyists and power-brokers, the sport which most obsesses political Washington is tennis.

Tennis matters here in a quite extraordinary way, and not only because the political alliance between President George Bush and Secretary of State James Baker was forged through winning successive doubles championships on the courts of the Houston Country Club back in the 1950s. The White House him on court. Although let down by a weak serve, he played hard, rushing to the net after his serve and volleying ferociously. His son Marvin became one of the best players in the city, and the father and son team were a match for most serious players.

Net gain: Two Democratic senators from the southern states, Bennett Johnson and John Breaux, are credited with a major coup. Lurking deep inside the Hart building of the US Senate is a vast indoor and air-conditioned tennis court whose existence few taxpayers have ever heard of. And if you want to understand how Washington tennis works in a political sense, look no farther than the energy bill to drill Alaska's pristine Arctic Wildlife Reserve. Close to the oilman heart of George Bush, the bill was steered through the Senate by Energy Committee chairman Bennett Johnson. Guess what they talked about between sets. The sooner Greenpeace starts fielding a tennis pro in its lobbying team, the better it'll be for its cause.

Various sources agree that Washington's brand of power tennis began when a tennis

Ritzenberg is now the pro at the St Alban's club, which is attached to one of the exclusive private schools, where ex-CIA Director William Webster plays with senators and Supreme Court justices. On the ladies' courts the Democratic party's foreign policy guru Madeleine Albright plays with Mrs Dan Quayle.

Courting the politicians: There are several high-prestige courts around Washington, of which the most discreet may be that put into

pro called Allie Ritzenberg launched a tennis clinic in the capital at the start of the Kennedy years, and the heady cocktail of power, macho sport and celebrity began to brew. Indeed, the former Senator Eugene McCarthy still half-seriously blames Ritzenberg for escalating the Vietnam War, since after each lesson in the grip of the topspin forehand, Defense Secretary Robert McNamara would go back to the Pentagon all buoyed up to despatch another couple of divisions to the fields.

<u>Left</u> and <u>above</u>, boys on the ball.

play by Congressman Steven Solarz when he was one of the most influential figures in the foreign policy establishment. There are also the Navy Yard courts, where Congressmen play without a fee, and the Congressional Country Club in the northern suburbs, the YMCA courts in Arlington and the private court at the vice-presidential mansion which George Bush made into a stellar setting in his eight years of residence.

Diplomatic tennis was pioneered by the legendary former Swedish Ambassador, Count Wilhelm Wachtmeister. A formidable player in his own right, Wachtmeister was also able to recruit the world champion Bjorn Borg to make up a doubles team with hopefuls like George Bush. Several of Washington's more interesting political friendships were forged on Wachmeister's court, including the long-standing mixed doubles team of former Secretary of State George Shulz and Katherine Graham, formidable dowager of the *Washington Post*.

'Skin deep: Throughout the winter months, the ritual Washington greeting on Monday mornings is "How 'bout them 'Skins." This requires no reply, but does identify you as a native. Ever since the Washington Redskins first reached the football Superbowl finals in

1973, won it 10 years later, and again almost 10 years after that, the team has been taken to that part of its bosom the city normally reserves for its expense account receipts.

The 'Skins cross every barrier of race and class and sex, and unite Washington in a remarkable way. This is partly because the city has twice woken up one morning to find it no longer had a baseball team.

It lost one to Minneapolis and another to Texas, and now has to make do with the Baltimore Orioles, who are an hour's drive away. Still, they are enough of a local team for President Bush to have taken the Queen

of England and the President of Egypt for a day at the ballpark. (Former Soviet President Mikhail Gorbachev was offered a ballgame, but chose horseshoe-pitching at Camp David instead.)

Named after the state bird, the Orioles have moved to a brand-new stadium worthy of Baltimore's most famous sporting son, the legendary Babe Ruth. But it is still in Baltimore. To the utter humiliation of the capital, even the expansion of the Major League did not help Washington's chances. The coveted new slots went elsewhere, since the decline in Washington's real estate boom left the city without the fat-cat investment guarantees that the Baseball Commissioners regular require.

The Redskins have sold out R. F. Kennedy stadium since before Jimmy Carter came to Washington. The waiting list for season tickets is now more than 10 years long. To hear the longest laugh in town, call their ticket office and ask if they have any spare seats. To attend a game, and have the privilege of eating lukewarm hot dogs while your neighbors tune in to the radio commentary and you peer at the midget activity on the field below, you will have to find a kindly local who will invite you along.

You may be rich and/or powerful and/or famous and/or beautiful enough to be invited into the private box of the owner. Otherwise you do what the rest of the city does and watch Sunday night football on television, and mourn the fact that the 'Skins have yet to find a quarterback worthy of their runners and receivers.

The much-maligned city government has created an admirable Recreation and Parks Department whose adult sports and street basketball programs are credited by some cynics as a major reason for the lack of local riots, however long and hot the summer. After the price of high-tech baseball shoes soared above $100 in 1990, however, there were two bizarre murders of young Washington blacks – apparently for their coveted designer footwear.

This caused surprise only among those who had never watched the intensity with which informal basketball games are played. The city runs over 130 playgrounds and recreation centers, and the Adult Sports Programme keeps a list of local league events, some of them close to professional standard. The Malcolm X recreation center, on Alabama Avenue and Congress Street SE, is one nursery of professional players, and while Potomac Gardens on 12th and G streets SE is locally more famous as a drug market, the basketball is brilliant. Go in daylight, but only take your disposable wallet.

Paddling the Potomac: Washington got its reputation as a maritime city when the British Army took advantage of the tide to come up the Potomac and burn the White House in the 1812 war. Then Richard Nixon spent his

has been sold off. There are marinas and, from the seafood restaurants beside the fish market on Maine Avenue, you can watch the boats cruise down towards the Chesapeake. For real sailing, you should start at Annapolis, where the US Navy has taught its young officers since the days of sail.

Do not even think about swimming in the Potomac River. It is dirty, polluted and dangerous. People have been swept to their deaths even while scrambling along the rocky banks near Great Falls, just up-river from the city.

There are crowded but pleasant beaches within an hour's drive of the city, at Sandy

summer evenings aboard the *Sequoia* presidential yacht. And the witnesses in the trial of Mayor Barry talked about the interesting houseboat parties he used to attend on the Washington marina. So the impression has spread that this is a serious marine center. Not exactly. You can hire boats, canoes and surfboards, but the Potomac's main use for water sports is to provide downriver access to the Chesapeake Bay. Even the *Sequoia*

Left, coach Allie Ritzenberg with socialite pupil Joan Braden. **Above**, former Olympic medalists on the Potomac.

Point state park, off Route 50, just west of the Chesapeake Bay Bridge, or ocean beaches farther away on the Atlantic side of the Delaware peninsula.

The city's 30 public swimming pools are usually full and can be rowdy, since naturally they have been placed mainly where the local population is less able to afford a private pool in the backyard. These private pools should be treated with respect: a *Washington Post* journalist won an acquittal after he shot and winged a teenager who clambered over the fence into his back yard for a secret dip one hot summer's night.

PLACES

"Driving around Washington, it seems like everybody knows where they're going but me," observed a resident of eight months' standing. In fact, even long-term Washingtonians with a fixed destination often find themselves navigating the city's traffic circles more often than they would like. Frustration is intense because, on a map, getting around ther District looks so simple.

Architect Pierre L'Enfant's 1793 design was a masterpiece of city planning. Based on a diamond-shaped grid, with the Capitol as its central point, the city is divided into four quadrants: northeast, northwest, southeast and southwest. North and South Capitol streets form the border between east and west, while the Mall and East Capitol Street serve as the division between north and south. The quadrants are mirror images of each other: numbered streets run north and south, lettered streets run east and west. Once the alphabet has been used up, east/west streets have two-syllable names: Adams, Bryant, Channing, etc. When these run out, three-syllable names begin: Albemarle, Brandywine, Chesapeake, etc.

Unfortunately, this elegant system is then invaded by rogue elements, like diagonal avenues – named for American states – and other streets which criss-cross in a disorganized fashion. Contemporary planners have added to the confusion by implementing one-way systems and changes of lanes during rush hours.

A simple way around all this is to walk, rather than drive. "Monument Washington" is perfect for pedestrians, although bear in mind that the historic appellation "The City of Magnificent Distances" still applies – things are further away than they look. Fortunately, Washington has more open spaces than almost any other town in America, so finding a place to rest footsore feet, either around the Mall or in areas like Georgetown or Dupont Circle, is rarely a problem.

Neither is finding a Metro stop, even outside the city in nearby Arlington or Falls Church. Beyond the suburbs are the green rolling hills of rural Maryland, where you can sail in the Chesapeake Bay or visit Baltimore and Annapolis. In Virginia are the cool, smoky Blue Ridge Mountains, perfect for hiking and camping, plus more sites of Civil War battles than any other state in America.

Washingtonians *do* appear as if they know where they're going, and are very determined to get there. With such a variety of pleasant places to choose from, can anybody blame them?

Preceding pages: the White House, founded in 1792, is the oldest public building in the capital; the Jefferson Memorial was completed in 1943; Georgetown was originally part of the state of Maryland; the Great Hall of the Pension Building. Left, the Washington Momument is the prevailing vertical in a largely horizontal city.

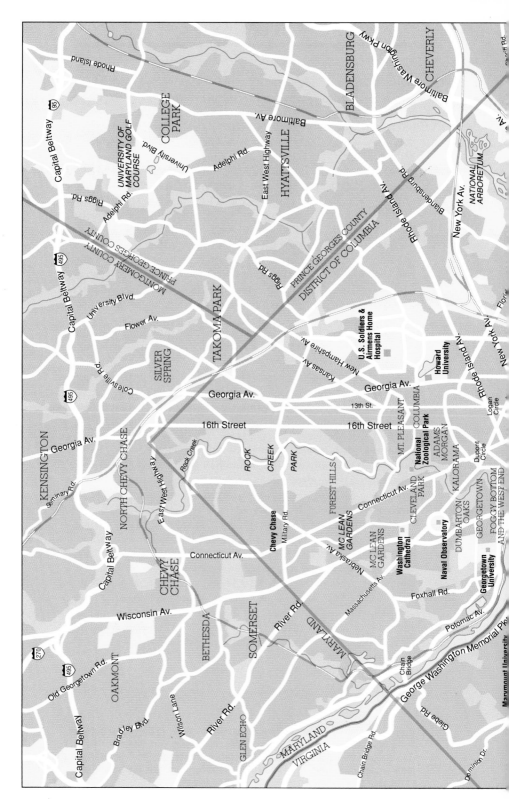

Rhode Island

CHEVERLY

BLADENSBURG

Baltimore Washington Pkwy

95

Capital Beltway

COLLEGE PARK

UNIVERSITY OF MARYLAND GOLF COURSE

University Blvd.

Adelphi Rd.

Riggs Rd.

Adelphi Rd.

East West Highway

HYATTSVILLE

Baltimore Av.

NATIONAL ARBORETUM

New York Av.

Blandensburg Rd.

Rhode Island Av.

495

Capital Beltway

MONTGOMERY COUNTY

PRINCE GEORGES COUNTY

PRINCE GEORGES COUNTY

DISTRICT OF COLUMBIA

University Blvd.

Flower Av.

Riggs Rd.

TAKOMA PARK

New York Av.

495

Colesville Rd.

SILVER SPRING

New Hampshire Av.

Kansas Av.

U.S. Soldiers & Airmens Home Hospital

Howard University

Floric

Rhode Island Av.

KENSINGTON

Georgia Av.

Georgia Av.

Georgia Av.

13th St.

COLUMBIA

MT. PLEASANT

National Zoological Park

Logan Circle

New York Av.

Seminary Rd.

NORTH CHEVY CHASE

16th Street

16th Street

ADAMS MORGAN

Dupont Circle

KALORAMA

Rock Creek

ROCK

CREEK

PARK

FOREST HILLS

CLEVELAND PARK

Connecticut Av.

DUMBARTON OAKS

East West Highway

Chevy Chase

Military Rd.

MC LEAN GARDENS

GEORGETOWN

FOGGY BOTTOM AND THE WEST END

CHEVY CHASE

Connecticut Av.

Nebraska Av.

MC LEAN GARDENS

Washington Cathedral

Naval Observatory

Georgetown University

Massachusetts Av.

Foxhall Rd.

270

Capital Beltway

Wisconsin Av.

BETHESDA

SOMERSET

River Rd.

MARYLAND

Potomac Av.

Marymount University

495

Old Georgetown Rd.

OAKMONT

Bradley Blvd.

Wilson Lane

River Rd.

GLEN ECHO

Chain Bridge

George Washington Memorial Pkwy

Glebe Rd.

MARYLAND

VIRGINIA

Chain Bridge Rd.

Dominion Dr.

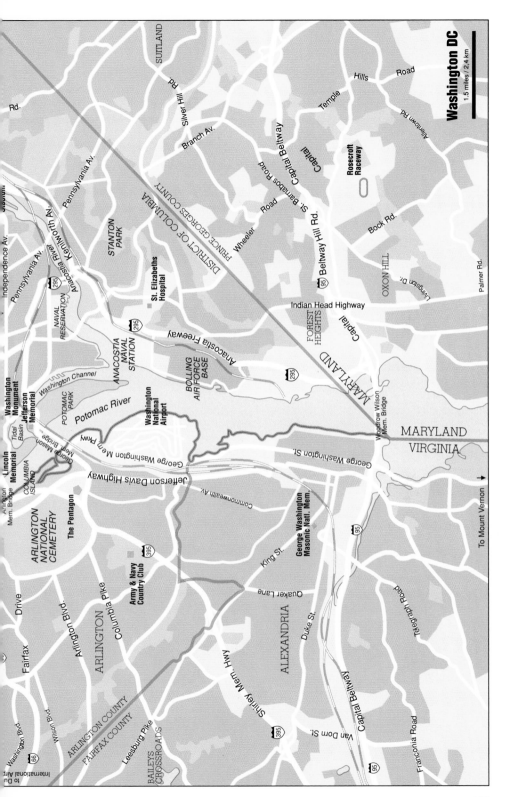

Washington DC

1.5 miles / 2.4 km

SUITLAND

Rd.

Hills   Road

Temple

Allentown Rd.

Silver Hill Rd.

Branch Av.

Capital Beltway

Capital

Rosecroft
Raceway

Wheeler   Road

St. Barnabos Road

Bock Rd.

Beltway Hill Rd.

95

OXON HILL

Livingston Dr.

Palmer Rd.

Rd.

Pennsylvania Av.

STANTON
PARK

Kenilworth Av.

PRINCE GEORGES COUNTY

DISTRICT OF COLUMBIA

Independence Av.

Pennsylvania Av.

295

Anacostia River

NAVAL
RESERVATION

St. Elizabeths
Hospital

295

Indian Head Highway

Capital

FOREST
HEIGHTS

295

MARYLAND

Washington Channel

ANACOSTIA
NAVAL
STATION

Anacostia Freeway

BOLLING
AIR
FORCE
BASE

Washington
Monument

Jefferson
Memorial

POTOMAC
PARK

Potomac River

Washington
National
Airport

Woodrow Wilson
Mem. Bridge

MARYLAND
VIRGINIA

Tidal
Basin

Lincoln
Memorial

COLUMBIA
ISLAND

George Mason
Mem. Bridge

George Washington Mem. Pkwy.

Jefferson Davis Highway

George Washington St.

To Mount Vernon

Arlington
Mem. Bridge

ARLINGTON
NATIONAL
CEMETERY

The Pentagon

Commonwealth Av.

George Washington
Masonic Natl. Mem.

95

Fairfax

Drive

Arlington Blvd.

Columbia Pike

ARLINGTON

Army & Navy
Country Club

395

King St.

Quaker Lane

ALEXANDRIA

Duke St.

Telegraph Road

Fairfax

Wilson Blvd.

ARLINGTON COUNTY

FAIRFAX COUNTY

Leesburg Pike

BAILEYS
CROSSROADS

Shirley Mem. Hwy.

395

Van Dorn St.

Capital Beltway

95

Franconia Road

Washington Blvd.

66

to Du
International Airp

133

THE WHITE HOUSE

A trip to the White House is almost imperative as a confirmation of national loyalty. To an American, it is on a par with a Frenchman visiting Napoleon's tomb in Paris, or a Briton checking up on Buckingham Palace – an essential in terms of "touching base." To a non-American, the White House offers an agreeable change from tours round the much larger and institutional buildings of tourist Washington.

Peak patience: During the high peak season, however, the more casual followers of cultural experiences would do well to understand that to penetrate the White House takes considerable determination, particularly if you are in the company of small children. Go armed with snacks if you don't care for the supplies at the kiosks close by – and bushels of patience. Also be warned that there are no public restrooms inside the White House; portaloos are available in the park on the Ellipse.

Entry to the White House is every citizen's right – every foreigner's, too – so tickets to the White House are free, and they run out quickly. The National Park Services ticket booth opens at 8 am and closes when the ticket supply for that day is taken. This happens pretty speedily during the summer. By arriving at 9 am, for instance, the earliest tour you are likely to be on is the 12 noon tour – number 13 out of 15 tours.

Once secured of a place, you are directed to the bleachers to await the signaling of your tour number. If you are looking at more than one hour's wait, it is probably better to walk to one of the hotels close by for a cup of coffee, or, if with children, up and east a few blocks to the shops on 14th and F streets NW. Make your way back to the site of the crowds 10 minutes before your tour is scheduled to leave. Then get in line to be shepherded by park rangers slowly towards the White House. For children,

all this walking can be extremely tiring even before you have reached the Executive Mansion itself. In peak season around 6,000 people are shuffled through the White House; during low season periods, the wait is usually no longer than an hour.

Once inside, security is similar to airport scrutiny, with metal detectors and bag surveillance. The tour itself – a self-guided shuffling behind the people ahead – lasts no more than 20 to 30 minutes. There are five public rooms on show: the East Room, the Green Room, the Blue Room, the Red Room and the State Dining Room. The tour exits along **Cross Hall** and through another large reception area with piano – the **North Entrance Hall** – onto the front steps of the White House.

On the ground floor, where the tour begins, are a **Library** and the **Vermeil Room**, housing a collection of gilded silver, the **China Room** and a **Diplomatic Reception Room**, on either side of which hang portraits of recent First

Left, high-level talks in the Oval Office. Right, White House in winter.

Ladies in strikingly similar stance. None of these rooms can be penetrated beyond a braided rope, and secret service men are everywhere to make sure that you adhere to the rules and behave with decorum. Given the assassination attempt on President Reagan and general fears of terrorism, it is a wonder the White House is open to non-invited visitors at all.

The security men are fairly prepared to answer questions, but they are somewhat daunting individuals. The only other indication, though, of the function of each room is on a floor placard, so it's wise to buy the guide on sale on the lower floor before starting the tour.

The White House, founded in 1792 and designed in the Georgian style by the Irish architect James Hoban, is the oldest public building in the capital. It is so-called because George Washington insisted on a stone facing to the brickwork. Sandstone was quarried from Aquia Creek in Virginia so soft that it had to be immediately whitewashed.

Another version of how the White House received its name is that, after the War of 1812, the stone was painted white in order to hide damage by fire. Although the nickname the "White House" was in use for many years, it was only recognized by Congress as the official title of the Executive Mansion in 1902.

The **West Wing** of executive offices and the **East Wing** entrance and *porte cochère* were added around the turn of the century by President Theodore Roosevelt. Under President Harry Truman, who worried that his bath might crash through the ceiling below during some crucial reception, the entire interior was gutted and reinforced, at a cost of $6 million, increasing the White House from 48 rooms to **54 rooms**. Almost nothing of the original building was left, particularly after lumps of stone from the building were engraved with masonic symbols and dispatched by President Truman to masonic lodges throughout the nation.

Demonstration of Wright Type B airplane, 1911.

During the four years of renovation from 1948 onwards, the Trumans lived opposite, in Blair House, now the president's guest quarters. Later, the interior of the White House underwent substantial change, starting with the efforts of Jacqueline Kennedy. In 1961 she formed a Fine Arts Committee to restore the rooms to their original style and grandeur. Upon discovering that the walls of the Blue Room may have been white during the tenure of Dolley Madison, she altered them to white silk.

Its current blue-bordered beige wallpaper was put up by Mrs Richard Nixon. Lady Bird Johnson, who preceded her, persuaded President Lyndon Johnson to establish the Committee for the Preservation of the White House, with its own curator – now an enduring White House post. Rosalynn Carter began an endowment for its decoration, while Nancy Reagan employed California decorator Ted Graber to make over the second and third-floor quarters.

Except for George Washington,

every president has lived in the White House. When the second American president, John Adams, took up residence in 1800, the house was still incomplete. During the War of 1812 with the British, the White House was severely burned and had to be restored by the original architect, James Hoban. President James Monroe instructed Hoban to add the **South Portico** in 1824. President Andrew Jackson raised funds for the **North Portico**, which was added in 1829.

The private part of the White House is, obviously, not open to the public. But the anecdotes of the private lives of some of its incumbents do slip out. Gossip column addicts were agog at the start of the Clintons' tenure to read of the stream of Hollywood personalities flowing through the White House. Barbra Streisand, it seemed, had an almost permanent room, until it became clear that this kind of expression of glamour and glitz was not what the public expected from the White House.

isenhower
nd Nixon
eet the
ress.

It had been more comfortable with Nancy Reagan's extravagant entertaining, or with Barbara Bush revelations that her family enjoyed being photographed in **Lincoln's bed**.

Some of the close family events that occur in the White House are deliberately made public – as when the marriage of President Nixon's daughter, Tricia, took place in the **Rose Garden**, designed by Jacqueline Kennedy as a present to her husband. And it is always amusing to mull over the recipes in books by ex-White House chefs, to glean a nuance of the tone of the White House under the related incumbents.

The rooms on view reflect the kind of elegance you expect from a house that is a public showcase, particularly when considering the caliber of "public" that is entertained here – the monarchs, the heads of state, the celebrities, the politicians. In the white and gold **East Room**, with its Art Deco **Steinway grand piano** supported by gilded eagles, are held the balls, the entertainments that follow state dinners, and most formal ceremonies. These ceremonies can strike a somber note: seven presidents have lain in state in the East Room, including presidents Abraham Lincoln and John F. Kennedy. In a lighter mood, both Alice Roosevelt and Lynda Bird Johnson were married here. And strictly for the record: President Richard M. Nixon chose the East Room to make his Watergate resignation speech.

The **Green Room** is full of early 19th-century furniture by the New York cabinet maker Duncan Fyfe and its walls are covered in green watered silk, put up by Mrs Richard Nixon. Thomas Jefferson is thought to have been the first to choose the color scheme, when he spread canvas on the floor of the then dining room and introduced guests to new culinary treats, including ice cream. Perhaps his disregard for propriety stemmed from having lost the competition to design the White House himself, another popular theory.

The **Blue Room**, a small, oval-

President Ronald Reagan stalked the corridors of power from 1981 to 1989

shaped chamber in which the President and First Lady often receive visitors, was designed as an elliptic salon by George Washington because he liked to review his visitors standing in a semi circle around him. At Christmas, this is where the First Family usually has a tree; over 100 years ago President Grover Cleveland chose this room as a wedding chapel for his marriage.

In the **Red Room**, where the First Lady likes to entertain guests, is a piano, its sheet music opened appropriately to "A Grand Old Flag" and "The Star-Spangled Banner." This is the room in which Dolley Madison held her well-known Wednesday-night receptions and musicals. The color of the room is inspired by a chair in the portrait of Dolley Madison.

The **State Dining Room**, whose 1902 wood paneling was painted a pale green under President Truman's incumbency, is still the antique ivory color selected by Jacqueline Kennedy to complement the gold curtains and gold

chandeliers. The room has seating for around 140 guests, plus a marble mantel inscribed with the White House prayer.

Out of bounds to the public are nine rooms on the second floor, the **Yellow Oval Room**, the **Treaty Room**, the **Queen's Bedroom**, the **Lincoln Bedroom**, the family bedrooms, the **President's Dining Room** and the family's **West Sitting Hall**. Beyond are bedrooms, utility rooms, billiard and storage rooms. From here, a few steps lead to the **Solarium**, where President Carter listened to classical music.

Nor is the West Wing open to the public, where the President's **Oval Office** lies – the room in which he receives important guests, rising from behind a desk made of the timbers from *HMS Resolute*. Also in the West Wing are the **Cabinet Room**, the **Appointments Lobby** and the **Roosevelt Room**, where staff conferences take place.

A list of American presidents can be found in the Travel Tips section.

Former First Lady Barbara Bush with Britain's Princess Margaret.

THE MALL EAST

When someone mentions the Mall, chances are that they are referring to that great, grassy, pebble-pathed pedestrian strip stretching between 3rd and 14th streets. Of course, this was not exactly what Pierre L'Enfant had in mind for the Mall. The city planner had envisioned something along the lines of a grand, mansion-lined and landscaped central boulevard running along the main east-west axis from the Capitol to somewhere near the present site of the Washington Monument. Unfortunately, his more ambitious plans were shelved, at least long enough for some of the land to be used for such unglamorous purposes as grazing fields for cows, a Civil War hospital, and a railroad route.

1901 plan: The colossal green expanse you see today, which is flanked by two narrow drives named for presidents Madison and Jefferson, bears the mark of the McMillan Commission, established in 1901 to translate L'Enfant's ideas into a new city plan.

The Mall has many moods, determined by the light, by the time of day, and by the seasons. When empty it is a reflective space where you can appreciate the scale and the grandeur of the monuments, and the precision of the planner. Best known as the front yard of the Smithsonian museums and the National Gallery, it also serves as a giant jogging track and a softball field for congressional leagues. Frequently the setting for concerts, festivals, gatherings, and all manner of happenings, it is also the traditional rallying point for protest marches and demonstrations.

Among the major events staged here is the annual Smithsonian Folklife Festival, which transforms the Mall into a sizzling circus of smells, tastes, sights and sounds from the US and cultures farther afield. If you don't mind picnicking blanket-to-blanket with the crowds, this is the place to be on the Fourth of July, where the gala celebration features a free concert by the National Symphony Orchestra and, of course, a fireworks extravaganza.

Silhouetted in late afternoon light, the sleek obelisk of the Washington Monument contrasts dramatically with the Norman-style towers of the **Smithsonian Institution Building**, aptly nicknamed **the Castle**. James Renwick, Jr, architect of the Renwick Gallery and New York's St Patrick's Cathedral, designed this red sandstone structure, which was completed in 1855 – the Smithsonian Institution's first building. Today it holds administrative offices and the Woodrow Wilson International Center for Scholars, as well as an **information center**.

It also contains a museum to, and the tomb of Smithsonian founder James Smithson, a wealthy Englishman who never even crossed the Atlantic. The illegitimate son of a nobleman, and a scientist himself, Smithson bequeathed

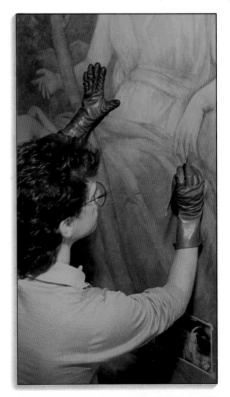

his $550,000 estate to the United States to found the Smithsonian Institution, "an establishment for the increase and diffusion of knowledge among men." The US Treasury continues to borrow this money at a perpetually fixed interest rate of 6 per cent.

The elegant Florentine Renaissance palace nearby – small-scale compared to the other Mall-side monoliths – is the **Freer Gallery of Art**. The Smithsonian's first art museum, opened in 1923, is an intimate collection of mainly Asian art donated by a self-made Detroit industrialist and art connoisseur, Charles Lang Freer. Freer's gift included his collection of etchings, plus the only collaborative assemblage of works by his friend, the painter James McNeill Whistler. Freer donated funds to the building as well as the collection; there was, however, a major string attached to the bequest: Nothing in the permanent collection could be loaned or sold, and the only outside pieces allowed into the museum were those purchased for that collection.

Between the Freer and the Castle, a copper-domed kiosk marks the entrance to the S. Dillon Ripley Center, part of the quadrangle complex on Independence Avenue opened in 1987, which also includes the **Arthur M. Sackler Gallery**, the **National Museum of African Art**, and the **Enid A. Haupt Garden**.

The garden itself is a magical mosaic of decorative sub-gardens, whose themes clearly reflect those of the surrounding museums. In fact, the whole complex is a marvelous harmony of form: the Sackler's diamond motif complements the spires of the Arts and Industries Building, while the African's circles relate to the Freer's arches.

While the descent to the subterranean galleries of the Sackler and the African is akin to entering a mausoleum, the galleries themselves are warm and the collections – each of which runs the gamut from ancient to contemporary – often remarkable. Highlights from the

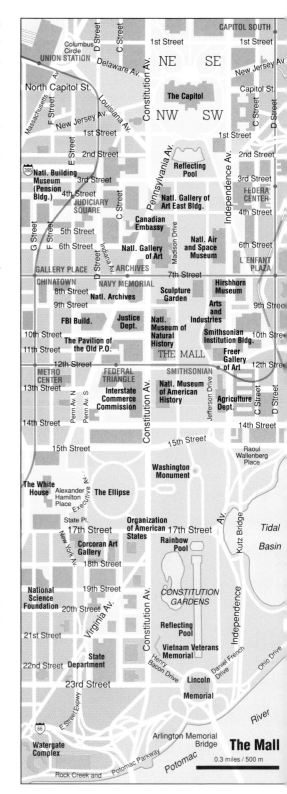

The Mall

0.3 miles / 500 m

Sackler Gallery include Ming dynasty furniture and a beautiful collection of jades; the National Museum of African Art gives cultural, as well as artistic, insight into the African way of life.

Whether or not you're interested in Asian or African art, you should at least go down to the galleries to admire the remarkable feat of engineering. Ninety-six percent of the quadrangle is below ground to a depth of 57 feet, which required waterproofing the entire structure and designing a special roof to support the 4-acre garden above – much of which is deliberately landscaped to conceal structural elements below. As if that weren't enough, the architect also had to figure out how to preserve a century-old linden tree.

The Philadelphia Centennial of 1876, which celebrated the Industrial Revolution, lives on inside the **Arts and Industries Building** – the cheerful Victorian structure flanking the quad's east side. When this 19th-century World's Fair closed, some 40 freight-car loads of leftover international exhibits were shipped to the Smithsonian, prompting the Institution to build the National Museum, as it was then called, to store all of the items – an episode which earned the Smithsonian its reputation as "the nation's attic."

Finished in 1881, the exposition-style building was the most modern museum in the country. Every item displayed in its dizzyingly busy interior was either exhibited at the Expo or produced during that era including furniture, jewelry, and even horse-drawn carriages. The museum shop is good for inexpensive Victorian-repro gifts and, in keeping with the mood, an old-fashioned carousel still turns and grinds on the Mall outside the museum's entrance just as it has since 1940.

The mood next door at the **Hirsh-horn Museum and Sculpture Garden** is decidedly different. DC's cooly contemporary museum-in-the-round has been aptly described by writer E.J. Applewhite as a concrete doughnut in a

walled garden. In the summer, there is an outdoor café among the bevy of enormous abstract sculptures.

It was the wish of Latvian immigrant and self-made millionaire Joseph Hirshhorn to donate his entire collection of 4,000 paintings and 2,000 sculptures – notable both for its size and its variety of late 19th- and 20th-century art – to the country that had served him so well. The bequest, which was twice as large as the collection amassed in 50 years by New York's Museum of Modern Art, made the Hirshhorn an instant treasure, long before it even had walls. Be sure to visit the landscaped, sunken sculpture garden across the drive.

If flight rather than artists' fancy is more your thing, the **National Air and Space Museum** next door should satisfy. The most popular museum in the world, it draws some 10 million visitors each year. Although the experts who conceived and designed the three-block-long glass and marble building lacked museum experience, it only

takes a glance around the main exhibit hall at the Mall entrance to realize that the concept, like the 90-foot-tall hangar-like structure, not only works – it soars. Suspended from the ceiling are such air-age stars as the Wright brothers' *Flyer*, Lindbergh's *Spirit of St Louis*, and the *Apollo 11* space craft.

And that's only the beginning. In addition to dozens of exhibit areas covering flight past, present and future, there is a planetarium, a hands-on interactive gallery on "How Things Fly," and a theater which features flight-related IMAX films projected on to a five-story-high and seven-story-wide screen. This latter attraction is guaranteed to thrill.

Cross the east end of the Mall, which is dominated by the imposing edifice of the Capitol, to Madison Drive and you will run into the West and East Buildings of the **National Gallery of Art**. Incongruous as they seem side by side – the one neoclassical and the other starkly contemporary – these structures

The "nation" attic": the Arts and Industries Building.

complement one another architecturally as well as artistically. While the National Gallery was chartered by Congress in 1937 and is operated by the federal government, it relies exclusively on private and corporate contributions for acquisitions.

The seed for a national gallery was planted by the industrialist and Treasury secretary Andrew W. Mellon, who built his collection of 121 Old Masters, including 21 paintings purchased from Russia's Hermitage Museum, with the idea that he would eventually give the collection away. In addition to these Old Masters is the high-tech **Micro Gallery**, an interactive multimedia computer system designed to help even techno-phobes find their way around the museum's vast collections.

The esteemed John Russell Pope was commissioned as architect for the **West Building**. Its dome happens to look distinctly like that crowning the Jefferson Memorial, which Pope also designed. A traditionalist, Pope chose a classical design, firstly, because official Washington was classical, and secondly, because he believed that it conveyed the appropriate image for a serious art gallery. One of the world's largest marble structures, it was to be the last of the District's heroic, neoclassical monuments. After perusing its 522,000 square feet of floor space, enjoying classical art by Raphael, Renoir, Gainsborough and others, you may want to rest your feet in one of the lovely garden courts, or have a bite in the garden café. Free (with an advance pass) Sunday evening concerts are held seasonally in the **West Garden Court**.

An underground concourse complete with a moving walkway, an ample museum shop, a café and buffet, and the Mall's only espresso bar, links the West with the **East Building**. When Mellon stipulated that the area to the east of the gallery be reserved for future expansion, the challenge of designing a structure for this odd, trapezoidal lot fell to the creative master architect, I.M. Pei.

vptian
ımise at
National
llery of Art,
st Building.

He resolved the problem by slicing the trapezoid diagonally and creating two interlocking, symmetrical triangles. He further balanced the site by lining up the central axis of the West Building with the midpoint of the triangular base forming the main block of the East. You don't have to be a mathematician to appreciate this bold and luminous building-as-sculpture, mercurial as the light that plays across its blade-sharp edges and planes.

Pei's brilliant use of triangular geometry infuses the interior with a sense of movement. Open balconies and bridges sweep across the atrium, decried by critics as "wasted space" or Pei-ian self-indulgence. The undeniably dramatic museum, which exhibits all manner of 20th-century art, from Henry Moore sculpture to pieces by Alexander Calder, is remarkable for its flexibility, accommodating the smallest and most intimate shows to the most international blockbusters. The Terrace Café overlooks the Mall and offers a more refined alternative to the Concourse eateries.

As you walk west, passing the tree-ringed ice rink (in season), which faces the National Archives on Constitution Avenue, the hulking **National Museum of Natural History**, subtitled the **National Museum of Man**, looms ahead. When the Hornblower and Marshall building opened in 1910, it was dubbed the "new" National Museum. Be forewarned that it is one of the more popular museums on the Mall, a fact you won't dispute if you choose to venture into the four-story-high rotunda on a typical summer day. As you wander through its three floors and labyrinthine halls, which literally exhibit everything under the sun, from dinosaur skeletons to the Hope diamond, the biggest blue diamond known to exist, bear in mind that all that you see represents only a fraction of the more than 81 million items stored here.

The pink marble box next door to the National History Museum is the **National Museum of American History**, designed by the Beaux-Arts firm of McKim, Mead and White, and eventually completed in 1964 by Steinman, Cain and White. Originally called the National Museum of History and Technology, it was created to house the Philadelphia Centennial leftovers that would not fit in the Arts and Industries Building. With its lively focus on *things* – more than 16 million objects – you will truly believe that you have wandered into the "nation's attic." Or garage, given that exhibits include a Ford Model T automobile and a Conestoga wagon like the kind that traveled to the West Coast "frontier" during the California Gold Rush. Other exhibits include a display of inaugural gowns worn by presidential wives; the first-ever typewriter; the flag which inspired Francis Scott Key to write the words to America's national anthem; and George Washington's false teeth. The museum shop is good, as is the cafeteria. There's an old-fashioned ice-cream parlor in the Palm Court.

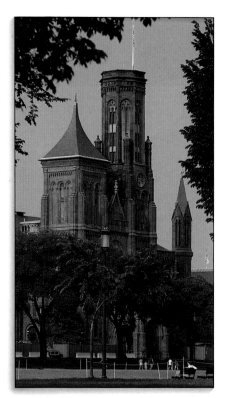

Left, the Smithsonian "Castle". **Right**, taking a shine to Mr Lincoln.

THE MALL WEST

South of Constitution Avenue and west of 14th Street to the banks of the Potomac sprawls an oasis of urban parkland, tree-shaded and watered, that comprises the westward extension of the Mall. Unofficially, it also takes in the **Ellipse**, the 52-acre oval field south of the White House, where the national Christmas tree stands each year. Set apart from the museum-lined corridor across the way, this is sacred ground – the heart of monumental Washington.

One of the most enjoyable ways to explore this area, apart from walking, is on a bicycle. Miles of paths weave through the trees, around the memorials, and along the riverfront. You may find, though, that you prefer to drive or to take a Tourmobile between the major monuments; distances are farther away than they originally seem once you strike out on foot.

The prevailing vertical in the horizontal city of DC is the **Washington Monument**. It is the essential memorial to the nation's first president, the District's quintessential symbol and landmark – and the invariable object of ribaldry. A few hundred feet west of the monument, you will find the Jefferson Pier marker, designating the monument's *intended* site at the intersection of the city's east-west and north-south axes – in line with the White House. The spot proved to be too marshy (Constitution Avenue was then part of the C&O Canal), so the monument had to be built on higher and drier ground, which threw the true east-west axis off by one degree to the south.

Ask a National Park Service ranger about the color change in the monument's shaft and you may be told that it is a high-water mark. Or that it is the height to which the monument is folded at night so planes don't crash into it. Actually, the color change marks the switch from Maryland to Massachu-

setts marble after a temporary halt in construction. When the discrepancy was noticed, building stopped again until a more compatible quarry was found. The obelisk was finally completed in 1884 with just under 900 steps leading to the observation deck at the top. It was the tallest structure in the world until the Eiffel Tower was completed five years later. It's very crowded during the day; the most romantic time to visit is on summer evenings when the monument is open until midnight. (*For more information, see "Washington for Kids," pages 183–187.*)

Down the slope and off to the side of the monument stands the small outdoor stage of the **Sylvan Theater**. On sultry summer nights it's a great spot to spread a picnic, share a bottle of wine, and enjoy a Shakespeare play, a rollicking musical, or a concert.

While you're in the vicinity, you might consider a detour down to the "new" **Bureau of Engraving and Printing** at 14th and C streets. Until

World War I the "old" bureau was housed next door in what is now called the Auditor's Building. All of the country's paper currency – about $20 billion a year – is produced here, along with treasury notes, postage stamps, White House invitations, and assorted other printed matter. You can tour behind-the-scenes and watch the stuff roll off the presses, a sure thrill for latent and blatant capitalists alike.

The bureau's neighbor at Independence and D streets, the privately funded **United States Holocaust Memorial Museum**, is a sobering tribute to the 6 million Jews and other victims of the World War II Holocaust. The story is told through documentary film, photographs, artifacts and oral histories. Particularly moving is the Hall of Remembrance, a hexagonal, skylit spiritual space for reflection and contemplation, where visitors can light memorial candles and where a perpetual flame burns for the dead.

After this, you may be ready for some fresh air and the serenity of the **Tidal Basin** nearby. Not a monument but undeniably monumental, this free-form "lake" was created in 1897 to trap the overflow from the estuarial Potomac River and drain it into the Washington Channel. A photographic cliché when the cherry trees are in bloom, it is nevertheless one of the city's beauty spots, great for picnicking, paddleboating, or perambulating.

Historic blossoms: The cherry blossom trees, Washington's most distinctive horticultural image, originally came from Japan. According to one local correspondent who has researched their background, since the trees were planted around 1912, there have been some local difficulties. When President Franklin D. Roosevelt ordered ground broken for the Jefferson Memorial in 1938, bulldozers went into the cherry groves and found some local matrons chained to the trunks in protest. During World War II, there were spasmodic ax attacks on this symbol of Imperial Ja-

A short stop for sightseeing.

pan, and such vandalism was then made a federal offense. Occasionally, a hapless tourist trying to break off some blossoms is giving a stern warning of imprisonment by one of the vigilant Park Police.

Bill Anderson is the chief scientist for the National Park Service, and it is his annual duty to stroll through the groves to establish which is the day to announce peak blossoming, which he reckons at 70 percent in bloom on 70 percent of the trees. Mr Anderson explains that this is a tricky calculation because the Japanese cunningly sent two varieties of cherry tree. Roughly two-thirds are Yoshino, and these bloom an average 10 days earlier than the other variety, the Kwanzan. March 16, in 1990, was the earliest day ever recorded for peak blossoming. Nevertheless, Washington's Cherry Blossom Festival kicks off the first weekend in April, blossoms or no blossoms.

If you want to join the annual pilgrimage to this spring cherry blossom mecca, park your car elsewhere and walk in, or use public transportation. A nocturnal stroll under the glowing trees, set off by stunning views of the monuments, is a magical experience, but it's best to exercise caution if strolling around once the sun has gone down.

The Basin's shoreline path will lead you to the steps of the domed and graceful **Jefferson Memorial**, arguably one of Washington's prettiest monuments, especially at night. Designed by John Russell Pope and landscaped by Frederick Law Olmsted, Jr, the monument-in-the-round recalls the Roman Pantheon, a nod to Jefferson's own fondness for that ancient structure and similar to the president's designs for his own home, Monticello. Built on the soft site of a dredged swamp, which characterized much of the Mall, the memorial, which was completed in 1943, required for reinforcement a foundation of concrete-filled steel cylinders sunk 135 feet down to bedrock. The domed building is ringed by 54 Ionic columns. Not

ounging by
e Lincoln
emorial.

everyone loved the monument. Critics decried its form as too "feminine," or as a "cage for Jefferson's statue," a 19-foot-high bronze sculpted by Rudolph Evans. The memorial marks the southern point of the Mall's north-south axis, with the White House forming the counterpoint.

To the south is **East Potomac Park**, a peninsula that dangles between the Potomac River and the Washington Channel, and which forms the southern half of a 700-acre riverside park. The views are superb, and you can watch planes take off and touch down across the river at Virginia's National Airport. This is also a good place to enjoy the springtime cherry blossom trees, where there are fewer crowds than around the Tidal Basin.

The peninsula's tip, **Hains Point**, holds a wonderful surprise: a giant figure breaking through the earth. The sculpture, *The Awakening* by J. Seward Johnson, Jr, was installed in 1980 as part of a citywide sculpture show.

Climbing on the sculpture is encouraged by the artist.

Stay a northwestern course through **West Potomac Park** and you will find the incomparable shrine to Abraham Lincoln: a neoclassical temple of gleaming, white marble cresting its acropolis. Familiar as its image, which graces the back of the penny and the $5 bill, Henry Bacon's design for a **Lincoln Memorial** – which was selected over John Russell Pope's – was dedicated on Memorial Day in 1922. It was a sad irony that day that one of the key speakers, the black president of Tuskegee Institute, was ushered away from the speaker's platform and seated in the segregated black section of the audience across the road.

Similar to Athens' Parthenon, the building is fronted by a colonnade of 36 Doric columns, the exact number of American states in the Union at the time of Lincoln's death. The columns slope inward to avoid looking out of proportion. Above the columns is a frieze with the names of these 36 states; higher still are the names of the 48 states that were in the Union at the time the monument was dedicated.

Daniel Chester French designed the famous figure of Lincoln, the tallest president, seated inside the memorial. If this marble Lincoln were to stand up, he would reach 28 feet. When it was discovered that Lincoln's naturally-lit face was nearly obscured, General Electric was called in to install special artificial lighting to create the shadows on his hair, brows, cheeks, and chin.

From the memorial, you can savor Lincoln's magnificent view across the **Reflecting Pool**, the elegant, 2,000-foot waterway and promenade inspired by Versailles and the Taj Mahal, to the Washington Monument and beyond to the Capitol. Attractive at any time, the scene is most dramatic in the light of dawn or dusk.

To the south of the Reflecting Pool is the **Korean War Memorial**, dedicated to all veterans or those killed or missing

The design for the Vietnam Veterans Memorial was one of 1,500 competition entries.

in the Korean conflict. The site features an American flag at the point of a triangle which thrusts into a circular pool. Nineteen statues of soldiers and a mural with many faces are also featured.

Sandwiched between the Reflecting Pool and Constitution Avenue is the green swath known as **Constitution Gardens**. After the last of the temporary wartime structures was demolished in 1966, President Richard Nixon proposed that the area be developed as a Disneyesque amusement park. Fortunately, the idea was soundly vetoed. Instead, you will find a tranquil setting of shady trees and bench-lined paths which meander alongside an artificial lake. A lovely little island in the lake contains a memorial to the signers of the Declaration of Independence.

The most subtle and emotionally powerful of the Mall's monuments, the **Vietnam Veterans Memorial**, stands just a short distance away through the trees to the west of the lake. It was a Vietnam vet who proposed the idea of a memorial, which Congress authorized in 1980. Selected from nearly 1,500 entries in an open design competition, the contemplative V-shaped wall of names – 58,183 casualties – in polished black granite was designed by Maya Lin, a 21-year-old Yale University architecture student and the daughter of Chinese immigrants.

To assuage the critics of Lin's abstract "rift in the earth," a representational statue of three soldiers and a memorial flagpole were erected.

Veterans' groups have set up makeshift shelters and tents near the memorial which are used as 24-hour vigil sites. In addition to selling mementoes and advertising their political grievances, the groups and shelters are there for the vets themselves, who come to reclaim the wall in the privacy of night. By day the wall belongs to the public – who file reverently by to gaze, to discover their own reflections, to touch a name, to leave flowers or a poem, or to make a wall rubbing.

ui Tin, ormer olonel in ne North ietnamese rmy who defected" 1 1990.

CAPITOL HILL AREA

From the long green sweep of the Mall, the **US Capitol** floats like a white mirage above the city. Icon of the federal republic and symbol of Washington, the Capitol has been the center of the city's political life since 1800 when the first joint session of Congress was called to order. Today, nearly 20,000 Congressional staff members, hordes of lobbyists and camera- and notebook-toting members of the media swarm like bees around the Capitol hive.

Capitol classic: L'Enfant designed the Capitol to be the geographical center of the city, the heart of the four equally developed quadrants, but the city developed primarily westward instead. Although the Capitol itself is surrounded by beautiful grounds and massive marble buildings, this grandeur doesn't extend far into the city's Southeast quadrant. The Capitol Hill neighborhood includes a small historic district of charming row houses, and a wedge-shaped residential area formed by Florida Avenue, Benning Road, Interstate 395, and the Potomac River in both Southeast and Northeast. Here, you'll find clusters of restaurants and bars, several notable attractions, and much of the city's lower-income housing. Caution is advised, however, especially at night, since these neighborhoods have contributed significantly to DC's high rate of violent crime.

The original US Capitol was designed by Dr William Thornton and its cornerstone laid by President George Washington in 1793. Not all stones were laid with such authority. After initial funding problems, plus one major fire (set by the British in 1814), nine architects, two roofs, and 70 years, the Capitol was finally completed and topped by its 19-foot-high statue of Freedom. The nearly 9 million-pound dome is not marble as it appears, but painted cast iron. In the spirit of democracy, the public is invited to tour the building and to stop by their representative's office for a pass for the House and Senate Galleries. Some members of Congress agree to picture-taking sessions, others to meeting groups of visitors from their home state. If American, VIP tours are also available by writing your representative in advance. If it's legislative action you're seeking, check the *Washington Post* for the day's schedule of committee meetings, then show up to see lawmakers trying as best they can to fulfill their agendas.

From the Capitol's **Great Rotunda** you can gaze up 180 feet to the interior of the Capitol dome where painter Constantino Brumidi's *Apotheosis of Washington* depicts George Washington and other colonial statesmen mingling with a bevy of loosely robed allegorical figures. You can also visit **Statuary Hall**, the handsome **Old Senate Chamber**, the **President's Room**, and the **Old Supreme Court Chamber**. Beneath the Rotunda is the **Crypt**,

which displays exhibits of the history of the Capitol and a sculpture of Lucretia Mott, Susan B. Anthony and Elizabeth Cady Stanton emerging out of a marble block. Local mavens have dubbed this work *Three Old Ladies in a Bathtub*.

On the Capitol's **West Terrace**, summer concerts are offered by the armed services bands. There is no more quintessential Washington entertainment than to sit on the Capitol steps, tap your feet to a Sousa march, and watch the sun set behind the Washington Monument.

Take time to stroll the **Capitol grounds** – a former alder swamp transformed into a shady parkland by the renowned landscape architect Frederick Law Olmsted, Jr, in 1874. Now encompassing 200 acres, the grounds include some 5,000 trees, some planted in the late 1800s. Look for the Olmsted-designed **grotto and spring house** designed for slaking the thirst of parched-throat filibusterers.

For more of the lush life, visit the **US Botanic Gardens** on the southwest side of the Capitol. This 1933 conservatory houses a great variety of tropical and desert plants – many of which are supplied to congressional offices. The gardens make a great stop on cold, rainy days and during special seasonal shows. Across the street, in a charming pocket park, is one of the city's most graceful statuary groups, the **Bartholdi Fountain**, designed by Frederic August Bartholdi (of Statue of Liberty fame) and installed here in 1877.

The favorite room of many a Washingtonian is the Main Reading Room at the **Library of Congress**, located inside the stunning "Victorian Rococo" Thomas Jefferson Building just behind the Capitol. In *Washington Itself*, author E.J. Applewhite compares the room to "the inside of a square Easter egg that Fabergé might have made for a Romanov" and also to "the interior of a Baked Alaska with pistachio and gold meringue executed in marble and bronze." It takes dedicated readers to concentrate on their research in this

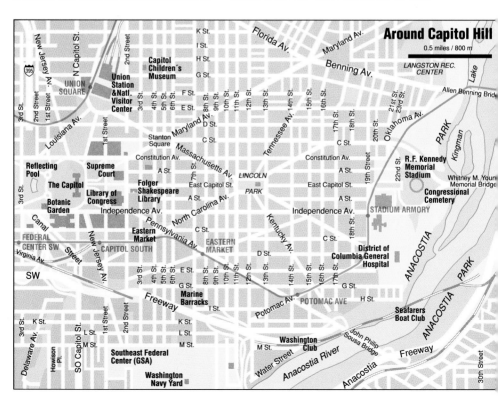

room with its 160-foot-high domed ceiling, clusters of richly veined marble columns, and its allegorical murals that chronicle the progress of civilization and human understanding.

You can visit the **Reading Room** as a researcher (if you're over 18 years old) or on a guided tour from the **Madison Building** across Independence Avenue. Equally dazzling are the library's collections: three buildings house some 90 million items featuring 27 million books and pamphlets in 470 languages, 12 million prints and photographs, 4 million maps and atlases, and a 7-million-piece music collection. Many of these items are on exhibit in the Madison Building. Some of the rarely-seen classics from the library's 100,000 motion pictures are shown in the 64-seat **Mary Pickford Theater**. Chamber music concerts, poetry readings, and lectures are presented in the library's other performance spaces throughout the year.

The severe exterior of the nearby Folger Shakespeare Library belies the cozy, Elizabethan-style interior of this great library, museum, and center of literary and performing arts. The Folger houses the world's largest collection of Shakespeare's printed works, including a set of precious First Folios from 1623. The Elizabethan and Renaissance worlds are brought to life in the **Great Hall** where many of the Folger's treasures are displayed. It's easy to imagine this hall full of mead-drinking, boar-eating revelers feasting at sturdy banquet tables.

The intimate Elizabethan-style **Shakespeare Theater at the Folger** presents performances of medieval and Renaissance music, and other educational programs. The handsome **Reading Room** is open to the public during events such as the Poetry Series, the PEN/Faulkner Fiction Readings, and Shakespeare's birthday celebration. Herbs and flowers grown in Shakespeare's time are planted in the secluded Elizabethan garden, a place to

The Supreme Court houses the smallest branch of the federal government.

contemplate "nature's infinite book of secrecy."

"Oyez! Oyez! Oyez!" With this dramatic cry the **US Supreme Court** is brought to order. This imposing marble edifice at 2nd and East Capitol streets houses the smallest branch of the Federal Government. The court employs 319 people to ensure that the executive and legislative branches abide by the US Constitution. Since the court reviews about 6,000 petitions a year, and hears oral arguments for about 125 of these cases, the court is likely the most efficient branch of government as well.

From the first Monday in October through April, the court hears oral arguments. In May and June it delivers its opinions. You can attend an entire session (seating is first-come, first-served) or get just a quick glimpse of the judicial process (ushers will seat you at a "three-minute chair"). Each attorney is given only 30 minutes for his argument. One veteran observer notes "It's like the theater to watch the attorneys scramble when they're asked to apply their reasoning to other cases and situations." In the off-season, the court room is open for tours.

North of the Supreme Court on Massachusetts Avenue is one of the city's great successes of architectural preservation: **Union Station**. This glorious Beaux-Arts train station was built in 1908 and fell into serious disrepair after World War II. In 1981, private and public funds totalling $160 million paid for the rescue job. In 1988 Union Station's former grandeur and the romance of the rail were restored. Today, some 40,000 visitors a day pass through Union Station's doors.

The entrance features a grand triple-arched portico modeled after the Arch of Constantine. In the Main Hall – inspired by the Roman Baths of Diocletian – Amtrak passengers, Metrorail riders, lunching Capitol Hill staffers, shoppers and visitors surge and flow in perpetual motion. Several cafés, first-class restaurants, a 9-screen movie

The Beaux-Arts Union Station was built in 1908

theater, and dozens of shops and fast-food stands keep the station lively day and night. East of the station, around North Capitol and F streets, you'll find a bit o' Ireland and tables o' politicians at The Dubliner, The Irish Times, and Powers Court restaurants.

Behind the station at 800 3rd Street is the **Capitol Children's Museum**. The exhibits here are designed to let children learn through experience as diverse as play-riding a bus or taxi or learning about the Mexican culture by making tortillas and hot chocolate. The museum's greatest accidental PR event is staged near closing time when parents begin coaxing and pulling their children away from the museum's captivating gizmos and gadgets.

Beyond the pull of the nine-to-five world of Capitol Hill is a neighborhood of townhouses and low-rise shops and restaurants. The south side of Pennsylvania Avenue, from 2nd Street east to Potomac Avenue, is lined with such long-standing watering holes as the Tune Inn and the Hawk and Dove, as well as pizza parlors and Greek, Thai and Japanese restaurants. On Massachusetts Avenue, between 2nd and 4th streets, you'll find rib-sticking German dishes at Café Berlin, American fare at Two Quail and American Café, French food at La Brasserie, and dessert at Bob's Famous Homemade Ice Cream.

A lively spot for breakfast or lunch is **Eastern Market** at 7th and C streets (just north off Pennsylvania). This block-long building dates from 1873 and houses vendors selling fresh produce, meat, poultry, seafood, and cheeses every day but Sunday. Prices aren't exactly cheap, but the old-market atmosphere and the quality of the goods are worth every penny.

Get in line at Market Lunch, a 20-year-old institution famous for its hearty breakfasts, crab cakes, and oyster sandwiches. On Saturdays and Sundays, vendors set up shop outside and sell baked goods, flowers, antiques, clothing, jewelry, and junk. Also on 7th

augural alls are eld in the ation's arbled hall.

Street is Roasters on the Hill, a friendly espresso bar where roasting, brewing, and serving coffee is an art.

On the south side of Pennsylvania you'll find the **Marine Corps Barracks** at 8th and I streets, home of the "Eighth and Eye Marines." Make reservations well in advance for the Friday evening Marine Corp parade held here in summer. With unmatched precision and patriotism, the Band, the Drum, and the Bugle Corps as well as the silent drill team assemble within the quadrangle for a ceremony that makes you proud to be American, even if you're not. The sight of a solitary, spotlighted marine playing "Taps" from the parapet of the main tower is guaranteed to send chills up your spine or bring tears to your eyes.

Ten blocks east of the barracks is **Congressional Cemetery**, at 1801 E Street. Opened in 1807, these burial grounds include the graves of senators, diplomats, prominent members of Congress as well as Capitol Hill architect William Thornton, "March King" John Philip Sousa, Civil War photographer Matthew Brady, FBI director J. Edgar Hoover, and Choctaw chief Pusha-mata-ha. Walking-tour maps are available.

A jaunt north on 19th Street brings you to the **R. F. Kennedy Stadium/DC Armory complex**. The five-tiered circular stadium seats 55,000 sports fans who flood here to root for the Washington Redskins. Since tickets are sold out for the next 26 years, and the waiting list is 42,000 long, you'll have to pay hawkers' high prices or watch the games on TV. Tickets are easier to come by for RFK's concerts and other events.

On Tuesdays, Thursdays and Saturdays the stadium's Parking Lot 6 is turned into the **DC Open-air Farmers Market** – one of the liveliest produce markets in the city. Next to the stadium is the **Armory Hall** where you can see everything from boat shows and "Holiday on Ice" performances to the circus and political conventions.

<u>Right</u>, Eastern Market.

DOWNTOWN

Downtown Washington is as much a concept as a locale. Geographically, it encompasses a wedge-shaped area roughly bounded by Massachusetts and Constitution avenues, and North Capitol and 17th streets. Speaking Metrowise, that translates to Farraguts North and West, McPherson Square, Metro Center, Federal Triangle, Gallery Place, Archives, Judiciary Square, and proximity to Union Station.

Behind the apparent facades and public faces of its various neighborhoods, downtown is defined by the beholder. It churns and burns with power, glitters with wealth, oozes with culture, and suffers with neglect (although this is changing). It is power-lunching at restaurants like **Joe and Mo's** and **The Palm**, or dealing with the panhandling on streetcorners. It is K Street's lawyers, Pennsylvania Avenue's bureaucrats, and 7th Street's artists. It is limos stretched curbside and yuppies at their happy-hour meccas. Side by side and overlapped, it is all downtown.

In the last few years, a revitalization of the area has taken place, starting with the opening of restaurants like **Planet Hollywood** and the **Hard Rock Cafe**, and concluding with the new 20,000-seat sports arena, the **MCI Center** (home of the Bullets basketball team and the Capitals hockey team). By the turn of the century, there will also be a state-of-the-art **Convention Center** at Mount Vernon Square, with the hope of putting the city on target as a convention and trade show host.

Connecticut Avenue, with its bevy of stores and restaurants, and the sumptuous **Mayflower Hotel**, is a good place to start a downtown expedition. Just off Connecticut on Rhode Island Avenue is the deceptively plain edifice of **St Matthew's Cathedral**, which President John F. Kennedy attended. The interior, a profusion of mosaic and marble, displays an altarside marker where Kennedy's casket rested during his funeral Mass in 1963.

On the corner of Rhode Island and 17th Street is the **B'nai B'rith Klutznick Museum**. Security was stepped up after a 1977 hostage-taking incident, when Muslim terrorists held 123 people for 39 hours. The small museum, which focuses on Jewish culture, has an impressive collection of ceremonial and folk objects.

The historic, red-brick building next door is the elegantly refurbished **Sumner School Museum and Archives**. Built in 1872, the original Sumner School, named for Massachusetts senator and abolitionist Charles Sumner, was the District's first school for black children. Along with the archives of the DC public schools and museum exhibits, the Sumner fills its former classrooms with art shows, concerts, poetry readings, conferences, and other special arts events.

Monopolizing the M Street block be-

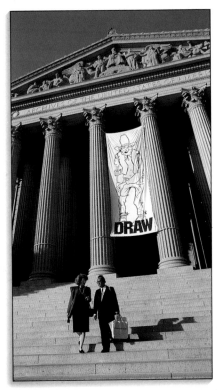

tween 16th and 17th streets is the imperious, three-building headquarters of the **National Geographic Society**. The Grosvenors, the conservative first family of the society, ironically hired Edward Durell Stone, the avant-garde architect of New York's Museum of Modern Art and the Kennedy Center, to design the modernist 17th Street building. Characteristically, the society documented the construction event with a time-lapse camera.

Explorers Hall regularly changes its exhibits, except for Geographica, the amazing high-tech, interactive journey through the vast world of geography. You can stock up on NGS publications in the shop, and if it's Tuesday, there's more than likely a free film showing at noon. For a complete listing of NGS events, pick up a calendar in the lobby.

If you continue east on M Street, past the **Jefferson Hotel**, you will pass the historic **Metropolitan AME Church** at 1518 M Street, a major underground railroad station for slaves defecting

from the south during the 19th century.

Across from the **Madison Hotel** on 15th Street are the offices of DC's hometown rag, the *Washington Post*, in print since 1877. One of the most influential newspapers in the country, the *Post* outshined them all with its legendary Watergate coverage. News junkies especially will appreciate a pre-arranged tour of the newsroom and pressroom. You can rub elbows with the press at the Post Pub or Peggy's Place around the corner on L Street.

If you walk south several blocks you'll run right into **Lafayette Park**, which squarely faces the White House. Thanks to that populist, Thomas Jefferson, this once-private presidential park is publicly enjoyed by chess players, office workers, tourists, and the homeless. Known locally as "Peace Park," it has also been a strategic site for demonstrations, tent cities, mock graveyards, and a vigilant string of protesters perpetually camped along the south side.

Among the landmarks ringing the

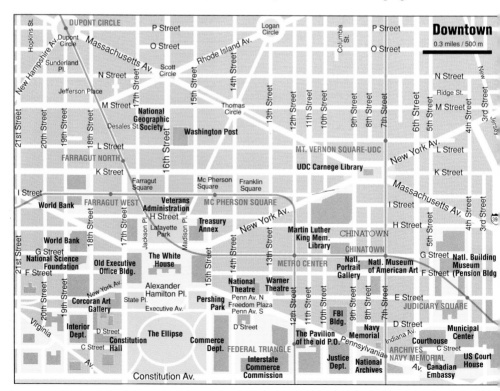

park, facing the **Hay-Adams Hotel** on the corner of H and 16th streets, is the pretty yellow-and-white **St John's Church**, with its adjacent **Parish House**. Completed in 1816, the so-cially-correct Episcopal church has been visited by every US president since James Madison, earning it the accolade "Church of the Presidents." Pew 54 is reserved as the "President's Pew," should he decide to drop by.

The brick town house diagonally across at H Street and Jackson Place is the 1818 **Decatur House**. Originally the residence of Commodore Stephen Decatur, a War of 1812 hero, and the first house built on the square, it has seen a succession of tenants over the years. Inside, six rooms are beautifully restored in Federal and Victorian styles. There's also a browsable museum shop.

Other landmarks, which you can only see from the outside, are the 1820 **Dolley Madison House** at H Street and Madison Place, and the 1824 **Blair House** at 1650 Pennsylvania Avenue, where visiting dignitaries and other presidential guests stay when they're in town on business.

Anchoring the block on the corner of Pennsylvania and 17th Street is the palatial **Renwick Gallery** of the Smithsonian's National Museum of American Art, devoted to crafts and decorative arts from the traditional to the contemporary and beyond. Built in 1859, it was the District's very first art gallery. When William Corcoran commissioned James Renwick to de-sign an avant-garde museum for his art collection, he unwittingly set an architectural trend responsible for the likes of the overdone French Second-Empire-style Old Executive Office Building across the street.

The Renwick's Grand Salon is stacked with paintings à la Louvre. Also notable is the six-sided Octagon Room, which was designed to display Hiram Powers' notorious nude, *The Greek Slave*. Victorian etiquette dictated that men and women view this sculpture

separately. The statue is now shame-lessly on display at the **Corcoran Gallery of Art** just down the street.

If you're in the market for art books or just appreciate a good browse, stop by the Franz Bader Bookstore at 1911 I Street. The **Bader Gallery** is down near the **Sheraton-Carlton Hotel** at 1500 K Street, a few doors from **Chapters**, a book-lover's bookstore.

The White House is bracketed by one of the oddest architectural couples around. Flanking its east side is the **Treasury Building**, the department's administrative home, looking every bit a classic Greek temple. Thirty-three years in the making and finally com-pleted in 1869, this handsome structure unfortunately mars Pierre L'Enfant's planned view of the Capitol from the White House.

Its flamboyant mate on the west side is the multi-tiered and mansard-roofed **Old Executive Office Building**. Com-missioned by President Ulysses S. Grant, and built between 1871 and

esident
ncoln's box
Ford's
eatre.

1888, it was for years the world's largest office building, with 566 rooms and some 10 acres of floor space. Generally regarded as an affront to the neoclassical style in vogue for federal buildings – epitomized by the Federal Triangle monoliths – architect Alfred B. Mullet's incongruous and costly Executive Office left him spent. His life ended tragically in litigation and suicide.

Pennsylvania Avenue jogs around the Treasury, is subsumed temporarily by 15th Street, and reappears by **Pershing Park** and **Freedom Plaza** headed straight for the Capitol. Thanks to a major development project along the avenue, this ceremonial boulevard between the "President's House" and "Congress' House" has received a much-needed face-lift in recent years, including a crop of attractive plazas and pocket parks, upscale restaurants, and clutches of cafés and chichi shops.

Renovation of some sadly neglected historic properties, such as the **Willard Inter-Continental Hotel** at 14th Street, has also improved the avenue's appearance. Host to the world's rich and powerful, this opulent, turn-of-the-century landmark hotel has been painstakingly restored. Indulge yourself with afternoon tea in the Nest or an aperitif at the in-the-round gentleman's bar. Handy to the hotel in the adjacent Willard Collection of posh shops and eateries is a Visitor Information Center.

Not nearly so luxurious as its neighbor, the spruced-up **Hotel Washington** at 15th Street offers a rooftop bar with a fabulous view. Be sure to go in the evening, for the panoramic sight of most of "tourist Washington" lit up at your feet. One block up, the Old Ebbitt Grill's clubby Victorian ambience is perfect for an Irish coffee after ice-skating at Pershing Park. Just two blocks from the **National** and **Warner Theatres**, it's a traditional stop for a before- or after-theater libation, snack, or repast.

If nearby **Federal Triangle** – that staid, neoclassical complex of power

The Pension Building; four-martini lunch.

architecture and bureaucracy which effectively "seals off" downtown from the airy Mall – has left you cold, the **National Aquarium** will provide some comic relief. The country's oldest aquarium, this 74-tank relic has been tucked away in the dark basement of the **Department of Commerce** since 1932. Children are fond of the wonderfully-named Touch Tank. The Commerce cafeteria is open to the public.

Alternatively, a good bet for a bite to eat is the Pavilion mall at the **Old Post Office**, the Romanesque-Revival palace at 12th and Pennsylvania. This magnificently restored 1899 landmark is a model cooperative of federal office and public space. The glass-elevator ride is reason enough to tour the belfry and the 315-foot clock tower, but wait until you see the 360-degree view.

In stark contrast is the much-maligned **J. Edgar Hoover FBI Building** across the street. Designed in the tradition of Le Corbusier's New Brutalism, the formidable – and costly – concrete hulk blatantly violated a Congressional charter to restore a semblance of human scale to the avenue. (*For more information, see page 176 and "Washington for Kids," pages 183–187.*)

For diversion of a different kind, detour a block up to 511 10th Street, where **Ford's Theatre National Historic Site** – which includes the **House Where Lincoln Died** across the street – memorializes Lincoln's last hours and displays an amazingly eclectic collection of Lincolniana in the museum downstairs. You can also catch a matinee or evening performance here.

From the FBI, a starboard tack will land you at the **Navy Memorial** in **Market Square**, whose twin edifices not only protect but frame the original visual line along 8th Street between the National Portrait Gallery and John Russell Pope's stately **National Archives**, which is located opposite.

The Archives' 21-floor federal repository contains 4 billion pieces of paper, along with mind-boggling numbers of

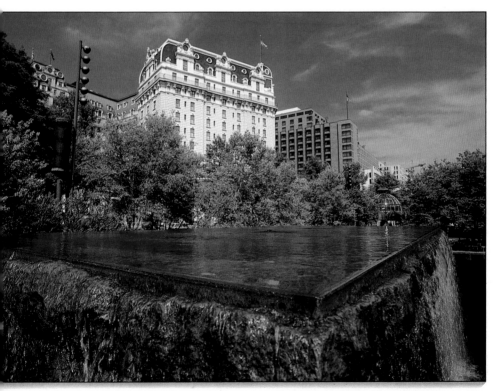

ershing Park nd the illard Hotel.

THE FBI

If Washington has a secret government, then the Central Intelligence Agency and the Federal Bureau of Investigation lie at its heart. But although the CIA discourages prying eyes, the FBI will escort you around its vast and bluntly ugly building for an hour-long visit. You will end up impressed, slightly better informed, realizing that you have been exposed to a hard-sell public relations exercise, and slightly deafened. This is because the tour always ends with an exhibition of marksmanship on the underground firing range, where agents blast away with .38 pistols and the historic Tommy Gun of the G-man days.

The tours begin in the J. Edgar Hoover building, named after the legendary first director who combined the stewardship of inter-state crime fighting and (much to the chagrin of the CIA) counter-espionage for 48 years, until his death in 1972. The FBI was actually created in 1908 by President Theodore Roosevelt in order to combat political corruption, but the organization remains

synonymous with the larger-than-life persona of J. Edgar Hoover.

Hoover built his career in rooting out "subversion," compiling the "Red Lists" of labor agitators, Bolsheviks, and socialist and anarchist immigrants into New York after 1918. A master of public relations, he impressed the public and Congress alike with a steadily-rising list of Federal crimes "solved" each year, many of which later turned out to be recovered stolen cars which had been driven across state lines.

Hollywood helped build up the image of Hoover's G-men, special investigating teams who tracked down gangsters in the 1930s like John Dillinger and George "Machine-gun" Kelly. Hoover also dreamed up the phrase "Public Enemy Number One" which helped make the FBI into national heroes. In World War II, the bureau tracked down Nazi spy rings, again grabbing maximum publicity, and during the Cold War years launched a renewed drive against Communists and the Atom-bomb spies.

Out of the 10,000 applicants who apply each year to be agents, only around 600 are hired. Special agents must be fit, college graduates aged between 23 and 35, and pass eight annual firearms tests.

In the 1960s, Hoover's hunt for subversives led him to target civil rights leaders and the organizers of the Vietnam anti-war movement. After the director's death, a US Senate committee reported that the FBI had used illegal and improper methods, burglarizing and spying on American citizens who were using their legal right to protest their government's policies.

This tarnish on the FBI's reputation has left a shadow on Hoover's name, and toned down the traditional reverence for him on the tour. So instead, you see some of Hoover's real achievements, like the building of a modern finger-printing system, (the bureau has more than 185 million sets of prints and claims that no two are alike), crime and pathology labs, and some of the more acceptable souvenirs of seven decades of crime-busting, including a sample from their collection of 35,000 guns.

Under the Freedom of Information Act, Americans can find out if the bureau holds a file or fingerprint card on them. For more details, write to the Director of the FBI at the J. Edgar Hoover building.

**FBI operativ■
shoots to
■ thrill.**

maps, film footage, photos, and tapes. This is where the Declaration of Independence, the Constitution and the Bill of Rights are kept, as well as, among other paper attractions, President Richard Nixon's letter of resignation. By appointment you can tour the National Archives behind the scenes.

If you turn north at the sweeping **Canadian Embassy**, where Pennsylvania and Constitution cross, and follow the staid corridor of courthouses around Judiciary Square to F Street, you'll run into the **Old Pension Building** – now the **National Building Museum** – a takeoff of the Palazzo Farnese and Diocletian's baths. (Congress proposed to install the Air and Space Museum here.) More memorable than this museum of building arts, though, is the building itself. Designed as the Civil War veterans' memorial by Union General Montgomery C. Meigs, its breathtaking **Great Hall** – the biggest room in town – contains the world's largest Corinthian columns. The Hall is rented

out for inaugural balls, and other events.

Standing alone in a space nearby at G and 3rd is the **Jewish Historical Society of Greater Washington**, housed in the small brick **Lillian and Albert Small Jewish Museum**, the site of DC's first synagogue. A few blocks farther east is the **Government Printing Office and Bookstore**, listed in the *Guinness Book of Records* as the world's largest in-plant printing operation, as well as **Georgetown University Law Center**.

The area around **Gallery Place** is considerably livelier than this. Galleries are springing up along the arts corridor of 7th Street. The maverick **Washington Project for the Arts** at 7th and D runs the most unique art bookstore around. If you're craving cool and can handle noisy, try **d.c.space** café/bar at 443 7th Street, or one of the nearby clubs. Wear black.

An ornate arch across H Street at 7th marks the heart of **Chinatown**. It's not New York or San Francisco, but there's

enough here to choose from. Dim sum is a Chinese New Year tradition.

Two wonderful, off-the-Mall Smithsonian museums, the **National Museum of American Art** and the National Portrait Gallery, share the **Old Patent Office Building**, the Parthenon look-alike at F and G streets between 7th and 9th. Appropriately, its marble halls show the words of Walt Whitman, that quintessential American bard, who read his poetry to wounded soldiers when the building served as a Civil War barracks, hospital, and morgue.

On the north side of the Old Patent Office, the museum houses the country's oldest collection of art – over 30,000 works by such talented Americans as Winslow Homer, Andrew Wyeth and Edward Hopper. The **National Portrait Gallery**, on the south side, is the home to the actual portraits of presidents and American heroes you've only seen in picturebooks until now.

If you've worked up an appetite

sweeping through two centuries of American art and history, try the Patent Pending cafeteria or a picnic in the shady central courtyard. Adjacent to the Old Patent Office is **Martin Luther King, Jr Library**, the main branch of the District's public library system, but also a museum, a venue for music concerts and art shows as well as being a researcher's haven; the library's Washingtoniana room has the biggest collection of information on the nation's capital to be found anywhere in the world.

If shopping is on your agenda, the revitalized heart of the downtown district around **Metro Center** is the place to browse through gleaming new malls and spruced-up department stores displaying the latest, or just the best, in fashion. You can also pick up discount day-of-performance tickets for most theaters at **TicketPlace**, a kiosk at F Street Plaza between 12th and 13th streets. Tickets for Sunday shows are sold on Saturday.

Several blocks north toward McPherson Square at 1250 New York Avenue, not far from the Washington Convention Center, is the inspiring **National Museum of Women in the Arts**. Ironically, the museum, which is uniquely and exclusively dedicated to women artists, occupies a former all-male Masonic temple. The pink-marbled entrance hall of Waddy Wood's Renaissance Revival structure is positively palatial, bordering on *frou-frou*. You can lunch tastefully amidst all this at the Palette Café.

Or, you can head over to the inimitable Café Mozart at 1331 H Street for a heaping helping of Viennese home-cooking and a stein of German beer. Oktoberfest specials run from mid-September "until the barrel runs dry."

More elegant, and redolent of the old South, is the restaurant at the historic **Morrison-Clark Inn**, up at 1015 L Street. For a taste of old England, stop by the **Henley Park Hotel** at 926 Massachusetts Avenue for a leisurely afternoon tea.

Left, the ayes have it
Right, The Palm's waitors celebrate its first waitress

WASHINGTON FOR KIDS

Washington, DC is one of the few American cities where, often, the point is to tour around with the entire family. Here are some capital ideas for parents on how to survive.

It's helpful when traveling with children to remember that the objective is to have a good time. When children are having fun, historical facts may not always sink in, but the love of traveling and learning will. Keep this in mind when the little feet start to drag and you question whose idea it was to make this trip in the first place. Just relax, and plan your days carefully.

Also, it's good to be aware that the famous symbols of Washington are monuments, and a pilgrimage to them is often just that from a child's perspective. While it's easy enough to *see* the white sights that line the Mall, getting right up to them is another thing. Liberal use of the Metro, the Tourmobile and an occasional cab can save time and tears.

Because kids tend to get hungry where refreshment lines are longest, take drinks and snacks with you. Nibbling on tour lines *does* make the wait more tolerable. A few food stands are located on the Mall, but it's best to plan ahead so you can schedule meal times that allow you to choose where you want to end up and where to eat.

Moan-free Mall: It's also a good idea to be prepared with pencil and paper, game and puzzle books to keep your kids occupied if there is a line or if you just want to relax on the Mall grounds. If you need to buy supplies, remember that hotel gift shops are often pricey. A good selection of toys, novelties and things-to-do books is available at the **Smithsonian shops**. Book stores located at the monuments are also a good bet for things of interest to kids.

The **Washington Monument** used to be a favorite stop, in part because of the climb up the 897 steps to reach the top of the structure, which is just over 555 feet tall. For safety and health reasons, access to the monument's highest point is now confined to the elevator, cutting the kid fun-quotient by more than two-thirds. The exception is the tours given by Park Rangers which take the elevator up and offer a hike down. Enquire at an information bureau to find out the times and days these occur.

If you do not opt for one of these tours, the waiting lines are legendary. Considering that the panoramic vista is often clouded with a Washington haze, a less demanding choice might be the view from the **Old Post Office Tower** at 12th Street and Pennsylvania Avenue. Surrounded by interesting food stands and novelty shops, the tower is not as high as the monument, but in some ways offers a more comprehensible view of downtown Washington.

The **Lincoln Memorial** is probably the most interesting to kids (who enjoy running up and down the steps), and a

Jefferson Memorial visit is enhanced by the pedal boats that are launched in its Tidal Basin. The **White House** tends to be of greater interest to adults than kids, plus the tour lines are consistently long (*see "The White House" chapter, pages 135–139*). The **Capitol** is best for those who have studied at least some US history, typically covered in American grade schools around the age of nine or 10. For children who are much younger, plan a shorter visit with the **Rotunda** as the highlight.

To help you see the most of Washington without becoming too exhausted, here are three sample day trips. These itineraries assume you will cover several major sights on your own and include suggestions specifically geared to children. Because kids like to *do* things and not merely look at displays, a combination of active and passive activities is included in the schedules.

DAY ONE: Start your trip with a plunge into one of the **Smithsonian's myriad collections**. Pick one or two museums from the following list and check the main entrance desk for special children's guides, orientation tours and information about the exhibits. It helps to let each family member make a selection on what to see.

Kids love the **Air and Space Museum**, particularly marching in and out of space capsules and playing with the interactive exhibits. While many of the exhibits are too detailed for kids under the age of 10, the notion of flight manages to catch nearly everyone's fancy. The **films** are also excellent, but tickets can be scarce and should be obtained as soon as you enter the museum. There is also a **planetarium** which may appeal.

The **Museum of American History** provides a fascinating overview of man and technology. Kids flock to the **automobile exhibits** and will certainly enjoy memorabilia from favorite TV shows in *A Nation of Nations*. If the **Hands-On History Room** is open, kids will enjoy dressing up in 18th-century clothing and playing with the crafts.

Puppy love.

At the **Museum of Natural History**, kids are intrigued by the **dinosaur bones** (and dinosaur shop), the **insect zoo** and the priceless **gem collection**. Much of the museum is an ode to the wonders of taxidermy, but things come more to life in the **Discovery Room**. Children can handle all kinds of animal objects here, but hours are limited as are the passes available for entry.

While on the Mall, younger children will enjoy a spin on the **carousel** near the Arts and Industries Buildings. Open daily May to September, the organ grinder's refrain is a perfect accompaniment to the frisbees, kites, picnickers and sunbathers you are bound to encounter in this part of town.

For lunch, head for **Union Station** where you will find an array of eateries and "fun" shopping that is easily reached by Metro. For your afternoon activity, you are a short cab ride from the Capital Children's Museum. Parking is available on side streets should you decide to drive.

The **Capital Children's Museum** at 88 3rd Street NE is a hands-on activity center where you can experiment on computers, build with almost life-size Lincoln Logs, and perform under strobe lights. There is an extensive exhibit on Mexican culture and the opportunity to participate in native crafts. Since the place is for kids, all types of behavior are tolerated: climbing aboard a **police motorcycle**, or sliding down a **fireman's pole** outfitted in genuine gear. There's room here for imaginative play with diverse exhibits to delight the toddler, pre-teen and adult as well. You can bring food or pick up a snack from the vending machines. Plan to spend a minimum of two hours here.

DAY TWO: Kids early on learn the importance of money. For them (and for adults) the fact that it comes from a printing machine – which can keep printing and printing – is a Must See. Don't spoil it and tell them you can't print what you need because most are just replacement bills headed for banks.

But do take them for the half-hour tour at the **Bureau of Engraving and Printing** located at 14th and C streets SW. You'll get to see the entire process – printing, cutting, stacking and counting – and also learn the up-and-down history of the $2 bill. Presses run 24 hours a day, all year round. The shop here sells **bags of shredded bills** and currency **sheets of uncut bills**. Both are great souvenirs for all ages.

Tour tickets are for specified times and should be picked up early on the day you plan to visit. If you have time before the tour, the Washington Monument and the Smithsonian museums are within reasonable walking distance.

For lunch and the afternoon, change your pace with a visit to the **National Zoo**. A short ride via Metro and a less than 10-minute walk takes you to the entrance at 3001 Connecticut Avenue NW. Home of traditional favorites, you will also find **Smokey the Bear** and **Ling-Ling** and **Hsing-Hsing**, the only panda bears in captivity in the US.

ugs-tra
citement
the Mall.

Given to the children of America by the People's Republic of China, the display includes children's letters on peace and international understanding.

Also aimed at children are several learning centers providing "touchy-feely" experiences: **Zoolab** is located in the Education Building near the main Zoo entrance, **Herp Lab** is in the Reptile House and **Bird Lab** can be found in the Bird House. Hours are changeable, depending on volunteers for staff, but a visit is worthwhile if the labs are open.

The zoo is a lovely setting with ample snack and lunch facilities, far from gourmet but certainly adequate. Toddlers' chairs on wheels are available for rent throughout the summer, but limited to weekends most of the other times.

When you have had enough wildlife, climb back aboard Metro for a short ride to the area called **Friendship Heights** and a visit to the **Washington Dolls' House and Toy Museum**. The miniature Victorian world you will find at 5236 44th Street NW will intrigue girls,

boys, the young and the old. Of special interest to kids are the **French** and **Spanish schoolrooms**, the **antique trains** and the wonderfully intricate **dolls' houses**. The collection can comfortably be viewed in half an hour. The museum also has an excellent shop for grown-up collectors.

Around the corner from the Toy Museum there is practical shopping as well as the upscale stores of the **Mazza Gallerie**. Complete the day with a meal at one of the many good local restaurants and a movie, all within walking distance of each other and Metro.

DAY THREE: You'll have to get up very early to go to the **Federal Bureau of Investigation (FBI)**. Tours through the building at 10th Street and Pennsylvania Avenue NW start at 8.45am, but there is already a line forming by 8am. A carry-out breakfast eaten on line would not seem inappropriate. Plan-ahead Americans can get around this by writing to their Congressman six to eight weeks in advance to schedule a tour time.

Amateur sleuths will learn about **crime detection, fingerprinting, blood typing, hair and fabric analyses** and much more. **Al Capone, Bonnie and Clyde** and other renegades are brought to life by your tour guide – who may turn out to be an actual FBI agent. The notorious **"Ten Most Wanted"** list makes the point that crime still continues, and the assortment of confiscated weapons will send chills up your spine. A shooting demonstration, performed by a real FBI operative, completes the tour.

If you've survived the line at the FBI, you'll be relieved that there is rarely a wait at the nearby **Ford's Theatre** and the **House Where Lincoln Died**. Situated across the street from each other at 511 and 516 10th St NW, these self-guided tours vividly tell the story of Lincoln's assassination. A visit to the actual spot where **the shooting** occurred and seeing the clothes that Lincoln wore on the night have their intrin-

Learning American history in the House Where Lincoln Died

sic interest. Besides the theater itself, which was restored and reopened in 1968 as a showcase for live productions, the **basement museum** offers exhibits on Lincoln's boyhood and his rise to the presidency.

Across the street at the **Petersen house**, where Lincoln died, the rooms look as they did on that tragic night in 1865. The exhibits humanize the Lincoln we have come to remember as Daniel Chester French's giant stone figure seated at the Lincoln Memorial.

For lunch or a snack, the **Old Post Office Pavilion** is close by, or you may prefer a meal in **Chinatown**, an easy 15-minute walk from the house and theater.

For an afternoon activity, a visit to the **Navy Museum** is a nice change from traditional sightseeing. Located in the Washington Navy Yard at 9th and M streets SE, the exhibits are constantly being updated but there is something of a vintage quality to their displays. Kids love it here because there are things to climb on both inside the building and outside. A replica of the gundeck of the *USS Constitution* provides the opportunity to ponder the seafaring vessels of America's early Navy. Cannons, missiles and periscopes provide a feast for curious minds.

Among the highlights is the *USS Barry*, a former destroyer now moored in the adjacent Potomac River. You can visit all parts of the ship – the captain's quarters, the mess deck, radio central, and even take a turn in the captain's chair in the pilot house surrounded by hand-polished brass fittings. Sailors are positioned throughout the ship and kids are encouraged to ask a lot of questions as they wander about.

The Navy Museum is not served by Metro and is best reached by taxi or car. There is parking on the grounds if you drive. Plan for at least a 1ˇ-hour visit; longer if you intend to stop at the nearby **Marine Corps Museum**. Though not as much fun as the larger Navy Museum, it will certainly appeal to military history buffs.

e National
o was
tablished
1889.

FOGGY BOTTOM AND THE WEST END

Croaking frogs, swampy lowlands, and a smoke-belching brewery – such were the salient features of Foggy Bottom in the mid-1700s. More than a century later, much of this soggy land along the Potomac River was filled in to accommodate the expanding city. Centered around **Washington Circle**, Foggy Bottom's slow and awkward growth created not a few disputes between developers and preservationists. The successes and failures of these groups have created a neighborhood seemingly at odds with itself.

Curious mix: Foggy Bottom and the adjacent West End are a mix of 19th-century town houses, the modern structures of George Washington University, the oddly-placed Kennedy Center (replacing the former brewery), the quirky Watergate complex, magnificent marble edifices, government buildings, new hotels, and a ganglion of poorly marked highways that speed traffic in and out of Virginia.

This section of DC – bounded by the Potomac River, Constitution Avenue, 17th Street, and N Street – is best on foot by day, and car by night, especially if you plan to take in the night life. Tourism really isn't big business in Foggy Bottom as it is on the nearby Mall. Entrances are often oblique, reservations for tours may be required weeks in advance, admission might be granted only by showing a photo identification. But the extra effort pays off in the form of smaller (if any) crowds and the feeling you're discovering some unusual attractions just off the beaten path.

To see Washington like a diplomat, begin at 23rd and C streets for a guided tour of the **State Department's Diplomatic Reception Rooms**. These five drawing rooms and dining rooms are where the Secretary of State entertains distinguished foreign guests several nights a week. The exquisite 18th- and 19th-century-style rooms contain a collection of donated antiques, including the mahogany desk upon which Thomas Jefferson drafted the Declaration of Independence; one of John Jay's punch bowls and a portrait by John Singleton Copley. The oddest item in the collection is the *Landing of the Pilgrims*, a work that depicts a British man-of-war flying the US flag, redcoats as pilgrims, and a dangerously rocky Massachusetts coast lined with welcoming Indians. More sublime scenes of the Mall and the Potomac River beyond are framed by the south rooms' graceful Palladian windows.

Secluded in a grove of elm and holly trees at the corner of 22nd and Constitution is the **Einstein Memorial** at the National Academy of Sciences. The memorial consists of a 7,000-pound bronze statue of Albert Einstein seated casually before a circular sky map. The granite map is embedded with 2,700 metal studs representing the planets, sun, moon and stars visible to the naked

eye. So endearing is this avuncular Einstein that most people can't resist climbing up onto his lap to pose for a photograph.

The seldom-visited **National Academy of Sciences** building features a Foucault's Pendulum in the ornate Great Hall, two-story-high window panels illustrating the history of scientific progress, and an auditorium where free concerts are frequently held.

The **Federal Reserve**, a block farther east on C Street, is an unlikely place to find video games and off-beat art, but in a town where whimsy is as rare as a balanced budget, don't ask questions. A first-floor gallery includes a game called "You Are the Chairman," which gives you the power to dictate the country's monetary policies. Don't worry if you hurl the nation into a depression – it's a surprisingly easy feat. The building's central corridor presents changing exhibits of 19th- and 20th-century art work, often as funky as "Post-Graffiti/ Fine Art" which included a painting

demonstration by an artist using a spray can. The Fed's board meetings (usually Wednesdays) are open to the public, so call ahead to determine the time and issues under discussion. Thursday's guided tours include the board room, the library, and a 20-minute film entitled *The Fed: Our Central Bank*.

The **Department of the Interior** building at 18th and C streets houses an eclectic museum displaying artifacts and information relating to the numerous conservation projects of this multifaceted organization. The **Indian Craft Shop** across the hall sells museum-quality turquoise and silver jewelry, baskets, sculpture, and other handicrafts made by American Indians.

In the exact geographical center of DC is the **Organization of American States**. The OAS, a largely ceremonial coalition of 26 Latin American and Caribbean countries, also occupies one of the city's most ornate Beaux-Arts buildings. The interior courtyard, with its pre-Columbian-style fountain and

A UN reception at the OAS building.

jungle of tropical trees, provides respite from the summer heat and a south-of-the-border getaway in the winter. Ascend the grand staircase to the **Hall of the Americas**, a magnificent room with barrel-vaulted ceiling and Tiffany chandeliers. Behind the building is the slightly neglected **Aztec Garden** and, on 18th Street, the OAS-operated **Art Museum of the Americas** – a treasure house devoted to contemporary art, films, and lectures.

Continental Hall at 1776 D Street serves as the headquarters and museum of the Daughters of the American Revolution. The **DAR museum** contains 34 period rooms furnished to evoke the state-by-state and historical differences in interior design in the United States. You'll see a California adobe-style parlor from 1850; a New Hampshire attic full of children's dolls and toys of the 18th and 19th centuries; and a nautical-style New Jersey room with a chandelier made from the recast anchor and chains from a British frigate.

The DAR's **Library of Genealogy and Local History** is the second largest in the country. Visit this 4-story library if only to gaze up at its skylight ceiling that sheds light over a cascade of balconies and onto the tomes perused by diligent researchers below. This room served as the DAR's convention hall until 1920 when the annual convention outgrew this space. In 1929, **Constitution Hall**, designed by architect John Russell Pope, opened next door on 18th Street to accommodate the DAR assembly. DC's second largest auditorium also hosts a variety of public lectures and concerts.

Just north of the DAR is the **American Red Cross** where you'll find a trio of stained-glass windows by Louis Comfort Tiffany in the upstairs board room. These beautifully iridescent, opalescent windows feature St Filomena, famed for her healing powers, plus gallant knights of the Red Cross and fortitudinous Una of Spenser's *Faerie Queene*.

d facades
d new
emmas.

One block north on 17th Street is the city's oldest and largest private art museum, the **Corcoran Gallery of Art**. The present gallery was built in 1879 to house the collection of Washington philanthropist and banker William Wilson Corcoran. As you enter the Corcoran, look up at the frieze where 11 names, chosen by the architect, are carved: PHIDIAS, GIOTTO, DURER, MICHAEL-ANGELO, RAPHAEL, VELASQUEZ, REMBRANDT, RUBENS, REYNOLDS, ALLSTON, and INGRES.

The trustees discovered too late that the much-lesser talent, Washington Allston, was an uncle of the architect's mother. Correcting in print what they can't in stone, gallery publications have replaced Allston with the more deserving Da Vinci. Inside is a comprehensive collection of 19th- and 20th-century American art as well as European carpets, tapestries, marble sculptures, and European paintings including those by well-known artists such as Rembrandt, Rubens, Renoir, and Degas.

Just west of the Corcoran is the **Octagon House**, designed by Dr William Thornton in 1798. This Georgian structure actually has seven sides with the rounded front portico forming the eighth "side." James and Dolley Madison stayed here after the British burned the White House in 1814; this is also where Madison later signed the Treaty of Ghent to establish the long-awaited peace with Britain. The house-museum, currently undergoing a $3.5-million restoration, is open for tours of its modestly furnished rooms and fine architectural exhibits.

The city's second largest land holder (next to the federal government) is **George Washington University**, occupying 20 square blocks from Washington Circle south to G Street. The school settled here in 1912 and, with much local controversy, expanded into the surrounding town homes converted into classrooms, dormitories, and office buildings. The university's well-known law library at 718 20th Street is an elegant brick and concrete structure and an improvement over GW's prosaic campus style.

If you see an ocean liner run aground in a row of townhouses, you're at **2000 Pennsylvania Avenue**, a thoroughly modern office building fronted by the **Lion's Row town houses**. The building now houses offices, Tower Records, several restaurants, and a number of other mall-type shops. Also in the neighborhood are the little-known private **international galleries** ("private" means you should call ahead) run by the arts societies of the **World Bank** and the **International Monetary Fund**, located respectively at 1701 and 1700, 19th Street. The World Bank gallery exhibits art from Bank-member countries; the IMF gallery showcases the best work of premier artists from around the world. One museum that is open (and free) is the **National Gallery of Caricature and Cartoon Art** at 1317 F Street, featuring cartoons dating from as long ago as 1747.

Tiffany window in the Red Cross building.

On the north side of Washington Circle, sandwiched between Georgetown and Downtown, is DC's newly developed **West End**. The main strip along M Street is dominated by glitzy hotels, new office buildings, and too few trees and pedestrians. Once you're inside the buildings, however, life is cozier.

The **Park Hyatt** hotel, at 24th and M, is noteworthy for serving one of the best afternoon teas in town – and for having a palm reader on hand for tea-time fortunes three days a week. Nearby, City Café offers an imaginative and tantalizing organic menu in an intimate dining room filled with tiny triangular tables.

The **Watergate complex** and the adjacent **Kennedy Center** have been described together as a "wedding cake and the box it came in." Now infamous as the site of the scandal that ousted Richard Nixon, this ultra-modern curvaceous complex of apartments, offices, shops and restaurants is currently popular for other reasons. The French restaurant Jean-Louis of the Watergate is housed here, as is the Watergate Pastry shop where you can feast on scandalously rich desserts.

The **John F. Kennedy Center for the Performing Arts** is the fulfillment of George Washington's dream to have a national cultural center located in the capital. Isolated from the rest of the city by careless urban planning and a tangle of roadways, this imposing monument contains six theaters presenting opera, ballet, musical theater, chamber music, jazz concerts, silent films, recitals, workshops, and children's theater.

If you are unable to attend a performance, take a free guided tour to see the inside of the theaters, the glamorous **Hall of Nations** and the **Hall of States**, and to learn whose generosity endowed each with enough funds to run the theaters. The tour includes the **Performing Arts Library** and the **Grand Foyer** which measures 630 feet long, 60 feet high, and 40 feet wide. The Roof Terrace affords spectacular panoramic views of the city.

e DAR's
nstitution
ll.

GEORGETOWN

Georgetown is the pedestrian heart of Washington. Shaded streets, brick and cobblestone sidewalks, row houses, and low-rise commercial buildings create an atmosphere that is quaint and on a distinctly human scale. Georgetown has the commercial bustle of a 19th-century port city, the youthful energy of a college town, the international style of a diplomatic community and the wealthy mien maintained by its resident population of senators, lawyers, social-ites, and members of the media.

It is also a place of traffic gridlocks and limited parking spaces, of rowdy just-legal imbibers cruising M Street and Wisconsin Avenue, and of Hallow-een madness and post-Redskin-victory mayhem. Georgetown hosts a not-trivial number of muggings, burglaries, and other crimes that make some quiet side streets unsafe after dark.

Port authority: Originally part of Maryland, Georgetown was settled in the mid-1700s on the banks of the Potomac River. Wharves, warehouses, and factories – many structures still extant – lined the riverbank of this flour-ishing port that shipped tobacco and flour world wide. The square-mile town, named after King George II, was soon populated by plantation owners from Maryland and Virginia, mer-chants from New England, and a great number of slaves and laborers. In the 1780s, Georgetown's gracious homes, inns and taverns made it an ideal staging area for the planning of the nation's permanent capital city.

George Washington, Thomas Jeffer-son, John Adams, and a slew of archi-tects, governors and foreign envoys fre-quented Georgetown, many establish-ing permanent homes. In the late 1780s Bishop John Carroll founded George-town Seminary – an institution that added to Georgetown's distinction. The seminary grew into **Georgetown Uni-versity**, the oldest Catholic college in the country. The gothic spires of the university's **Healy Building** dominate the skyline of Georgetown from its perch at 37th and O streets.

Georgetown thrived as a cosmopoli-tan city, industrial center, and shipping canal terminus until the advent of the railroad and the growth of the new capi-tal after the Civil War. With its status eclipsed and its territory swallowed by Washington in 1871, Georgetown fell into neglect but never lost its sense of a separate identity. Georgetown is ringed like a walled city by Rock Creek Park, the Potomac River, Georgetown Uni-versity and Whitehaven and Dumbar-ton Oaks parks. Though most of the trade here is conducted in shops and restaurants along M Street and Wiscon-sin Avenue, Georgetown's waterfront retains some of its earlier bustle.

The 185-mile-long **Chesapeake & Ohio Canal** begins in Georgetown and is easily accessible from several points here. Commuters, strollers, dog walk-

ers and weekend athletes use the serene and shaded canal and its towpath. **Mule-drawn boat rides** from the Foundry Mall take you back to a more leisurely age.

Right on the Potomac River at 31st Street is **Washington Harbour** – a modern monstrosity housing not-so-notable shops, eateries and offices. But it's worth a visit if only for its computer-choreographed central fountain, sculptures and riverside promenade.

At 30th and M streets you'll find the **Old Stone House**, one of the city's oldest and quaintest buildings. Built in 1765, this six-room house served as a carpentry shop and home for its original owners. The architecture and furnishings reflect the modest lifestyle of the pre-Revolutionary days. Behind the house is a small and wonderfully wild garden where fruit trees and densely planted borders of flowers bloom with abandon spring through fall. This is a perfect retreat for lunchtime picnickers and weary pavement pounders. Just

around the corner on 31st is **Booked Up**, an antiquarian bookstore owned by writer Larry McMurtry. Just one small musty room contains about 30,000 first editions and rare books arranged on shelves in no particular order – possibly to encourage browsing. You can find books and booklets for under $10 and, if you're looking for a first edition in the $11,000 range, this is also the place.

At the west end of M Street is the oft-promoted **Georgetown Park** mall. This $100-million Victorian-style mall is a success story of architectural preservation, but its 85 international boutiques and specialty shops can't hold a candle to the more interesting (and less pricey) stores along M and Wisconsin streets. These streets are lined with opportunities to buy everything from expensive Italian suits, cheap shoes, surplus military wear, antiques, household goods, coffees and spices, and American crafts. The best cure for shopper's syndrome (exhaustion) is afternoon tea in the pretty **Garden Terrace** of the

Mule-drawn boat rides a available on the canal.

Four Seasons Hotel at 2800 M Street.

The greatest charm of Georgetown is its architecture – street after street of elegant town homes – best seen on foot. Don't miss two of the finest rows of Federal homes lining the **3200-3300 blocks of N Street**; "**Evermay**," a spectacular private residence you can admire from the sidewalk at 1623 28th Street; four whimsical **Victorian town homes** on the 3000 block of Q Street; and stately **Marbury House**, at 3307 N Street, where Jacqueline and John F. Kennedy lived at the time he was elected president.

One of the grandest residences in the neighborhood is **Tudor Place** at 1644 31st Street. From 1805 to 1983, this neoclassical mansion was lived in by succeeding generations of the same family. Martha Custis Peter, a granddaughter of Martha Washington, purchased a city-block's worth of property with $8,000 left to her by the Washingtons. Martha and her husband Thomas hired Dr William Thornton, architect of the original US Capitol and the Octagon House, to design their home. As a friend of Thomas Jefferson, Dr Thornton created a gracious home with some clever Monticello-esque features.

Visitors will find rooms eclectically decorated and graced with formal neoclassical portraits, Civil War-era daguerreotypes, moderately masterful paintings by "artistic" family members, and modern snapshots.

Just north of Tudor Place is **Dumbarton Oaks**, a museum-house and garden that is beautiful in every season. The 1801 home and property were purchased in 1920 by Mr and Mrs Robert Woods Bliss as a "country retreat in the city." Mr Bliss, a former ambassador to Argentina, was a serious collector of Byzantine and pre-Columbian art. His wife Mildred, and noted landscape gardener Beatrix Farrand, designed 10 acres of formal gardens. In 1940, the Blisses donated their property, library, and collections to Harvard University, which subsequently opened it to the

he hair of e dog...

public. The lavish **Music Room** served as site for the 1944 discussions that led to the ratification of the United Nations.

The museum's **pre-Columbian collection** is housed in eight exquisite glass pavilions designed by Philip Johnson. The glass invites the leafy green outdoors in to envelope the brilliant gold jewelry, jade statues, and stone masks on display.

What was envisioned for Dumbarton Oaks' neglected grounds was nothing short of brilliant. The old barnyards, cow paths, and steep slopes were replaced by **terraced gardens, boxwood hedges, 10 pools, nine fountains**, an **orangery**, a **Roman-style amphitheater**, a pebble garden, and three seasons of blooming flowers. A full-time crew of a dozen gardeners work year-round to maintain the gardens, whose beauty and number of visitors peak with the blooming of bulbs, forsythia, and cherry trees in the spring.

Nearby **Oak Hill Cemetery** provides the perfect classroom for an education in urban landscaping, local history, and the architecture of the afterlife. In continuous use since 1849, this comfortable place includes the graves of John Howard Payne (author of *Home, Sweet Home*), statesmen Edwin M. Stanton and Dean Acheson, and socialite Peggy O'Neill. The gate house offers a brochure with a map locating the graves of other Washingtonians. A stroll down the brick paths and mossy steps leads you past a **Gothic-style chapel**, a miniature **Temple of Vesta**, marble obelisks, **pensive angels**, and forlorn women carved in Phidian robes.

By night, Georgetown is where you'll find the city's greatest variety and densest concentration of restaurants and bars, from well-established French restaurants and top-rated hotel dining rooms to trendy nouveau Italian spots, upper-crust pizza joints, cafés, bakeries and pubs of all types. You can choose from Moroccan, Mexican, Indian, Thai, Vietnamese, Indonesian, Japanese, Ethiopian and American cuisines. For

Georgetown Park Mall.

superlative suppers, Au Pied du Cochon is Georgetown's only 24-hour bistro; **Martin's Tavern** is Georgetown's oldest tavern; F. Scott's is the neighborhood's ultra-chic bar and restaurant featuring Big Band dancing. The posh **Aux Beaux Champs** at the **Four Seasons** hotel is Georgetown's only four-diamond restaurant.

Since many Georgetown eateries stay open until the wee hours, you can enjoy a movie then a postmortem discussion over a late supper. The **Key** and the **Biograph theaters** – the city's two remaining repertory theaters – provide plenty of food for thought with foreign films, animation festivals, locally made art films and off-beat films.

While the Georgetown bar scene tends to be fairly run-of-the mill (J. Paul's, Paul Mall, Garrett's, Third Edition), a few nightclubs are worth seeking out. **Blues Alley** is DC's oldest and most prominent jazz club where stars such as Dizzy Gillespie, Wynton Marsalis and Nancy Wilson perform.

■nch party Paolo's.

Reservations are a must for this intimate club tucked in an alley off Wisconsin below M Street. The better tables are given to patrons who show up early for dinner. Geared to the international set, the nightclubs around here offer entertainment like salsa and merengue dance bands, live Persian music, and dinner-theater performances of the type performed by the political satire revue "Capitol Steps." If you're dancing until the wee hours, a couple of them serve continental breakfast Saturday and Sunday mornings 1–4am.

The **Bayou** is a casual 500-seat club at 3135 K Street offering nationally known rock 'n' roll, jazz and blues performers, as well as drinks and pizza. The **River Club** at 3223 K Street is an art-deco-style supper club playing swing music and rock 'n' roll. If you still have energy to burn, you can wander over to **3600 Prospect Street** to gaze down the **75-step staircase** where the priest in the film *The Exorcist* met his ill-timed fate.

DUPONT CIRCLE TO ADAMS MORGAN

Dupont Circle – where Connecticut, Massachusetts, and New Hampshire avenues intersect – is the heart of the artsy neighborhood that goes by the same name. Since the 1960s the circle has been a rallying point for demonstrations, a stage for ad hoc concerts and impromptu happenings, and now party-central for the bike-messenger crowd. When the sun shines, the circle is a veritable theater-in-the-round, whose colorful cast of characters includes chess players, lunchtime picnickers, lovers and potential lovers, the generally wacky and weird – and the down and out.

An antidote to Washington's monumental and decidedly conservative tendencies, Dupont Circle is comfortably human-scaled and playfully trendy, with a European touch. Art galleries are scattered throughout, along with a myriad of outdoor cafés, bistros, and bars such as the **Childe Harold**, a smoky, down-under neighborhood institution frequented by writers, and **Kramerbooks and Afterwords Café**, Dupont's Grand Central for browsing, cruising, or shmoozing. You'll also find funky shops, chic boutiques, and bookstores. Foreign and art films are frequently the bill of fare at the neighborhood **Dupont** and **Janus theaters**. This is also the active hub of DC's gay community.

Architecturally, Dupont Circle is a delight and a treasure. The town houses lining its shady side streets are infinitely, and often whimsically, outfitted with English-style gardens, keyhole porticoes, stained- and leaded-glass windows and – if you look up – slate roofs, turrets and copper bays.

Two palatial landmarks front Dupont Circle, both typical of the turn-of-the-century Beaux-Arts mansions built by Washington's upper crust during the neighborhood's fashionable heyday.

The ornate Patterson House at number 15, now the **Washington Club** – a private women's social club – temporarily housed the Calvin Coolidges during White House renovations in 1927. When Charles Lindbergh returned from Paris, he got his presidential welcome here. The **Sulgrave Club**, another private social club housed in the triangular manse at Massachusetts and P Street, was named after George Washington's English ancestral home.

If you follow New Hampshire Avenue to 18th Street, you'll find an unusual pocket park cornering Church Street. With its backdrop of 19th-century ruins from the original Gothic-style **St Thomas' Episcopal Church**, it conjures romantic images of the English countryside. Toward the middle of this narrow, gas-lighted Victorian street is the **Church Street Theater**, a "rental house" to local and non-local companies, which stages plays, dance and readings from works of literature.

Another impressive Beaux-Arts

eceding
ges:
iscling in
Adams
organ Day.
ft, wall art
the style
Toulouse-
utrec.
ght,
dies' Tea
Embassy
w near
pont
rcle.

landmark commands the corner of 18th and Massachusetts. Now the headquarters of the **National Trust for Historic Preservation**, the original McCormick Apartments, built in 1917, were once *the* prestige address in town. Each of its six apartments – one per floor – featured such amenities as silver- and gold-plated doorknobs, wine closets, and silver vaults. Andrew Mellon, one of many notable residents, amassed the art collection here which spawned the National Gallery of Art. The Trust bought the building in 1977 from its think-tank neighbor on Massachusetts Avenue, the **Brookings Institution**.

While you're in the neighborhood, N Street between 17th and 18th offers a few choice options for imbibing or dining. The Victorian **Tabard Inn**, with its homey ambience, is particularly cozy in winter when the fire is going. If an English pub suits your fancy, try the **Union Jack** in the **Canterbury Hotel** next door, which offers an impressive choice of draft and bottled brews from the UK and Ireland, as well as authentic pub grub. Across the street, the portals of the **Iron Gate Inn** open on a romantic high-walled garden, leading back to a secluded courtyard and the carriage-house restaurant. If none of these appeal, you'll surely find something a few blocks up 17th Street.

When the German brewer and entre-preneur Christian Heurich came to Washington in 1871, he founded the successful Heurich Brewing Company, and subsequently built a 31-room, Romanesque-Revival castle on the corner of New Hampshire and 20th. Today, the lavish **Heurich Mansion** is the headquarters for the **Historical Society of Washington DC**, which preserves every authentic detail of this Victorian house-museum, even down to the wall paint. The top floor has been converted into an invaluable research library. There's more Washingtoniana for sale downstairs in the bookstore. When you leave, walk down Sunderland Place for a peek at, or better yet, a picnic in the **Dupont Circle.**

secret garden which is located out back.

In the late 1980s Heurich's grandson reincarnated the family business as the Olde Heurich Brewing Company. While the new designer version of the family lager is now bottled in Utica, New York, DC claims Heurich as its own – and only – brew.

Fittingly, Massachusetts Avenue west of Dupont Circle is known as **Embassy Row**, where Washington's diplomatic community is concentrated. Colorful flags and coats-of-arms of more than 130 nations decorate the embassies and chanceries, both on and off the avenue. While most of the embassies are not open to the public – the opulent **Indonesian Embassy** at 2020 Massachusetts Avenue is a must-see exception – there is plenty of ambient pomp and beauty around here to make for a good walking tour, especially in the spring months.

When diplomat Larz Anderson and his wife planned their 50-room palace at 2118 Massachusetts Avenue, it was with the idea that it would become the future headquarters for the **Society of the Cincinnati**, an elite fraternity founded by Revolutionary War officers and comprised exclusively of the male descendants of these gentlemen. The facade of the **Anderson House** only hints at the impossibly opulent interior of this turn-of-the-century house-museum, filled with the couple's astounding international collection of art and furnishings, and the ghosts of privilege and power. The library holds reference works on the American Revolution, local history, and genealogy. Free concerts are also held here.

The prestigious and private **Cosmos Club** occupies the former Townsend mansion across the street. A few blocks up on Florida Avenue is the austere **Friends Meeting House**, built in 1930 for Quaker President Herbert Hoover. The plain interior has a traditional "facing bench," designed for "weighty" Friends to pronounce their messages. If you have worked up a thirst, head over

to the Brickskeller Down Home Saloon at 1523 22nd Street, where you can choose from more than 500 brands of beer from around the world.

Of all the museums in Washington, the **Phillips Collection** at 21st and Q streets, across from the **Ritz-Carlton Hotel**, is without a doubt the homiest. Indeed, the country's oldest museum of modern art started out in 1921 as a two-room gallery in Duncan and Marjorie Phillips' brownstone. There is no more intimate or hospitable place to visit resident old friends – Impressionists, Post-Impressionists, American Modernists, and some Old Masters, or take in a special exhibit. And there are few more perfect ways to spend a fall or winter Sunday afternoon than to sip a glass of wine at the café next to the museum shop downstairs, and enjoy a free concert in the grand music room. This is a popular tradition; claim your seat early.

In a different vein, a block up on R Street is the **Fonda del Sol Visual Arts Center**. A community-oriented multi-media museum with a Hispanic focus, it was founded by a group of pan-American artists and writers to highlight the region's multicultural heritage. The gallery primarily showcases work by contemporary artists and craftspeople, but it also has an eclectic collection of folk and pre-Columbian art.

One block to the east is the little-known **Art, Science and Technology Institute**, home of the **Holography Museum of the 3rd Dimension**, which is devoted exclusively to the laser-made holographic arts. It has been described as the most off-the-wall show in town.

West of here, Massachusetts Avenue makes an elegant turn at **Sheridan Circle**, the embassy-ringed and tightly secured nucleus of the **Kalorama** neighborhood. Formerly a diplomat's country estate, the name means "beautiful view" in Greek. A few blocks to the north, the quiet streets of this exclusive neighborhood, epitomized by **Kalorama Circle**, are a feast of elegant Tudors, Normans, and Georgians dating

Adams Morgan architecture South American festival dancer.

from – and epitomizing – the 1920s.

In front of the **Romanian Embassy**, a curbside memorial marks where a car bomb killed Allende-appointed Chilean ambassador Orlando Letelier and, unintentionally, passenger Ronni Moffitt, on September 21, 1976 – a job linked to Chilean secret police and army officials in the Pinochet regime.

Moving clockwise around the circle to number 2306, you find the **Alice Pike Barney Studio House**, a special, and little-known landmark. At the turn of the century, Barney, a flamboyant artist, playwright, and producer – in the words of Betty Ross, "a genteel Bohemian with a social conscience" – decided to liven up Washington's dull cultural life, and so she commissioned Waddy Butler Wood to design an all-purpose home and studio, where for years she ran the only Paris-style salon in town. In 1960 Barney's daughters gave the well-used Studio House to the National Museum of American Art. It can be seen by appointment.

Wood also built the stately Georgian-style **Woodrow Wilson House** nearby at 2340 S Street, where Woodrow and Edith Wilson retired the day Warren G. Harding took office in 1921. The 28th president bought the house as a surprise for his second wife, presenting her with a piece of earth from the garden and the front door key, in Scottish tradition. Hidden in the far right corner of the garden is a narrow stairway that winds down to Decatur Place.

Just next door is the **Textile Museum**, a fabulous private museum dedicated exclusively to the display and study of international textile arts, both historic and contemporary. Its collection of Oriental carpets is unmatched in the world, thanks to museum founder George Hewitt Myers, who became hooked after buying his first rug for his Yale dorm room. He opened the museum in 1925 next door to his home and kept right on collecting. Today its collection includes some 1,400 carpets and 13,000 textiles, and the museum's

muted galleries feature permanent and special exhibits. The gift shop has a superb collection of books on textile arts, along with crafts, jewelry, and yarn. The small research library contains more than 13,000 volumes. Curators will personally advise about your own textiles, but it's best to call ahead.

You'll pass **Mitchell Park** if you continue up the hill, named for Mrs E. N. Mitchell who, in 1918, bequeathed the land to the city in exchange for the perpetual care of her pet poodle's grave. You can find dear Bosque's grave – an unmarked and unimpressive cement block encircled by a blue chain – in the playground.

Across from Mitchell Park is a charming architectural interlude, a sweet spot, a secret garden called **Decatur Terrace**. The formal stairs and fountain, which the neighbors generously refer to as the "Spanish Steps," link 22nd and S streets.

If bizarre strains of the Middle East come to you while hiking through Rock Creek Park, you're not hearing things – or rather, you are: It's the **Islamic Center** at Massachusetts and Belmont Road, the spiritual and cultural mecca for Washington's Muslims. Designed by Italian architect Mario Rossi, a convert to Islam, it's also Embassy Row's most exotic structure. For the slight inconvenience of removing your shoes, you can enter the mosque's ornate sanctuary, brimming with colorful Turkish tiles, Persian carpets, Iraqi stained glass, and an Egyptian chandelier.

In the mid-1950s a neighborhood organization was formed to promote cooperation among racially segregated residents. The group took its name by combining the names of two area elementary schools: the all-white Adams and the all-black Morgan. The Adams Morgan organization left its name as a legacy to and symbol of this uniquely diverse community. Every September in honor of **Adams Morgan Day**, the neighborhood throws a giant street party, with music stages, ethnic

Drinks in th jungle.

food booths, crafts, and major crowds.

Along with the artists and bohemians, who moved in in the 1960s, came an influx of Hispanic refugees and immigrants, establishing Adams Morgan as DC's Latin quarter and Greenwich Village, rolled into one. The entire community comes out to celebrate itself, joined by thousands, during the **Hispanic Festival**, which is traditionally held the last weekend in July and features pan-Latin food, the sizzling sounds of salsa and marimba bands, wonderful African crafts, and a colorful parade of nations.

If you're looking for the heart of Adams Morgan, you'll find it at the "T" intersection of **18th Street and Columbia Road**. The closest Metro stop is Woodley Park. Simply follow Calvert Street across the **"Duke" Ellington Bridge** – named, of course, for the pre-eminent jazzman and native son – and you're here.

The plaza by the Perpetual Savings Bank is the village green of Adams Morgan. By day on Saturdays, when the neighborhood is a delight to explore, it becomes a **farmer's market**. On summer evenings you can expect to see anything from Andean pan-pipers to West African stilt-walkers, a kids' bucket-drum combo to a Delta-blues harmonica player, young rappers to Michael Jackson types.

Exotic aromas: Inevitable development – disparaged as "Georgetownization" – has transformed the once higgledy-piggledy stretch of 18th Street into a funky-hip quarter, where exotic aromas – especially Ethiopian and Eritrean – waft from the myriad ethnic restaurants, and the young and the restless come to see and be seen on crowded weekend nights. The flavor here is decidedly Left Bank à la Washington, an international smorgasbord of sidewalk cafés, trendy bars and clubs, bookstores and specialty shops, antique and rummage stores, and galleries.

Alas, Adams Morgan is in danger of becoming a victim of its own success.

imanjaro
tures
ican
formers.

Clubs, bars and restaurants spring up with regularity, only to close down or be taken over by someone else a few months later. Some of the best original haunts have closed down for good, and on weekends the narrow sidewalks are packed with people; don't even think about looking for a parking space for your car, but arrive and leave by taxi. There are, however, a few places that haven't changed: the **Kilimanjaro Restaurant and Nightclub** down on California Street features the live and recorded sounds of top pan-African performers, and has for some time.

East of 18th Street, Columbia Road changes abruptly. Salsa blares from boom-boxes, Latino shops, and vendors' booths, and Spanish is the language of the street.

North of here Adams Morgan flows into the residential neighborhood of **Mount Pleasant**. The heart of Washington's poor and dispossessed Hispanic community is also undergoing block-by-block gentrification. In the spring of 1991 a clash between black police officers and Hispanics here escalated into two days of riots that spilled into Adams Morgan. Seedy as it is, the main artery of Mount Pleasant Street offers the **African Room**, an intimate and authentic West African restaurant and disco, but take your car or a cab. Don't walk around at night.

If you're looking for a quiet refuge away from the fray, wander over to **Meridian House International**, which crowns the ridge between Crescent Place and Belmont Street, off 16th Street. Set on the magnificently landscaped hillcrest are two historic mansions designed by the ever-versatile and prolific John Russell Pope.

The one is a very French Louis XVI-style château, whose lovely pebbled garden is lined with pollarded Spanish linden trees, while the other recalls an English country manor. Both now belong to this international educational and cultural foundation, whose galleries and concerts are open to the public.

Cities restaurant.

214

BACHELORS AND BARGAINS

If you want to buy a car, a plane, a restaurant or a hot date for the evening, look no further. Although Washington may lack a shopping thoroughfare as grand as Fifth Avenue or as elegant as the Champs Elysées, the city hold its own when it comes to unusual auctions.

The most entertaining is an annual event where some of the capital's most eligible bachelors are offered to the highest bidder. The bachelor puts together a "dream date" which can range from brunch and a Redskins game to a lavish weekend in the Bahamas. A brochure details his vital statistics: height, weight, hobbies, favorite movie, plus a one-word description of his own choosing.

Come the big night, black-tie contenders parade around a stage so women can bid on "Mr Sensitive" or haggle over "Mr Controversial." Sources are coy as to whether any of these dates lead to eventual romance, but on at least one occasion a bachelor rescinded after seeing his fate, and paid the sum on offer out of his own pocket. All proceeds go to charity, of course.

A different kind of auction is held every two months in Franconia, Virginia, about 12 miles south of DC. Here, flashy cars and gold jewelry seized from Washington's drug dealers are up for grabs. About 200 people usually attend, half of them from the car and jewelry trade, and the rest being the well-informed public. Prices tend to be "way below retail, more like a wholesale dealer's price," according to one organizer.

Other confiscated and abandoned vehicles are sold by the Washington DC police pound, on the first and third Tuesday of each month, at 5001 Shepherd Parkway, SW. You can ask what vehicles they have in stock by calling ahead. The rule is you can start the engine, put the car in gear, but not drive it. You can look under the hood, and check the oil and water, but no test-drives. If the car blows up as you drive it from the pound, that's too bad. The best buy in memory was a three-year-old Porsche that went for $4,200, probably because of the extra air conditioning from a couple of bulletholes.

There are bargains galore through the US Marshal's Forfeited Property sales service, which sells everything confiscated by the FBI and the Drug Enforcement Administration under the tough Anti-Drugs law of 1986. Under this law, the property on which drugs are found, whether a car, a plane, a boat or a building, is forfeit.

The 18th-century manor of Shelburne Glebe, with 774 divinely-landscaped acres, was sold by the marshal's office for $5 million – reckoned to be about half its market value – after being confiscated as part of the property of Christopher Reckmeyer, a convicted drug trafficker.

A well-maintained 1981 Cessna 402c went on the block at Harrisburg airport for $150,000; an equivalent model was advertised in the aviation trade press the next month for $325,000. For reasons of geography, the bulk of these auctions are held in Florida, Texas and California, where most of the seizures are made. How about bidding for the Savannah Moon, a four-star restaurant with 240 seats in South Miami? Yours for $375,000 in cash, complete with liquor license. Or you may be interested in the Paso Fina ranch, just outside Miami, with 20 mature horses and five colts. It could go for a song, as no minimum bid is listed. ∎

gible for
tion.

THE UPPER NORTHWEST

"Out in the country" was how heat-and-humidity-weary Washingtonians described Upper Northwest until well after the Civil War. Here, in this rural retreat above Rock Creek, woodland was dense and temperatures were 10 to 15 degrees cooler than downtown. On hot summer evenings, Presidents Van Buren, Tyler, Buchanan, and Cleveland came here by carriage from downtown to their gracious country "cottages."

Tempting triangle: With the completion of the first trolley bridges over Rock Creek at the turn of the century, the city expanded northward. Cleveland Park and Woodley Park became fashionable year-round communities and luxury hotels and grand apartment buildings soon graced broad Connecticut, Wisconsin, and Massachusetts avenues. Today, Upper Northwest – a triangle of land formed by 16th Street, Massachusetts Avenue, and DC's western border with Maryland – retains much of its original rural appeal. Despite commercial centers rapidly rising and expanding around Metro stations, unspoiled swaths of woodland, sylvan parks, and tree-lined streets give gracious sanctuary to Mother Nature and her worldly residents.

Threading through the entire neighborhood is the city's largest park and prime natural attraction, **Rock Creek Park**. The park's 1,754 acres were purchased by Congress in 1890 for its "pleasant valleys and deep ravines, primeval forests and open fields... its repose and tranquility, its light and shade..." About 4 miles long and up to a mile wide, the park includes extensive trails and paths for hiking, a marked bike route, picnic areas, recreation fields, tennis courts, an 18-hole golf course, a nature center, planetarium, and horse center.

Historical sites in the park include **Pierce Mill**, a restored 1820s gristmill where you can purchase a sack of cornmeal or wheat flour ground on the premises; Civil War-era **Fort De-Russy**, located at Oregon Avenue and Military Road; and the nearby 1880s **log cabin of Joaquin Miller**, "Poet of the Sierras." **Carter Barron Amphitheatre**, an open-air theater within the park, features a summer festival of pop, rock, and jazz. The **tennis center** is the site of top-level tournaments, to which Washingtonians flock. For an old-fashioned motor tour, follow the 10-mile-long **Beach Drive** which winds its narrow way through the entire park. West of Rock Creek Park, roadless **Glover-Archbold Park** and **Battery-Kemble Park** let you escape the sounds of the city. Narrow trails through this jungly park join the **C&O Canal towpath**.

The main Upper Northwest thoroughfares – Massachusetts, Wisconsin, and Connecticut avenues – slice through the neighborhood on a northwest course into the Maryland suburbs. Just after you cross Rock Creek on

THE C&O CANAL

Slicing a narrow liquid strip through the northwest sections of Washington is a piece of Victorian-era true grit. The C&O Canal, which begins in affluent Georgetown and lopes its way alongside the Potomac River for 185 miles until reaching the Allegheny Mountain town of Cumberland, Maryland, is a relic from another time. Once an ambitious transportation scheme which went awry, today it survives as a playground for outdoor-loving Washingtonians.

The Georgetown section of the canal is well-preserved and upbeat. During warm weather months, restored canal boats are drawn by mules plodding their way along the towpaths, and guides in period costume entertain their audience with tales of the rise and demise of the canal system.

The journey is slow, but not too slow. On board, the smells of dankness and fresh mint intermingle, and the mules vie for towpath space with joggers in headphones and designer gear. Soon after, the vista opens up with views of the Potomac and, behind the

river, high-rise suburban buildings. Here and there on the banks is a large cardboard box which looks suspiciously as if it has been used as a temporary home.

About 10 miles farther up the canal lies the wealthy commuter community of Great Falls, which also offers vintage boat rides. In this much more rural setting, passengers may catch a glimpse of a white-tailed deer or a raccoon. An abandoned goldmine, in operation from the 1860s through the 1940s, lies nearby, and hastily dug graveyards in the hills pay tribute to those who labored to build this extensive waterway but fell prey to diseases along the way.

Serious aficionados of canal wildlife time their visits for either early or late in the day, when chances improve for glimpsing the area's more exotic inhabitants – turkey vultures, the great horned owl, beaver and, rumor has it, even bears.

Less than 10 miles beyond Great Falls, the canal abruptly runs dry. It remains so with the exception of a brief rewatered section near its terminus 150 miles away in Cumberland. As originally conceived, the canal was to have stretched well beyond Cumberland all the way to the Ohio River, hence its name: the Chesapeake and Ohio Canal. There, the plan went, canal boats would load up with bulky raw materials and carry them eastward to the Chesapeake Bay and beyond. But it never happened.

In fact, so the story goes, the C&O Canal had its problems from the start. On July 4, 1828, President John Quincy Adams turned the first shovelful of dirt only to encounter roots and then rocks. Seventy-four lift locks later, in 1850, the canal reached Cumberland, but there it halted, having cost slightly more than $11 million.

Construction was plagued by labor shortages, great unrest, and frequent flooding from the nearby Potomac. Materials were difficult to come by, there were never enough funds, and there were constant legal battles to be fought with the upstart Baltimore and Ohio Railroad.

In fact, the dawning of the railroads sealed the fate of the C&O Canal forever as a viable means of carrying goods. The B&O Railroad was inaugurated the very same Independence Day as the canal, rendering this languid mode of transportation obsolete before it had even fully begun.

Cruising
■ **the canal.**

Massachusetts from downtown you'll spot the **British Embassy** on the left. There is a larger-than-life statue of Winston Churchill giving the "V for Victory" salute (some joke that he's hailing a cab). The base of the statue contains a time capsule to be opened in 2063, the centenary of the conferring of Churchill's honorary US citizenship by President John F. Kennedy.

The British chancery and residence, an adaptation of an English country house, was designed by British architect Sir Edward Lutyens in 1931. The embassy's celebration of the Queen's birthday – a garden party with strawberries and Devonshire cream, plus a sprinkling of notables – is a highlight of Washington's spring social season.

Massachusetts Avenue then curves in a gentle arc around **Observatory Circle** to distance rumbling automobiles from the sensitive instruments housed in the **US Naval Observatory**. The Observatory charts the position and motion of the celestial bodies, measures the earth's rotation, determines precise time and maintains the nation's master clock. Free weekly night tours allow visitors to look through the 26-inch refractor telescope used to discover the Martian moons in 1877.

Also on the Observatory grounds is the Victorian-era **house of the Vice President of the United States**, originally built for the superintendent of the Naval Observatory. This turreted, informal-looking home is a far cry from the White House, for it is little known, little publicized, and seen even less. The house was co-opted from the Navy in the 1970s, as it was felt that an official home located on the grounds of a military post would be easier – and less expensive – to protect than a private residence elsewhere in the city. Needless to say, the VP's home is not open to the public.

Dominating the city's skyline from the crown of Mount Saint Alban at Massachusetts and Wisconsin avenues is the towering **Cathedral Church of**

ie National athedral as built om 300 illion tons Indiana mestone.

St Peter and Paul, also known as the Washington Cathedral or **National Cathedral**. The corner stone of this magnificent Gothic-style cathedral was laid in 1907 by President Theodore Roosevelt. Eighty-three years and 300 million tons of Indiana limestone later, one of the world's largest ecclesiastical structures was officially completed. The cathedral serves as the seat of the Episcopal Diocese of Washington, but it welcomes people of all faiths to its services, concerts, and annual festivals. This is truly a national cathedral – a fact made gloriously evident through the stunning, quite modern stained-glass windows that tell stories about American history and American heroes.

The **Space Window** in the nave commemorates the scientists and astronauts of Apollo 11 and includes a piece of moonrock retrieved on that mission. Other windows depict the home life of Martha and George Washington at Mount Vernon, Lewis and Clark's explorations of the American Northwest, the struggle for religious freedom in Maryland during the 17th century, and the events of World War II. Thomas Jefferson, Robert E. Lee, Abraham Lincoln as well as his mother and step-mother are glorified in other scenes.

Allow plenty of time not only to study these radiant windows, but to gaze at the nave's soaring vaulted ceiling, to explore the several small chapels, and to gaze at the kaleidoscopic **West Rose Window** as it glows in the setting sun. The best views of Washington and of the cathedral's exterior carvings are from the 70 windows in the **Pilgrim's Observation Gallery** in the west tower. The crypt level includes the London Brass Rubbing Center, the Rare Book Library, and the gift shop. A stroll on the peaceful cathedral grounds will lead you through a 12th-century Norman arch into the medieval-style **Bishop's Garden**, to the Herb Cottage shop, and greenhouse.

The largest Greek Orthodox church in the United States graces the block just

The Vice President's House.

south of the National Cathedral. **Santa Sophia** is famous for its stunning and intricate mosaics that decorate the edifice and interior dome of the church. The best time to visit the church, and to hear the a cappella choir singing from the circular balcony, is during Sunday morning services.

Farther north on Massachusetts at **Ward Circle**, is **American University**, an independent university chartered by Congress in 1893. The public is invited to attend on-campus lectures, concerts, movies and art exhibitions.

From Ward Circle, take Nebraska Avenue northeast to Connecticut Avenue, then head south a few blocks to **Politics and Prose**, a bookstore specializing in the books and interests of local authors. Readings, book-signing parties, and wine-and-cheese receptions are held regularly here. Farther down Connecticut, you'll pass the urban Van Ness campus of the **University of the District of Columbia** and the silvery UFO-style **Intelsat** building,

the headquarters of this international satellite communications company.

Continuing south leads you into **Cleveland Park**, a residential neighborhood recently designated an historic district. Named after President Grover Cleveland who spent the summers in the area , Cleveland Park is dominated by grand turn-of-the-century homes, mostly in Queen Anne or Georgian revival styles. Stroll down Newark Street to Highland Place, then onto Macomb Street to see a panoply of porches, turrets, Palladian windows, gabled roofs, balconies, and white picket fences.

At Connecticut and Ordway is the **Uptown Theater**, an art-deco gem that features epic-size movies on a big screen. Traffic gets tangled in front of the theater when private premier shows lure stars and fans. Across the street, in a convenient strip of shops are the Uptown Bakery (real bread, coffee, and pastries), Vace (real Italian deli with take-out), and Gallaghers (a real friendly neighborhood pub).

A bit farther north on Linnean Avenue is **Hillwood**, the estate of the late Marjorie Merriweather Post, Washington socialite and heiress of the Post cereal fortune. Hillwood is a rather quirky place, comprising a 40-room **Georgian mansion**, a **museum of decorative arts** and wonderful gardens. The inside of the house can be visited only by joining the two-hour guided tour to view 18th-century French decorative objects and masterpieces of Russian Imperial Art, many pieces collected when Mrs Post and her fourth husband served as the first American envoys to Moscow after the Russian Revolution.

If you prefer to go it alone, you can explore Hillwood's other buildings and **25 acres of grounds**. Here you'll find a *dacha* housing Russian folk art; an Adirondak-style cabin featuring American Indian artifacts, the greenhouse protecting thousands of orchids, and the pleasantly airy café building offering light fare and an afternoon tea with scones. The grounds also have formal Japanese and French gardens and a sweeping view over Rock Creek all the way to the Washington Monument. Don't miss the pet cemetery where Mrs Post's two dogs – Café au Lait and Crème de Cocoa – are buried amid dogtooth violets, weeping dogwoods and forget-me-nots.

Woodley Park, just south of Cleveland Park, also served as a summer retreat for a number of US presidents. The neighborhood takes its name from Woodley manor (now Maret School, at 3000 Cathedral Avenue) that served as a summer home for presidents Van Buren, Tyler, Buchanan, and Cleveland. Woodley Park's most famous residents these days, however, are **Marilyn Monroe** (painted on a huge mural at Calvert and Connecticut) and Ling-Ling and Hsing-Hsing, the two giant pandas living at the **National Zoological Park**.

Established in 1889 by the Smithsonian Institution to protect an acquired herd of buffalo, the zoo now features some 4,000 animals living in semi-natural environments on 163 wooded acres. The zoo's main trails have been beautifully re-landscaped according to the original plans of architect Frederick Law Olmsted, Jr. These paths link together a dozen looping side paths that lead to outdoor and indoor caged habitats supporting **rare blue-eyed white tigers, lowland gorillas** and other fabulous animals. Two recent additions to the zoo include the animal **Think Tank**, which helps to understand the way scientists investigate thinking, and the **Pollinarium**, inside the greenhouse.

For the "peaceable kingdom" experience of the zoo, visit the grounds in the morning before the buildings open or in the evening hours after the buildings close. This way, you can enjoy the meandering pathways before crowds of homo sapiens and baby carriages create mile-long conga lines. Many of the animals are fed and are most active in the morning before 10am.

Left, writer Niem Cheng a local resident. **Right**, a St Albans student strums.

LOGAN CIRCLE AND THE NORTHEAST

Picture Logan Circle – that Victorian-ringed rotary intersected by Rhode Island and Vermont avenues – as the focal point for the vast, amorphous area north of downtown and Capitol Hill, and east of Dupont Circle, that extends through the northeast quadrant. Bounded on the west by 16th Street, it is raggedly defined on the south by Massachusetts Avenue, North Capitol Street, Florida Avenue, and Benning Road to the Anacostia River. The Maryland border contains the rest.

Once fashionable: Beyond the pale of "tourist" Washington, this area unfortunately embraces some of DC's most troubled neighborhoods. Public transportation will get you to most sights, but take the car, if you have one. The once fashionable neighborhood of Logan Circle, with its remarkable concentration of three- and four-story Victorian mansions and townhouses, became synonymous in recent years with drug dealers, small-time pimps, and prostitutes. One of the city's more creative strategies for eliminating the latter problem was to round up the women and march them to the state of Virginia.

It was also near here that DC's inimitable former mayor Marion Barry was arrested for crack cocaine possession at the **Vista International Hotel** on **Thomas Circle**. Of late, tighter controls and impressive restoration efforts seem to have reversed the trend and Logan Circle is clearly on the yup-and-yup. Still, it's wise to confine your wanderings around here to daylight hours.

Housed in a pristine Victorian house one refurbished block off the circle at 1318 Vermont Avenue is the **Bethune Museum-Archives for Black Women's History**, named for the pioneering civil rights activist and educator Mary McLeod Bethune, who founded the National Council of Negro Women here in her one-time residence. Don't expect to see a "preserved" home or even a single personal article. This no-frills museum is dedicated to telling the history of black women, but its exhibits are surprisingly lean.

West of the circle, scattered along the somewhat seedy stretch of 14th Street now trendily tagged the "Uptown Arts District" – a reference to the city-supported cultural revival of this area – you'll find three of DC's funkiest and most enterprising alternative theaters, along with a growing batch of unpretentious restaurants and cafés.

On the corner of 14th and P streets, the **Studio Theatre** occupies an old car warehouse – complete with an industrial-sized elevator capable of transferring fully assembled sets from studio to stage – which has been outfitted as a state-of-the-art theater. The city's third-largest producing company after Arena Stage and the Folger, Studio productions range from classic to contemporary, and feature artists from around the country, not just local performers.

The more adventurous **Woolly Mammoth Theatre** just across the way on Church Street goes for the cutting-edge of contemporary drama, running new and preferably offbeat works by young playwrights, recent off-Broadway scripts, and avant-garde classics, all performed by a first-rate core company. As for the theater itself, it's rudimentary – 132 fold-up chairs and painted wood floors – but cozy.

A few blocks up the street is the **Source Theatre Company**, the smallest of the three. You're never more than six rows away from the actors in this stark, black theater. The Source spotlights work by new playwrights, and you can sometimes catch a late-night comedy show here. A regular summer event, the month-long **Washington Theatre Festival** showcases new plays by local – and variable – talent, staged here and at venues around town.

The ambience changes considerably when you get to 16th Street, two blocks to the east. Perfectly and impressively aligned with the White House, the wide, terraced boulevard was designed as *the* approach to the District by car. It also runs alongside the city's central meridian, which was surveyed in 1816 as a possible alternative to the prime meridian at Greenwich – an unviable idea, as it turned out. The line's presence is recalled around **Meridian Hill**.

Once considered as the site for a new presidential residence, Congress instead purchased 12 hillside acres between Florida Avenue and Euclid Street for a public park. Not just a green space, **Meridian Hill Park**, also known as Malcolm X Park, splendidly recreates the formal gardens of 17th-century France and Italy. Sadly, it's best not to visit this lovely spot alone, even during daylight hours.

Among the myriad houses of worship along 16th Street, which range from Baptist to Buddhist, Universalist to Unification, Swedenborgian to **Scottish Rite**, the latter – not a church, but nevertheless sacred – between R and S

Bethune Museum; dressed in Sunday best.

streets, is without a doubt one of the most remarkable. The Masons commissioned the capable John Russell Pope to design their **House of the Temple** in the image of the Tomb of Mausolus, one of the world's Seven Wonders. Every inch of this colossal, sphinx-flanked temple, which you can tour, is masonically significant and symbolic, down to its very proportions and the sequences of its front steps, which represent the sacred numbers of Pythagoras.

As you veer northeast, you will run into a hive of activity on Georgia Avenue around U Street, where the 150-acre, city-worn campus of **Howard University** begins. This prestigious and predominantly black institution, established in 1867 by civil rights champion Oliver O. Howard, has produced such high-caliber alumni as Andrew Young and Thurgood Marshall. If you can find it, the small **art gallery** in the **College of Fine Art** has a wonderful collection of African art and exhibits the work of major black American artists, as well as those by students, faculty, and alumni.

Prize-winning chapel: Once you cross North Capitol Street, you're in the city's northeast quadrant in the up-and-coming neighborhood of **Brookland**. The Catholic Church has a decided presence along this stretch of Michigan Avenue. In fact, it has a monopoly on the neighborhood's attractions. At **Trinity College** – a Catholic women's college founded in 1897 – the prize-winning Byzantine **Chapel of Notre Dame** boasts a 67-foot dome, marvelously filled with a La Farge mosaic depicting a scene from Dante's *Divina Comedia*. You may have to hunt for someone to unlock the door, however.

Just beyond sprawls the gray-stone campus of **Catholic University**. Founded in 1887, it is the only university established by American Roman Catholic bishops. The majority of its board members belong to the clergy. Catholic's **Hartke Theatre** is known not only for the quality and range of its productions, but for star alums like Jean

eighborhood rackhouse.

Kerr, Jon Voight, and Susan Sarandon.

It is the magnificent **Basilica of the National Shrine of the Immaculate Conception**, though, with its mosaicked and gold-crowned dome, which commands attention here. The hemisphere's largest Roman Catholic church, and the seventh-largest church in the world, this Byzantine-Romanesque monument consumes three acres donated by Catholic University, a gift sanctioned by Pope Pius X – who sent $400 along with his blessings. Dedicated to the Virgin Mary, the Marian shrine was constructed in fits and starts between 1920 and 1959 with funds from American parishes.

The basilica's ground floor holds the original dark and clammy **Crypt Church**; the sarcophagus of Bishop Thomas J. Shahan – the only person buried here; a hall of donors; and the tiara of Pope Paul VI. It all pales, though, compared to the glittering **Great Upper Church**, whose mosaic-covered walls contain an entire Italian quarry. Not to be missed are the three oratories and 57 unique chapels.

A right turn at Monroe Street will take you past **Colonel Brooks Tavern,** *the* neighborhood watering hole and good-time restaurant, which also serves up Dixieland jazz some nights of the week. If you're up for greasy southern soul food and ambience, try Murry & Paul's up on 12th Street, Brookland's old-fashioned Main Street.

At least you won't go hungry if you venture out here for a performance at the **Dance Place** at 3225 8th Street, the enterprising force behind DC's contemporary, avant-garde, and ethnic dance scene. Undaunted by its move from more central Adams Morgan – Dance Alley between 18th Street and Columbia Road keeps the legacy – it still stages the best in local, national, and international troupes each weekend, with special performances for Black History month in February and an annual African Dance Festival in June.

A pilgrimage to Brookland is incom-

A pointed encounter a Logan Circle

232

plete without a visit to the **Franciscan Monastery**, at 1400 Quincy Street. The Franciscans built themselves this hilltop American headquarters and named it Mount Saint Sepulchre. A sort of monastic theme park modeled after Istanbul's Hagia Sophia, it contains replicas of holy shrines, grottoes, and Roman catacombs.

Byzantine in style with Renaissance touches, the blindingly opulent monastery church, completed in 1899, contains stained-glass windows from Bavaria and a five-ton bronze altar canopy. In season the meticulous cloister garden is redolent with the scent of roses.

Much more modest in comparison is **St Anselm's Abbey**, the well-hidden Benedictine monastery at 4501 South Dakota Avenue and 14th Street. The monks annually host a spring flower show and sale on the grounds of the monastery.

n-executive ighborhoods en suffer.

South of Brookland at 800 Florida Avenue, **Gallaudet University**, the world's only college for the deaf, holds its own against the surrounding mean streets. Still, you can safely tour within the walled grounds of the Gothic-style campus, which were designed by Frederick Law Olmsted, Jr, the architect of New York's Central Park.

Not far to the east, by the banks of the Anacostia River, lies the **National Arboretum**, surprisingly undiscovered even by most locals. In fact, so little known is it that you can feel as though you have the entire rolling refuge of 444 acres of gardens and woods to yourself – except when the 70,000 azaleas, the arboretum's most prolific planting, are in bloom.

For an olfactory treat, be sure to smell the historic roses and specialty herbs opposite the bonsai exhibit, and then wander over to the surreal-looking stand of 22 Corinthian columns salvaged from the old portico of the US Capitol building. There are no concessions, so think about packing a picnic if you plan to spend any amount of time here – as you should.

SOUTHWEST WATERFRONT AND THE SOUTHEAST

Alive, alive-o! The heart of DC's Southwest and Southeast neighborhoods is the waterfront marina. At the **Maine Avenue Fish Market** along the Washington Channel, dozens of vendors hawk fresh seafood from the Chesapeake Bay and the lower Potomac and Delaware rivers. Boat-side stands are piled with everything from bluefish, rockfish and red snapper to soft-shell crabs, eels, and conch.

A fishy story: The market is open daily, year round, but go on a summer weekend when vendors are shouting, families are hauling away bushels of still-snapping blue crabs, and cars are squeezing in and out of the parking lot. Even if you're not planning a feast, stop by to savor the scene and a plate of freshly shucked clams or oysters. This is one area of town where you're likely to find a cab driver who'll get you to your destination on time. If he's stopped locally before picking you up, chances are the cabbie will have a crate of dripping seafood tucked away in the trunk of the car. It's in *both* your interests for him to step on the gas pedal pronto.

Not all of this part of DC is this lively, however. When the Federal City was laid out in 1791–92, the Southeast and Southwest quadrants north of the Anacostia River were slated as mixed residential and commercial areas. The mismanaged City Canal, which once flowed along Constitution Avenue, was intended to bring some of Georgetown's trade here. But the stinking canal and a new railroad depot sent the wealthier residents packing and created a squalid neighborhood of substandard buildings and high crime.

Beginning in the 1930s, a series of redevelopment plans were introduced, then abandoned or partially realized. As a result, much of this area is dominated by a jumble of "innovative" architect-designed buildings of little interest to most visitors. The rest of Southeast DC, separated from the city by the **Anacostia River**, developed slowly and independently from the nation's capital, though the neighborhoods here are populated largely by federal and District government employees.

Both the **Washington Channel** and the riverfront are lined with private yacht clubs and boat yards. From the pier at 6th and Water streets you can board the 145-foot *Spirit of Washington* for a scenic cruise on the Potomac River. This line offers a variety of day and nighttime cruises along the river, plus daytime excursions to George Washington's home, Mount Vernon.

The waterfront is also popular for dining. Several cavernous restaurants along Maine Avenue and Water Street specialize in seafood and panoramic views of the Washington Channel, marina, and downtown monuments. The Big Six – Le Rivage, Pier 7, Hogate's, 700 Water Street, Phillips, and the

eft, a scaled-down ale at aine venue arket.

ight, sailor om the ashington avy Yard.

Gangplank seat from 75 to 725 diners and also offer a variety of entertainments such as happy hours, comedy acts, dancing, and live jazz.

Nearby **Arena Stage** at 6th and M streets, is one of the best places in DC for first-rate dramas, comedies, and musicals – both classic and contemporary. From its humble beginnings in the old vat room of the former Heurich Brewery (where the Kennedy Center now stands), the company performs in a complex that includes the 800-seat **Arena Theater** (in the round), the 500-seat **Kreeger Theater**, and the 180-seat cabaret-style **Old Vat Room**.

Southwest of the Arena, occupying the mile-long peninsula near the confluence of the Washington Channel and the Potomac and Anacostia rivers, is **Fort McNair**, one of the oldest active military posts in the US. Though the original 18th-century fort and arsenal were destroyed and the buildings of the Army War College (now expanded into the **National Defense University**) are

not open to the public, the grounds and views of **Hains Point** and the waterfront make a pleasant visit for military history buffs.

Farther up the Anacostia River in Southeast is the **Washington Navy Yard**. This historic precinct served as a naval gun factory during the 19th century. The precinct comprises the **Marine Corps Museum** and the **Navy Memorial Museum**, both accessible from the 9th and M streets entrance. The Marine Corps Museum galleries include combat art, uniforms, weapons, and technology. Also on display is memorabilia of John Philip Sousa, master of the Marine Band from 1880 to 1892 and composer of about 140 military marches. The Navy Memorial Museum's 5,000 artifacts trace naval history from the Revolutionary War to the age of space exploration.

On the south side of the Anacostia River is **Anacostia**, one of the city's less affluent neighborhoods best visited by car and with a degree of caution. Incorporated in 1854 as one of Washington's earliest subdivisions, **Old Anacostia** retains certain historical and architectural appeal. Between Good Hope Road, Martin Luther King Boulevard and 14th Street, you'll find the **Old Market Square**, several 19th-century churches, and pleasantly embellished frame houses.

On a tree-shaded hilltop at 14th and W streets stands **Cedar Hill**, the stately home of black abolitionist, presidential advisor, and writer Frederick Douglass. The 21-room house speaks volumes of the life and times of Douglass and his family from 1877 to 1895. During this period, this self-educated former slave worked as the US Marshal and recorder of deeds for DC, and minister to Haiti.

Many of Douglass's original possessions are on display, including his impressive personal library of 1,200 volumes and gifts from President Lincoln, Harriet Beecher Stowe, William Lloyd Garrison. Cedar Hill is not a sanitized period home, but a home that keeps

Cedar Hill, home of black statesman Frederick Douglass.

Douglass's memory very alive. At 1901 Fort Place is the **Anacostia Museum**, one of the Smithsonian Institution's off-the-Mall museums. This innovative museum documents the history, culture, and contributions of notable African Americans.

Around Anacostia you'll also find five of the nearly 50 forts built in a ring around the city at the outbreak of the Civil War. **Forts Stanton**, **Davis**, **Dupont**, **Chaplin**, and **Mahan** now form a chain of city parks where the forts' original earthworks can be discerned. Fort Dupont, the best preserved of the group, also includes recreational facilities and hiking and biking trails.

With just a little bit of imagination you can visit Monet's gardens at Giverny… at **Kenilworth Aquatic Gardens**. Just off the Anacostia Freeway in DC's northeast corner, this 12-acre sanctuary, founded in 1882 near the marshlands of the Anacostia River, features pond after pond of exotic water lilies, lotuses, and aquatic plants in a natural outdoor setting. Summertime promises the most blooms, and early mornings are the best time to visit since you can see the night-blooming flowers before they close and day-bloomers as they open. This garden is a joy just to wander in, filtering color and light as if to please an Impressionist painter.

The gardens are also a treat for amateur naturalists. Behind the visitor center there are three ponds of labeled species where you can familiarize yourself with the tropical lilies and ancient lotuses (the rest of the gardens are label free). The most extraordinary lilies are the Victoria *amazonica* from South America which have platter-like leaves up to six feet across. The quieter you (and your children) are on your visit, the better your chances for spotting the resident toads, turtles, muskrats, green herons, red-winged blackbirds, and migrating waterfowl. Whatever you bring to Kenilworth – a camera, paints and an easel, or a picnic – you'll leave this watery area with a sense of tranquillity.

Barbershop Anacostia.

AROUND WASHINGTON

The Capital's rapidly expanding Virginia and Maryland suburbs offer almost as many attractions and distractions as the city itself. Surrounding the District on four sides, the suburbs hold dozens of residential neighborhoods, parks, museums, restaurants, parks, and commuter traffic that are urban enough to be within DC's borders.

Southern perspective: This fact often makes the transition between the city and suburb almost indistinguishable, especially inside the Interstate 95 Beltway around the city. The most popular sights are in towns and parks in Montgomery County in Maryland, in Fairfax and Arlington counties and the City of Alexandria in Virginia. Since Arlington County and a section of Alexandria were part of Washington from the late 18th to mid-19th century, the historic homes and museums here chronicle the history of the nation and of its developing capital city during this vital period, but with a slightly southern perspective. Beyond the Beltway the suburbs become more rural and the influence of the federal government becomes less pronounced.

You can visit most of the nearby suburban attractions by public transportation, car or bike. Expect traffic congestion on most roads during the morning and evening rush hours, as commuters plunge headlong to or from DC. One way you can usually beat the traffic is on the **W&OD bike trail,** which runs 45 miles from Alexandria west into Loudoun County, or on the **Mount Vernon Trail** which parallels the Potomac River from the Lincoln Memorial south to Mount Vernon.

Before leaving DC proper, be sure to stop in the middle of the Potomac River on 88-acre **Theodore Roosevelt Island**. Walking paths criss-cross this wooded wildlife haven and lead to a 23-foot-tall statue of President Theodore

Roosevelt. Just south is **Lady Bird Johnson Park**, a 121-acre man-made island planted with some 1,000 flowering dogwood trees and a million daffodils. Within this park is the **Lyndon Baines Johnson Memorial Grove** where white pines, dogwoods, rhododendrons, and azaleas surround a monolith of pink Texas granite.

As you cross Memorial Bridge into Arlington, **Arlington House** dominates the hill before you. Arlington House was the home of Robert E. Lee and his wife Mary Anna Randolph Custis, great-granddaughter of Martha Washington. The couple lived here from 1831 until Lee resigned his commission in the US Army to defend his native Virginia in the Civil War.

During the war, hundreds of Union Army soldiers occupied the property and cut most of the 200 acres of virgin oak forest for fortifications and firewood. In 1864, after Mrs Lee refused to pay the property tax in person, the Federal government confiscated the

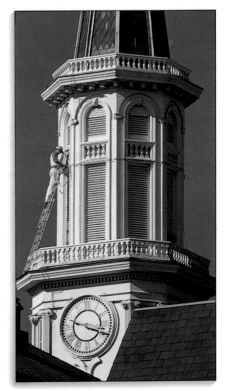

estate and established what is now Arlington National Cemetery on the grounds. The house has been restored to its mid-19th-century appearance to offer a glimpse of pre-war Southern gentility. Walk the scenic route to the house via 200 easy steps north of the main gate of the cemetery.

The rolling hills of **Arlington National Cemetery** hold more than 213,000 graves and represent America's history of war – from the Revolutionary War to the Persian Gulf War. The simple white headstones, set in even rows as far as the eye can see, make a moving testament to the US's military sacrifices.

Unless you are visiting a relative or friend buried here, access to the graves is limited to Tourmobile buses departing from the Visitors Center or, even better, your own two feet. Unless you can't, walk. Lines for Tourmobiles are often interminably long and the narrated tour covers only the central cemetery. Your experience here will be enhanced by a solemn, strolling pace.

The **Tomb of the Unknown Dead** of the Civil War marks the grave of the 2,111 soldiers who died on nearby Virginia battlefields. The mast of the **battleship *Maine*** marks the grave of 229 men who died in the explosion preceding the Spanish-American War. The **Tomb of the Unknowns** (formerly the Tomb of the Unknown Soldier), carved from a 50-ton block of Colorado marble, holds the remains of four US servicemen, one each from World Wars I and II, and the Korean and Vietnam Wars. The **Changing of the Guard**, which takes place here every half-hour in summer, every hour in winter and also throughout the night, is on every visitor's list of things to see while in Washington.

Others buried here include Pierre L'Enfant, Oliver Wendell Holmes, Rear Admirals Robert E. Peary and Richard E. Byrd and presidents Taft and Kennedy. **John F. Kennedy's grave**, with its simple, eternal flame glowing in **Dulles International Airport...**

all weathers, still attracts crowds of visitors. The **tomb of Robert F. Kennedy** is not far away in a grassy plot.

At the cemetery's north end stands the **Iwo Jima Memorial**. The 100-ton bronze statue depicts the raising of the US flag on Iwo Jima, the World War II battle site where more than 5,000 marines died. On Tuesday evenings during summer, the Marine Silent Drill Team and Drum and Bugle Corps hold a public sunset ceremony here.

Just south of Arlington Cemetery is one of the world's largest office buildings, the **Pentagon**. This five-sided, five-storied headquarters of the Department of Defense covers 3,705,793 square feet and provides offices, restaurants, and shops for more than 23,000 civilian and military employees. Hour-long tours, conducted by backward-walking guides, feature corridor after corridor of combat art, portraits of high-ranking officials, aircraft models, and, finally and oddly, a massive slab of the Berlin Wall. What makes a Pentagon tour fascinating is the very fact that you *can* tour this building. Be sure to use the Metrorail or Metrobus as visitor parking is poorly marked and inconvenient.

West of the Pentagon you'll find Arlington's high-rise office complexes of **Rosslyn** and **Crystal City** and its lower-rise residential neighborhoods. The immigrant Asian population here has created a wealth of Vietnamese, Cambodian, Korean and Thai restaurants, many located in what is called **Little Saigon** on Wilson Boulevard.

Back along the Potomac River is **Washington National Airport**. Just 3˅ miles from downtown, this airport suffers from traffic congestion – both automobile and airplane – so use the Metro and expect flight delays. For a close-up view of the planes taking off and landing, there are two open parking areas along the GW Parkway: **Roaches Run**, north of the airport, and the **Washington Sailing Marina**, south of the airport. The marina offers lessons and rentals in sailing and windsurfing as well as renting out bicycles. The marina's Potowmack Landing restaurant has outdoor seating with great views of the river and DC.

The parkway continues south into **Old Town Alexandria**, a charming eight-square-block historic district of 18th- and 19th-century buildings and a colonial port atmosphere. Alexandria was founded in 1670s and soon became a prominent trading center that once rivaled the ports of New York and Boston. You'll find Alexandria similar in many ways to Georgetown, but this Virginia port city, founded in the 1670s, is smaller, sleepier, and serves up more southern hospitality. Begin your amble at the **Ramsay House Visitors Center** on King Street where out-of-town visitors can pick up a free parking pass for the metered on-street spaces.

To get a background in Alexandria's history, stop by the local history exhibits at the **Lyceum museum** on South Washington Street or the **Carlyle House**, a grand Scottish-manor-style

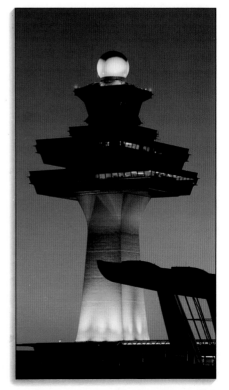

was
signed by
ro
arinen.

home on North Fairfax Street and one of the first homes built in Alexandria. Signs proclaiming "George Washington Slept Here" are common and questionable from New York to Georgia, but Alexandria's claims are *bona fide*.

In 1765 Washington built a townhouse here at **508 Cameron Street** (a replica of the original home now stands in its place) and Washington celebrated his last two birthdays in the ballroom of what is now **Gadbsy's Tavern Museum** on North Royal Street. The museum preserves an original tavern (1770) and the City Hotel (1792) that was a center of political, business, and social life in early Alexandria. Next door, the 200-year-old **Gadbsy's Tavern Restaurant** offers hearty 18th-century victuals served by waiters in period dress and character.

Alexandria's favorite native son, Robert E. Lee, lived in a red-brick house on Oronoco Street from 1812 until his West Point enrollment in 1825. This gracious home, now called the **Robert**

E. Lee Boyhood Home, is handsomely furnished throughout with early 19th-century antiques.

Alexandria's art scene is as vital as its history, with more than 20 Old Town galleries and the **Torpedo Factory Art Center**. A munitions factory during both world wars, the Torpedo Factory houses the studios of 150 artists who create, display, and sell their works on the premises. Stroll north from here to the **Alexandria Waterfront Museum** in the TransPotomac Canal Center and to the nearby whimsical sculpture called *Promenade Classique*.

Farther south on the GW Parkway you'll arrive at **Mount Vernon**, the beautiful estate of Martha and George Washington during the years 1754 to 1799. Situated on a bluff above the Potomac River, the white Georgian mansion has been meticulously restored to its appearance during the last years of Washington's life.

The home contains much of the original furniture, including **Washington's death bed**, his sword and clothing, and articles belonging to his family. The **stables, kitchen, gardens, slave quarters** and **greenhouse** have also been carefully preserved. Well-tended period gardens and the **Washingtons' burial vault** are a short walk from the mansion. About 10,000 tourists a day visit the estate during peak season – so be sure to get an early start.

An easy drive west of DC toward Vienna, Virginia, is **Wolf Trap Farm Park**, America's only national park for the performing arts. The much-loved **Filene Center** stage draws some 6,800 picnic-toting patrons here in summertime for concerts (opera, ballet, modern dance, jazz, stand-up comedians) in both covered and lawn seating. The intimate barns at Wolf Trap hosts a variety of performances from October through May. Continuing west to the foothills of the Blue Ridge Mountains, is **Washington Dulles International Airport**, a graceful sweep of a building designed in 1962 by Eero Saarinen.

Pulitzer Prize-winning resident Stanley Karnow.

Between the Potomac River and MacArthur Boulevard in Maryland is **Glen Echo**, an arts and performance center remembered by generations of Washingtonians as a countryside amusement park at the terminus of DC's old trolley line.

Now a National Park, Glen Echo seems caught in a twilight zone where applause from theater audiences, squeals from roller-coaster riders, and plinking tunes of the merry-go-round always echo. Many of the restored amusement park buildings serve as either art studios and classrooms, a children's theater, or a ballroom dancing center. Nearby is the **Clara Barton National Historic Site**, the 36-room home of the founder of the American Red Cross.

No visitor should leave the Washington area without paying homage to the natural feature that determined the location of the capital city. The spectacular and turbulent **Great Falls of the Potomac** can be viewed from parks on both Maryland and Virginia shores. Here, the Potomac River makes its final plunge down a series of rapids and cataracts en route to the Chesapeake Bay. On the Maryland side, off MacArthur Boulevard, the falls are part of the **C&O Canal Historic Park** that includes the towpath, restored canal locks, and the 1828 **Great Falls Tavern** (which is now a museum).

On the Virginia side, off Georgetown Pike, **Great Falls Park** offers more dramatic views of the 76-foot falls from an observation area and from massive boulders above the river. The best time to visit is during spring floods when the volume of water often exceeds that of Niagara Falls.

Swift currents and slippery rocks are responsible for several drownings each year; caution is strongly advised when venturing near the water. The park's extensive trails parallel the river, cut through woodland and swampy areas, and also offer views of the Potomac River and the chasm of Mather Gorge.

ount
ernon,
eorge
ashington's
me from
'54 to 1799.

DAY TRIPS:
MARYLAND

To the north and east of Washington, DC lie ample opportunities for day trips. You can follow the path of the 17th-century pioneers through the Blue Hills to the Cumberland Gap, and Deep Creek Lake. There is a major Civil War site at Antietam, near the old town of Frederick with its many antique shops. For summer sun and swimming there are the beaches of the Eastern Shore of Chesapeake Bay and, if you don't mind the driving, more beaches in the state of Delaware. Along the way is the delightful and historic coastal town of Annapolis, and the port of Baltimore.

BALTIMORE: The city on the Chesapeake Bay is the site of the nation's oldest monument to George Washington. It also boasts Edgar Allen Poe, the waspish man of letters H. L. Mencken, and the baseball hero Babe Ruth as favorite sons. As Baltimore is only a 45-minute drive from Washington, it can't be too many decades before it becomes a formalized extension of the capital, as the suburbs creep towards each other along the Beltway.

Baltimore is an elderly, distinguished city that has undergone some drastic revitalizing, particularly around the old run-down **Inner Harbor** area, now a throbbing tourist attraction. The wide pedestrian area that swings round the waterfront hums with action – jugglers, trick cyclists and magicians giving impromptu performances to the crowds that it draws from out of the vast mall behind. You can rent rowing boats, pedalos and sailboats from spring through to fall, or stare back towards the new and challenging high-rise buildings embracing the harbor from across the bows of the submarine *USS Torsk* – one of the fastest submarines launched during World War II.

Housed in one of these high-rises is the **National Aquarium**, a great introduction to the underwater world. You

begin the visit on the top story of the pyramid-shaped building, and gently wind your way down the middle of a glass-fronted, 220,000-gallon **Open Ocean tank** that mirrors the marine life you would find at equivalent depths in the sea – brightly colored fish on the top floor, the sharks down in the murky depths on the ground. There is a **Hands-On pool** where children can touch starfish, anemones, shellfish and sea vegetation, as well as other tanks that present specific marine habitats.

Across the other side of the harbor is the Maryland **Science Center** and Davis Planetarium. Although in summertime there are lines to get into the National Aquarium, they are better managed than those at the Science Center, so be prepared for a disorderly wait. But children generally find it worthwhile, particularly when they can watch – or volunteer for – live demonstrations that set their hair standing on end or show how they can emit electric sparks from their bodies. It is a predomi-

Preceding pages: bird-watching; fishing near Great Falls; checked out for the season. **Left** and **right**, Maryland is full of gracious homes.

nantly hands-on experience, with excellent displays that explain many of modern science's inventions and discoveries in an easy-to-understand fashion. There are also permanent exhibits on the life of the Chesapeake Bay, geology and energy exhibits, plus thought-provoking temporary shows. Also housed in the building and almost more fun than the scientific section is the awe-inspiring display of stars and planets in the night sky of the **Davis Planetarium**, as well as a cinema screen, five-storys high, showing IMAX theater movies that almost push you into the action.

ANNAPOLIS: A city dear to George Washington's heart, Annapolis is the capital of Maryland – though it likes to style itself "The Sailing Capital of the United States." Dedicated visitors should start at the Tourism Council of Annapolis and Anne Arundel County for information and maps.

Nothing has changed in the 18th-century heart of the town, though Annapolis has grown enormously beyond the city center. It is a charming place to cover on foot, particularly along the **waterfront**. This still presents a soothing vista of masts and sails, since the harbor has always been too shallow to accept anything but small vessels. Unless you are a boat enthusiast yourself, it can be a place to avoid on the last weekend in April and in October when the city hosts America's largest sail and power boat shows and all other movement grinds to a halt.

The **Maryland State House**, built in 1772, is the oldest state capitol building in continuous use in America. This is where George Washington resigned his commission as commander-in-chief of the Continental Army in 1783; where the Treaty of Paris that officially ended the Revolution was signed in 1784; and where Thomas Jefferson was appointed the first United States ambassador to France. Its cypress-beam dome is the largest wooden dome in the country. The elegant plasterwork in the central

Baltimore's Inner Harbor

hall cost the life of Thomas Dance, the craftsman who executed it, when he fell 90 feet from the scaffolding.

Other interesting sites include the **Old Senate Chamber**, where a bronze plaque marks the place where George Washington stood to deliver his farewell address, the **House of Delegates** and the **New Senate Chamber**, both with skylights designed by Tiffany.

There are three private houses that can be visited that date from the period when George Washington spent much of his time in Annapolis. The **house of William Paca**, a signatory of the Declaration of Independence and governor of Maryland, was built in 1765 and is furnished with period furniture and paintings. In the restored terraced garden is a fish-shaped pool. **Hammond-Harwood House** was built between 1773 and 1774 and has one of the most beautiful carved doors of the time. Opposite is the **Chase-Lloyd House**, begun by Supreme Court Justice Chase in 1769, and continued by Edward Lloyd IV, a wealthy planter, who took over in 1771 when Chase ran out of funds. This house is on three floors with a formidable hall of Ionic pillars and a so-called "floating" staircase.

If there's time, the **Naval Academy** is worth a tour. Now the base for 4,000 midshipmen (and some 450 women), its 329 acres include, among other interesting sites, the Chapel in which are found the remains of the father of the US Navy, revolutionary hero John Paul Jones. One-hour guided tours begin at the Visitor Information Center in **Ricketts Hall**. If you don't have long in Annapolis, be sure to take one of the 1˘-hour walking tours with Historic Annapolis Inc. that leave from the Old Treasury Building in State Circle.

CHESAPEAKE BAY AREA: For some reason, Washingtonians seem only to truly believe they have been to the beach if they have spent 3˘ hours – or more frequently 5˘ hours with the extra time spent in a traffic jam – getting there. But there are two alternatives to the Atlantic

Maryland's
history
continues top
fascinate.

shore haul, where it is just as possible to get sunburnt and sand in your sandwiches without the stress of the drive. One is the Eastern Shore, with its small and evocative old colonial towns; the other is the beaches of the Bay.

On the **Baltimore side** of the **Bay Bridge**, the string of small beaches is less imposing than on the other side, with gentler waves and unthreatening currents; these beaches do attract jellyfish, however. At many of the beaches there are special nets to keep these out of the swimming areas. Compensation for these inconvenient creatures is the generous supply of beach amenities, like paddle-boat rentals, barbecue grills and picnic tables, or swings and playgrounds for children. Right by the Bay Bridge on the last Route 50 exit before the bridge is **Sandy Point State Park**, which is good for picnicking, fishing and swimming. **Rocky Point Waterfront Park**, at Back River Neck and Barrison Point roads, Back River, offers a large beach, lifeguards, boat rentals,

fishing, horseshoe pits, volleyball court and picnic areas. **Bay Ridge Beach**, at Herendon Avenue, Bay Ridge, Annapolis, is a privately owned public beach with nettle nets at sea, a swimming pool and a baby pool, snack bar, regular bar and wooded picnic area.

The **Eastern Shore** is one of Washington's best kept secrets. While energetic young people tear across the Bay Bridge in their open jeeps, radios blaring, heading for the Atlantic coast resorts of Rehoboth and Ocean City in Delaware, the relaxed and unassuming towns of the Eastern Shore lie closer to home and are for the most part ignored. On the far side of the Chesapeake Bay from Baltimore and Annapolis, this is where the gentry of more gentle times came to take the sea air. It's an area of farms and marshlands, wild bird sanctuaries and road-side produce booths, seafood restaurants and small beaches dusted with shells.

Cambridge, a small town of some 11,000 people, is characteristic of the **A rural retreat.**

Eastern Shore. Founded in the 1680s, it sits between the **Choptank River** and a **National Wildlife Refuge** stretch of tidal marshlands and woods favored in winter by tens of thousands of migrating ducks and Canada geese. Start at the Dorchester County Office Building for a guided walking tour.

There is plenty to see on a pleasant day out, from cowgirl **Annie Oakley's** house at the end of Hambrook Boulevard, to the early 18th-century **Meredith House** and **Neild Museum** with its smokehouse, antique doll collection, crafts and furniture. The **Brannock Maritime Museum** on Talbot Avenue shows a history of the Chesapeake Bay, in particular its oyster industry. Local restaurants are good, too, with most specializing in local crab.

Just two hours from Washington is the old but still active village of **St Michaels**, a center of boating activity located where the **Miles River** meets the Chesapeake Bay. Apart from the very attractive **harbor**, the **Chesa-**peake Bay Maritime Museum** is the main focus for visitors, an extensive waterfront edifice with a lighthouse and several old local sailing ships and vessels to see. There are two oyster dredgers from the 1850s. In summer you can see some of the larger ships, their sails billowing, racing in the warm breeze. There are a few recommended restaurants in town, too, for food and drink after the sun sets.

You can take two worthwhile trips from St Michaels – one to **Oxford**, taking the Oxford-Bellevue ferry, supposedly the oldest privately owned ferry in the United States. In the town you can visit the **Maritime Museum** on Morris and Market streets. The second trip is to **Tilghman Island**. Here you can chat with the fishermen of the Chesapeake Bay as they work on their boats and nets.

St Michaels is not far from **Easton**, an old colonial bay-side town full of antique shops and old book stores. This is an area of strong religious background.

fe in the ay area.

In 1777, the Eastern Shore Quakers vowed to "disunite" any member of the congregation who still employed slaves. In Easton, William Penn preached at the **Third Haven Meeting House**, built in 1682 and possibly the oldest frame house of worship still in use. There are numerous historical manor houses and dwellings around Easton, but most of them are scattered outside the town itself. Contact the Historical Society of Talbot County for information, guides and maps.

ATLANTIC OCEAN BEACHES: Washingtonians head for **Ocean City** in Maryland, and quieter **Rehoboth, Dewey Beach, Bethany Beach** and **Fenwick Island** in Delaware to avoid the heavy humidity of summer. Just 3ˇ hours from Washington, on the southern Atlantic shore, Rehoboth in summer is a jumping hot bed of noise, music, T-shirt emporia, beach beauties and Adonises.

Along the boardwalk is a run of stores selling saltwater taffy, hot dogs and souvenirs and a small fun fair with airplane rides and dodgem cars. On Saturdays there are band concerts and talent opportunities for summer visitors. As well as the usual resort fast foods, there are a number of up-market restaurants just behind the main drag, not necessarily charging upmarket prices, and striving to serve original and pleasantly presented dishes.

If you prefer your seaside experience a little less brash, the beach at **Cape Henlopen State Park** is in a protected nature reserve and simply offers you hundreds of yards of open beach and empty sand dunes. Be warned with small children that the surf along all of this coast is sometimes quite strong and the current can be vigorous. However, all of the beaches are well manned by efficient-looking lifeguards.

DEEP CREEK LAKE AREA: Washington's other water sports center, 4 hours west from the capital and turning itself into a skiing resort in winter, is Deep Creek Lake in the heart of the Appalachian Mountains. Built in 1925 as a reservoir,

Both bay and ocean beaches can be easily reached.

it encompasses 3,900 acres of fresh water that provide a paradise for fishermen and watersports enthusiasts.

There are sailboats, power boats and canoes for rent at the several marinas around the lake, with regular weekend sailboat races and water skiing events, including the Barefoot Skiing Championships. From May to October there are sponsored fishing contests with prizes for the biggest largemouth bass, bluegill, chain pickerel, walleye and more. The woods that reach down to the lake offer cool and quiet trail walks.

West of Deep Creek Lake is the town of **Cumberland** which began as Fort Cumberland, a crucial frontier outpost during the French and Indian War. George Washington defended the town and you can visit his one-room log cabin headquarters – the only remains of the fort – in **Riverside Park**.

A handsome town of fine buildings, parks and gardens, Cumberland is full of antique and curio shops. **Washington Street** is where the rich coal and rail

barons lived, in mansions ornately executed in all styles from Federal to Georgian Revival. The **History House** on Washington Street is full of household gadgets, technical machinery and toys of the 19th century. Nineteen fully furnished rooms illustrate life in 1867, while another room depicts an early 1900s schoolroom. In the basement is the old servants' quarters, with kitchen and pantry, while elsewhere in the house are rooms displaying 19th-century costumes, veterinary, medical and dental equipment. One of the oldest buildings on the street is the **First Church of Christ Scientist**.

But the railway station, with its displays of memorabilia, is where you should start. Not only because this is where you can collect a pamphlet for a self-guided walking tour of the town, but because this is where the train departs. An old restored locomotive huffs and puffs its way through the beautiful **Cumberland Gap** to the town of Frostburg on a splendid 3-hour round trip.

creation
cilities are
cellent.

There is a layover in Frostburg, with enough time to eat in the terminus, browse through its gift shops, take a turn at the video games, or watch how the railroad turntable works from the observation room. There is even time to venture into **Frostburg** itself for a brief walk around the town before boarding the locomotive for the ride back.

ANTIETAM NATIONAL BATTLEFIELD: The battle of Antietam, when the South's General Lee tried to follow up his victory at Manassas by invading the northern states, was the scene of the greatest and bloodiest carnage of the entire Civil War. It all took place in a single day. More than 23,000 men were slain and "lay in rows precisely as they had stood in their ranks a few moments before," according to Union General Joseph Hooker.

Clara Barton, founder of the American Red Cross, was among those who tended the wounded. After the Manassas battle in Virginia, Lee sent **Stonewall Jackson** to seize the vital river crossing and arsenal of Harper's Ferry, and lead his soldiers into Maryland in the hope of forcing the evacuation of Washington and swinging the slave-owning state of Maryland to the Southern cause. Unfortunately, his battle plan fell into the hands of Union General George McClellan. When the Confederates marched into the little town of Sharpsburg they walked straight into 87,000 Union soldiers. Though the resulting carnage left both sides wondering who had won, and whether the cost was worth the victory, the battle was a crucial turning point in the Civil War.

After the South's defeat, it lost its very real hope of winning diplomatic recognition and the support of European countries. President Lincoln took the battle as an apposite moment to denounce slavery officially. One week after the battle, on September 23, 1862, a draft of Lincoln's Emancipation Proclamation was published in the press.

The 26-minute film at the **Visitor Center**, set in the rolling Maryland pastureland where the battle occurred, gives the best orientation to start your tour. It takes you from **Dunker Church**, where fighting commenced, to the cornfield which saw most of the military action, and to **Bloody Lane** where, in four hours, 5,000 soldiers lost their lives. Unless you are a sturdy hiker (and the Visitor Center provides maps if you are), you will need to tour by car as the site is large and enclosed inside a network of minor roads.

Perhaps the most dramatic spot is **Burnside's Bridge**, where a handful of Georgian sharpshooters held off Burnside's infantry division, shooting them down as they tried to cross a narrow stone bridge. Burnside's scouts did not find a ford across the river until it was too late. You can still see the Georgians' fox-holes on the hill above the bridge. A map and brochure detail the events at the 11 stops you make along a drive of 8ˇ miles. Renting a cassette tape is also illuminating.

Left, sails to the wind. Right, armchair equestrian.

DAY TRIPS: VIRGINIA

Washington was founded as a geographical compromise midway between the Northern and Southern states. And, as a result, it is wonderfully placed for day trips that bring the visitor very different flavors of the surrounding countryside, its turbulent history and cultural progress.

To the west of Washington lie the Blue Ridge Mountains of Virginia. Its Shenandoah Valley is perfect for fall drives to admire autumn leaves the equal of any leaf color view in New England. To the south and west are the poignantly moving battlefields of the Civil War, each with detailed on-the-spot explanations and diagrams; near Charlottesville are monuments to America's more peaceful development: Thomas Jefferson's house and the University of Virginia, two of the most civilized establishments to be found on any continent.

MONTICELLO: Located on the top of a foothill of the Blue Ridge Mountains close to the town of Charlottesville, Monticello is perhaps the only historical house in America that entirely expresses the character of its owner. While there may not be an enormous amount to see in the way of a personal collection of treasures and possessions, nonetheless the spirit of Thomas Jefferson infuses the entire estate. Jefferson built Monticello between 1769 and 1809 as a house to retire to, an expression in brick and mortar of his ideals and sensibilities.

This classical tribute to the architects of ancient Greece and Rome was a haven from politics. But while reflecting Jefferson's love of the graceful symmetry and spareness of line found in those ancient civilizations, Monticello also incorporates many of Jefferson's own innovative ideas: in his study is a desk-cum-chaise he designed that allowed him to write while lying down; on the

long windows are sliding double glass doors to keep in the heat and nearby are silent "dumb waiters" that travel between floors to carry light parcels upstairs or down.

His garden, too – carefully restored according to Jefferson's detailed gardening notes – expresses the civilized nature of the man, laid out in a perfect balance of shape and showing where he practiced his experimental gardening and cultivation techniques. Here the president grew 20 varieties of his favorite English pea, and more than 250 different kinds of vegetable.

CHARLOTTESVILLE: The **University of Virginia** is yet another manifestation in stone of the beliefs and principles of Thomas Jefferson. Charlottesville is the graceful Virginia town, set against a backdrop of rolling foothills, where, in 1817 along with James Madison and James Monroe, Jefferson laid the cornerstone for the university. The former president was 75 years old when he drew up the blueprints for these elegant

grounds with their classical buildings united by a covered colonnade of lyrical arches and pillars. Here, too, can be seen the influence of ancient Roman architecture – particularly in the **Rotunda**, modeled after the Roman Pantheon – and the designs of the Italian Renaissance architect, Andrea Palladio. Begin at the Thomas Jefferson Visitors Center at the intersection of Route I-64 and 20 South for maps, leaflets and a driving tour map of historic sites.

FREDERICKSBURG: This peaceful town is not only famous as the place where George Washington grew up, but for the devastating Civil War battles fought around it. Over 750,000 troops clashed in the fields beyond Fredericksburg, but the town of Washington's boyhood is a tranquil, civilized place where more than 350 buildings were constructed before 1870. It is here, rather than at Mount Vernon, where he was supposed to have thrown a dollar – not across the mile-wide Potomac, but the 300-foot wide Rappahannock

River. The soon-to-be president also threw, not a dollar, but a Spanish doubloon instead.

Fredericksburg is full of history. The best place for an overall picture before a tour is the Visitors Center on **Caroline Street** which has a film show, maps and block tickets for a nearly 50 percent saving on entry to many historical sites. On **Charles Street** is the house of Mary Washington, the president's mother, in which she lived for the last 17 years of her life. It is furnished with period pieces, and the garden restored to its original 18th-century form. Costumed guides show visitors both. Look out for the ornamental plasterwork in the **Great Room** and Mary Washington's needlepoint. Tea and gingerbread cooked according to Mary Washington's own recipe is served in the kitchen building by folks in period dress.

In the **James Monroe Law Office** on Charles Street can be seen correspondence between Monroe and Jefferson, Washington and Benjamin Franklin; White House china and cutlery from the period, and pieces of furniture President Monroe acquired for the White House, some of them from France and said to have belonged to Marie Antoinette. Tea and wassail, a traditional hot mulled wine, served by period costumed waitresses are available at The **Rising Sun Tavern**, built in 1760 by George Washington's brother Charles as a residence and turned into a tavern in the 1780s.

CIVIL WAR SITES: Enthusiasts of the War Between the States will find no shortage of sites to visit within an easy day's trip from Washington. One of the bloodiest battles was at Antietam in Maryland (*see the preceding chapter*) but 60 percent of the engagements were fought on Virginia soil. Between December 1862 and May 1864, more than 100,000 soldiers in Confederate and Union forces were found dead or wounded on the fields of what is now the **Fredericksburg and Spotsylvania National Military Park**.

Four devastating major battles of the

Abraham Lincoln reviews the war situation at Antietam, 1863.

Civil War – the Battle of Fredericksburg, December 11–13, 1862; the Battle of Chancellorsville, April 27–May 6, 1863; the Battle of the Wilderness, May 5–6, 1864; and the first confrontation between General Robert E. Lee and General Ulysses S. Grant, the Battle of Spotsylvania Court House, May 8–21, 1864 – were fought on an area that stretches beyond the 6,000 acres of woods and meadows that make up the military park.

This is an area punctuated with trenches and gunpits. When viewed listening to the taped narrative available from the Visitor's Center it makes for an immensely moving experience. It is hard to imagine that this gentle countryside was once the scene of the most appalling carnage; it is difficult to tell which is more sobering, the closely-wooded country around **Chancellorsville** where the enemy got frighteningly close before being seen, or the open killing field of Fredericksburg itself. General Robert E. Lee's troops shel-

tered almost invulnerably behind a country wall and mowed down line after line of advancing Union soldiers, almost 10,000 men in a matter of hours.

At Chancellorsville is the small building in which General Stonewall Jackson died after being mortally wounded by his own troops as he reconnoitered Union troop movements. It is now called the **Stonewall Jackson Memorial Shrine** and commemorates his life and military career.

A mapped driving tour follows a loop that includes most of the major battles, while there are also maps for a 7-mile hiking trail, both available at the park Visitor's Center.

Don't be concerned that this – or any other Civil War site – may be an experience too arduous for young children. Tours can be taken by car or on foot, and are so well explained in on-site placards and the Visitor's Center's films and literature that boredom can be easily kept at bay if you pick the right pace for your offspring. However, not all the

rain trestles guarded by roops at Manassas Bull Run), 863.

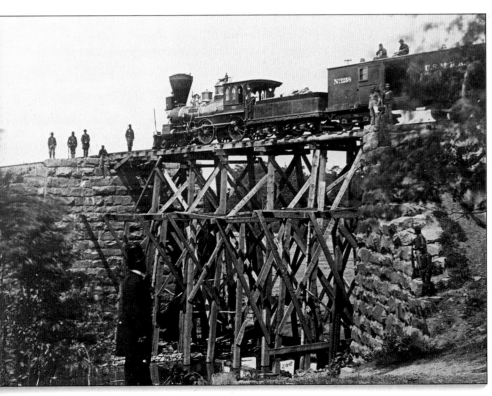

sites are within easy access to refreshments, so arm yourself with a small store of drinks and snacks.

Twenty-five miles west of Washington lies **Manassas (Bull Run) National Battlefield Park**, the site of two of the largest and most bloody battles of the war. Both forces sought control over a strategic railroad junction. Known by the Unionists as **Manassas** after the nearby town and by the Confederates as **Bull Run** for the local stream, this is where the first major land battle was fought on July 21, 1861.

It is also where General "Stonewall" Jackson earned his nickname for holding firm against advancing Unionists at a critical point in battle – "standing like a stone wall," in General Lee's words. Washingtonians came out with picnic hampers to be entertained by what they anticipated would be an easy and picturesque victory, certain the Union would never send troops into the South. But they quickly turned tail, and their carriages and coaches joined the desperate flight after what is now thought of as the first example of "modern" warfare.

The Visitor's Center is an evocative spot from which to picture the nearly 30,000 soldiers killed or wounded in 1861 and 1862. The **Battlefield Museum** here has audiovisual exhibits on the battles that can be seen on the driving or walking tours; follow markers which begin at the Visitor's Center. There are quite a number of edifices that were part of the battle still to be seen: the **Stone Bridge** over Bull Run stream where the Union soldiers opened fire to launch the first battle; the **raised railroad** where General Jackson's troops maintained ground during the second battle; and the **Stone House tavern** that was used as a field hospital.

It was at **New Market Battlefield Park** on May 15, 1864, that 247 young cadets, all of them under 20 years old, were summoned in desperation from the Virginia Military Institute in Lexington to give vital support to Confederate General Breckinridge, whose

men were being decimated by the forces of Union leader General Sigel. The young cadets fought with such skill and courage that they helped the Confederates vanquish the more experienced and larger opposition force. A walking tour takes you round the parkland, following the development of both sides of this important battle.

The battlefield park is smaller than the other two, only 160 acres. Right in the middle of the field is the **Hall of Valor**, in memory of the cadets, a museum that gives both sides of the Civil War story in film, dioramas, and exhibits. Outside in the park there are replicas of cannons, plus a farmhouse from the period whose outhouses have been restored to display a 19th-century working farm with garden and blacksmith's. This is where, in May, a **re-enactment of the battle** is staged in full costume by nearly 1,000 players.

For the battle-weary there are the **Endless Caverns**, whose extraordinary caves are dramatically lit to display the different caves' intricate and colorful formations, and the **Bedrooms of America Museum**, with 11 rooms of furniture that illustrate the development of American bedrooms between 1680 and 1930.

THE SKYLINE DRIVE: Between the towns Front Royal and Waynesboro lie 105 twisting miles through the tree- and flower-covered summits of the **Blue Ridge Mountains**. There are dozens of overlooks from which to gaze upon the **Virginia Piedmont** and the **Shenandoah Valley**, to take photographs or, with a copy of *The Park Guide,* to set off on one of the many trails, short or overnight, that start on the Drive. Those with less energy can simply enjoy the colors.

During the summer, these are soft greens in a bluish haze, punctuated by flowers. But the Skyline Drive really comes into its own in the fall when the colors of the changing leaves are spectacular. This is a relatively recent bonus. Though originally this land had been covered in thick forest, by 1935 when the **Shenandoah National Park** was created, the trees had been cleared, the streams fished out and the wild game decimated by the local settlers. In 1976, the efforts of the park's conservationists to reforest and regenerate natural growth were so successful that Congress declared roughly 40 percent of the park an **official wilderness**. Under the protection of the National Park System, the forest has been reclaimed and returned to its natural state.

The Park Services offer several good restaurants, accommodations in overnight log cabins, campgrounds and lodges, as well as many ranger-conducted activities, likes hikes, talks and campfire get-togethers. The **Dickey Ridge Visitor's Center**, open during the summer months, can provide information and tips on camping in the Shenandoah Valley. The name Shenandoah, by the way, is an Indian word which means "Daughter of the Stars." An ancient belief is that the valley used to be a lake, and that, once every 1,000 years, the stars would sing around it.

Nine miles west of the 211 entrance onto the Skyline Drive, the **Luray Caverns** are the largest underground caverns in Virginia. The tour takes one hour over a 1«-mile exploration of some of the weirdest and most impressive stalagmites and stalactites to be seen anywhere. The only **Stalacpipe Organ** in the world is here, with the ceiling hangings tuned to concert pitch and tapped by an organist using rubber-tipped plungers. The **Skyline Caverns** at Front Royal are a smaller version of the Luray Caverns, but nonetheless boast some unique anthodite formations.

Because of its 35 mph speed limit, it takes almost 4 hours to drive the length of the Skyline Drive without stopping. The northern Front Royal entrance is 1˅ hours from Washington. The Drive is inside the Shenandoah National Park and there is a small admission per car.

WILLIAMSBURG: This can hardly be considered a comfortable day trip, for although it is only a 3˅-hour drive from

The green, rolling hills of Virginia.

Washington, you need a whole day in Williamsburg to do this historic town justice and will probably feel too tired for the journey home again. It is not impossible, however, to do the return trip in one day if time is limited.

The best way, though, would be to arrive in Williamsburg just before the Visitors Center closes at night and buy all the admission tickets for the following day in order to avoid the long lines that build up early in the morning. Then settle for the night in one of the reasonably priced chain motels and hotels close by. (Don't forget to bring a swimsuit – many have pools.)

Williamsburg should not be missed by anyone spending a reasonable amount of time in the capital. It is a kind of stylish upmarket theme park, taking you on a journey 200 years back in time with more elegance and credibility than you could imagine possible. One of America's very first planned cities, Williamsburg was constructed between 1698 and 1705, after the abandonment

of Jamestown as the Virginian capital.

Because it was conceived as a gentle country town, each house on the main street was surrounded by half an acre of land to allow for the smokehouse, stable, dairy, orchard and slave quarters that were common to genteel families of the time. It was a prosperous market town, lying between the **College of William and Mary** at one end and the **Capitol** building, the regional seat of government, at the other. The royal governor, the Crown's representative in the colony of Virginia, lived in a grand residence constructed between the two. With the Revolution, and the town under heavy enemy fire, the new Commonwealth government moved to Richmond, thus initiating the demise of Williamsburg.

Restoration of the town began in the late 1920s and is an on-going project. **Colonial Williamsburg** now comprises about 85 percent of the original settlement. Visitors wandering through may think they have been caught in a time warp. The houses, shops and hostelries open for anyone to wander through are peopled by citizens in 18th-century dress, applying themselves quietly to the trades of the time with traditional implements. They will willingly explain what they are doing – in 18th-century English. Here are ordinary people, supposedly, going about their ordinary daily business.

Eating in Williamsburg is fun. The taverns all serve excellent food, some offering traditional colonial fare, indoors and out, and the minstrels, waiters and waitresses are all in colonial dress. The experience presents a thoroughly convincing and pleasurable opportunity for anyone to imagine almost exactly what life would have been like in early colonial Virginia.

If you travel to Williamsburg with children, you should plan to stop at **Busch Gardens** on your way. An amusement park with a European theme, the gardens are located 5 miles east of Williamsburg.

Left, the governor's palace. Right, shopping for that little colonial something.

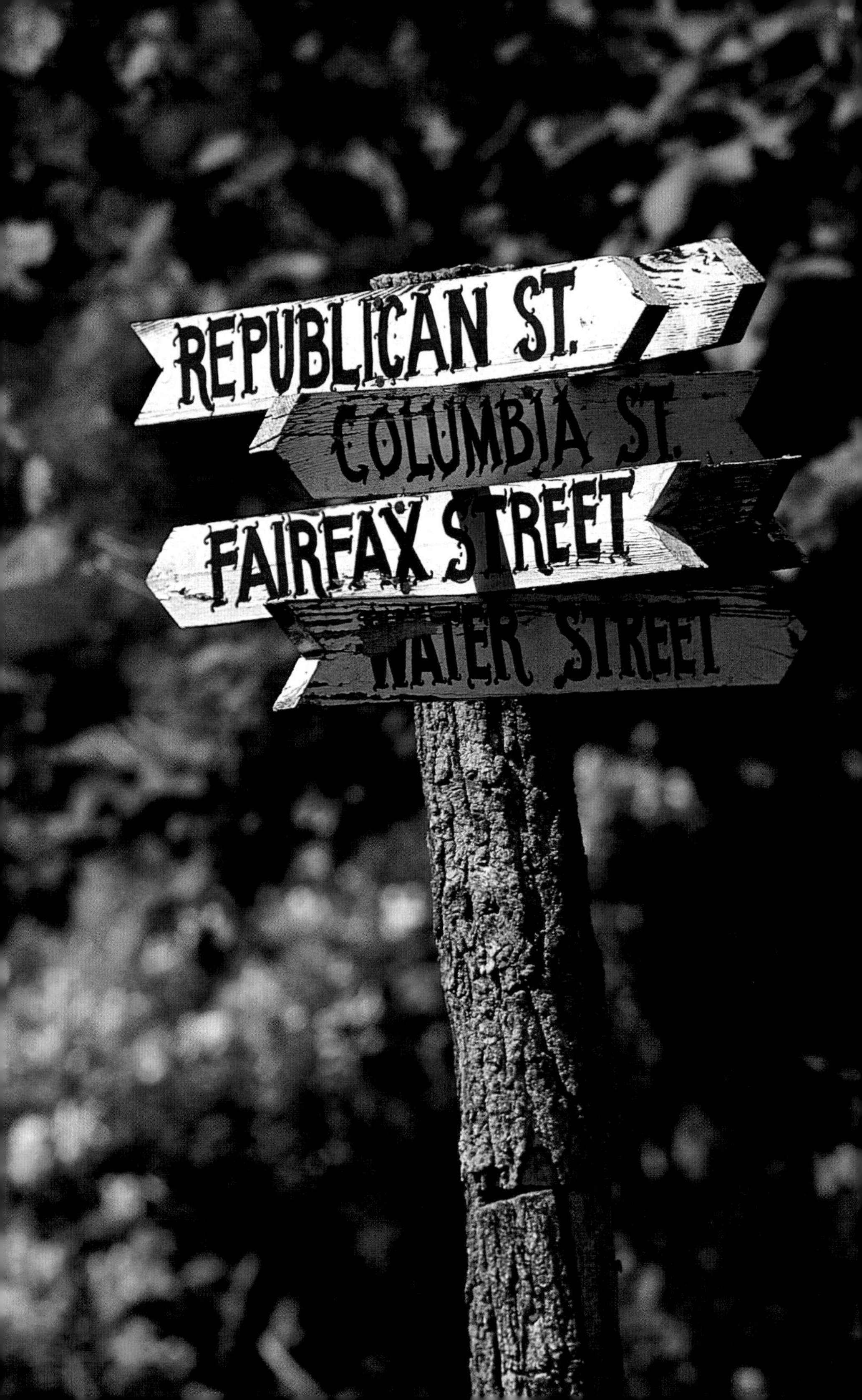
REPUBLICAN ST.
COLUMBIA ST.
FAIRFAX STREET
WATER STREET

INSIGHT GUIDES
Travel Tips

FOR THOSE
WITH MORE THAN
A PASSING INTEREST
IN TIME...

Before you put your name down for a Patek Philippe watch *fig. 1*, there are a few basic things you might like to know, without knowing exactly whom to ask. In addressing such issues as accuracy, reliability and value for money, we would like to demonstrate why the watch we will make for you will be quite unlike any other watch currently produced.

"Punctuality", Louis XVIII was fond of saying, "is the politeness of kings."

We believe that in the matter of punctuality, we can rise to the occasion by making you a mechanical timepiece that will keep its rendezvous with the Gregorian calendar at the end of every century, omitting the leap-years in 2100, 2200 and 2300 and recording them in 2000 and 2400 *fig. 2*. Nevertheless, such a watch does need the occasional adjustment. Every 3333 years and 122 days you should remember to set it forward one day to the true time of the celestial clock. We suspect, however, that you are simply content to observe the politeness of kings. Be assured, therefore, that when you order your watch, we will be exploring for you the physical—if not the metaphysical—limits of precision.

Does everything have to depend on how much?

Consider, if you will, the motives of collectors who set record prices at auction to acquire a Patek Philippe. They may be paying for rarity, for looks or for micromechanical ingenuity. But we believe that behind each $500,000-plus

bid is the conviction that a Patek Philippe, even if 50 years old or older, can be expected to work perfectly for future generations.

In case your ambitions to own a Patek Philippe are somewhat discouraged by the scale of the sacrifice involved, may we hasten to point out that the watch we will make for you today will certainly be a technical improvement on the Pateks bought at auction? In keeping with our tradition of inventing new mechanical solutions for greater reliability and better time-keeping, we will bring to your watch innovations *fig. 3* inconceivable to our watchmakers who created the supreme wristwatches of 50 years ago *fig. 4*. At the same time, we will of course do our utmost to avoid placing undue strain on your financial resources.

Can it really be mine?

May we turn your thoughts to the day you take delivery of your watch? Sealed within its case is your watchmaker's tribute to the mysterious process of time. He has decorated each wheel with a chamfer carved into its hub and polished into a shining circle. Delicate ribbing flows over the plates and bridges of gold and rare alloys. Millimetric surfaces are bevelled and burnished to exactitudes measured in microns. Rubies are transformed into jewels that triumph over friction. And after many months—or even years—of work, your watchmaker stamps a small badge into the mainbridge of your watch. The Geneva Seal—the highest possible attestation of fine watchmaking *fig. 5*.

Looks that speak of inner grace *fig. 6.*

When you order your watch, you will no doubt like its outward appearance to reflect the harmony and elegance of the movement within. You may therefore find it helpful to know that we are uniquely able to cater for any special decorative needs you might like to express. For example, our engravers will delight in conjuring a subtle play of light and shadow on the gold case-back of one of our rare pocket-watches *fig. 7*. If you bring us your favourite picture, our enamellers will reproduce it in a brilliant miniature of hair-breadth detail *fig. 8*. The perfect execution of a double hobnail pattern on the bezel of a wristwatch is the pride of our casemakers and the satisfaction of our designers, while our chainsmiths will weave for you a rich brocade in gold *figs. 9 & 10*. May we also recommend the artistry of our goldsmiths and the experience of our lapidaries in the selection and setting of the finest gemstones? *figs. 11 & 12.*

How to enjoy your watch before you own it.

As you will appreciate, the very nature of our watches imposes a limit on the number we can make available. (The four Calibre 89 time-pieces we are now making will take up to nine years to complete). We cannot therefore promise instant gratification, but while you look forward to the day on which you take delivery of your Patek Philippe *fig. 13*, you will have the pleasure of reflecting that time is a universal and everlasting commodity freely available to be enjoyed by all.

Should you require information on any particular Patek Philippe watch, or even on watchmaking in general, we would be delighted to reply to your letter of enquiry. And if you sen

fig. 1: *The classic face of Patek Philippe.*

fig. 4: *Complicated wristwatches circa 1930 (left) and 1990. The golden age of watchmaking will always be with us.*

fig. 2: *One of the 33 complications of the Calibre 89 astronomical clock-watch is a satellite wheel that completes one revolution every 400 years.*

fig. 5: *The Geneva Seal is awarded only to watches which achieve the standards of horological purity laid down in the laws of Geneva. These rules define the supreme quality of watchmaking.*

fig. 3: *Recognized as the most advanced mechanical regulating device to date, Patek Philippe's Gyromax balance wheel demonstrates the equivalence of simplicity and precision.*

fig. 6: *Your pleasure in owning a Patek Philippe is the purpose of those who made it for you.*

fig. 7: *Arabesques come to life on a gold case-back.*

fig. 8: *An artist working six hours a day takes about four months to complete a miniature in enamel on the case of a pocket-watch.*

fig. 9: *Harmony of design is executed in a work of simplicity and perfection in a lady's Calatrava wristwatch.*

fig. 10: *The chainsmith's hands impart strength and delicacy to a tracery of gold.*

fig. 11: *Circles in gold: symbols of perfection in the making.*

fig. 12: *The test of a master lapidary is his ability to express the splendour of precious gemstones.*

✣
PATEK PHILIPPE
GENEVE
fig. 13: *The discreet sign of those who value their time.*

your card marked "book catalogue" we shall post you a catalogue of our publications. Patek Philippe, 41 rue du Rhône, 1204 Geneva, Switzerland, Tel. +41 22/310 03 66.

See the World with a different eye

Getting Acquainted

Telephone numbers prefixed by 800 are toll free in the US and "1" should be dialed first. When dialing Washington numbers from inside Washington, the prefix 202 should not be used.

The Place

Washington is not a large city, barely 10 miles across at its widest, with a population of just under 1 million. Most of the tourist attractions are in downtown Washington near the Potomac River. It is divided into four quadrants – northwest (NW), northeast (NE), southeast (SE) and southwest (SW). Check the quadrant on any address to prevent heading for a similar address in a different quadrant.

Streets that are numbered run north-south, one set to the west of the Capitol and a second set to the east. Lettered streets run east-west, with much of the alphabet repeated south of the Capitol. There is no J Street, sometimes said to have been a deliberate snubbing by designer of the city, Pierre L'Enfant, of unpopular Chief Justice John Jay, so if counting, bear in mind that K is the tenth letter. Named streets also generally run east-west.

Time Zones

Washington is in the Eastern Standard Time zone. When it is noon in Washington, it is 9am in Los Angeles, 5pm in London, 8pm in Moscow and 2am in Tokyo. The clock goes forward one hour on the first Sunday in April for Daylight Savings Time and one hour back on the last Sunday in October to return to Standard Time.

Climate

Washington's summers can be extremely uncomfortable to the uninitiated, with high humidity accompanying high temperatures. There are often viol lent summer storms. Winters are cold usually with plenty of snow, though as in summer – the weather is unpre dictable and can produce unexpected warm days. The most clement sea sons are fall, when the air is warm bu not oppressive, and the very brief spring around April, when the weathe is still fresh.

Monthly Averages

January	44.6° F	7.0° C
February	44.4° F	6.8° C
March	53.0° F	11.6° C
April	64.2° F	17.8° C
May	74.9° F	23.8° C
June	82.8° F	28.2° C
July	86.8° F	30.4° C
August	84.4° F	29.1° C
September	78.4° F	25.7° C
October	67.5° F	19.7° C
November	55.1° F	12.8° C
December	47.8° F	7.1° C

The People

Culture & Customs

Washington is not a spontaneous city The policy of filling up days with mee

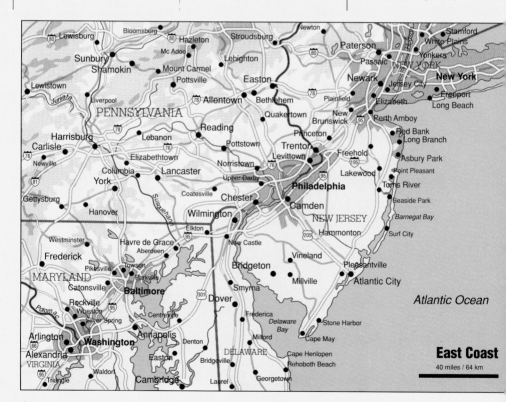

Atlantic Ocean

East Coast

40 miles / 64 km

ings and agendas, which starts at the top with "power Washington," filters down into everyday life, too. It can be difficult to get in touch with people by telephone, to arrange to meet up at the last minute, or to get an instant decision about anything.

If you have business to attend to, be sure to arrange all appointments before you arrive. If you're in Washington for pleasure, but want to arrange a special tour of a museum, or see a certain collection in one of the libraries, write to the appropriate person well in advance. Otherwise you will lose precious days on your arrival in town simply trying to organize your visit.

Language

The native language is English, but in large parts of Washington and over the Potomac in Arlington, Virginia, other languages are spoken, in shops and restaurants. Foremost are Spanish, Chinese, Vietnamese, and other languages of South and North East Asia.

How the US Government Works

The American experiment in democratic self-government entered its third century in 1991 with the bi-centennial of the Bill of Rights. These rights are now codified in 10 amendments to the Constitution and were drafted shortly after the Constitution itself to settle lingering anxieties about the limits of the state's powers over the lives of individuals.

Educated in the social theories of such European Enlightenment thinkers as John Locke, Thomas Hobbes, and Jean-Jacques Rousseau, the founders shared a deep mistrust of any concentration of power, having recently overthrown the rule of a despotic English king. The system of Thomas Jefferson, James Madison and Alexander Hamilton was designed to ensure that no institution or faction could seize control of the apparatus of government.

The system is a federal one, so the national government's powers are limited. Most criminal law, for example, is written by the state legislatures. When Americans refer to the **Federal government** they mean Washington, DC. The government has three branches, each able to limit the powers of the other two. This is known as the separation of powers and the system of checks and

balances. The three branches are organized by function: the legislative, executive, and judicial branches.

The **legislative** power is vested in **Congress**, which consists of two bodies, the House of Representatives and the Senate. Both are elected directly by the people and act according to majority vote. They are organized into committees, which consider, amend and send to the entire membership bills which win a majority of committee members. Bills which fail in committee can be resurrected by a majority of the entire membership of the House or Senate.

Membership in the **House of Representatives** is apportioned according to population. The total number of Representatives is fixed at **435**, and they are allocated to each state's proportion of the total national population. Each decade a census determines the official population and congressional seats are adjusted accordingly. In 1990, for example, it was found that population had shifted out of New York and into California. New York lost several seats; California gained. The state legislatures had the tricky task of redrawing district boundaries.

House members are elected for **two-year terms** and appear to always be campaigning for re-election. With this frequency of accountability and the relatively definable nature of their areas, their votes are meant to represent the interests of specific constituencies. Thus a Representative from the plains of Nebraska would advocate certain agricultural policies to benefit wheat farming, while a Representative from Chicago might concentrate on mass transit or urban health care issues.

The House is led by the Speaker, elected by a majority of the members and therefore leader of the majority party. Bills can be introduced in either body of Congress, but only the House can initiate appropriations of funds, the real business of policies.

The **Senate** is considered the senior body. Senators represent larger constituencies and are elected for **six-year terms**. They are meant to operate on a broader scale than House members, thinking more of the nation as a whole. Each State has two Senators, so a very large population like Texas has no more Senators than a tiny state like

Wyoming. This was another of the founders' schemes for balancing things out. The small colonies feared dominance by the large ones, and this allocation was designed to guarantee that small state interests would not be submerged.

The Senate is nominally run by the Vice President of the United States. But the Vice President's power in the Senate is limited to voting only when there is a 50/50 tie. The majority and minority leaders, elected by their memberships, exert the real power, as do the committees which conduct the detailed analysis and the behind-the-scenes politicking that actually run the government.

When a bill passes majorities of both bodies, it is sent to the President for signature and can then become law. Frequently a bill has been amended by each body in different ways, so it is then referred to a "conference" committee in which Representatives and Senators hammer out the differences and reintroduce the bill for final approval.

The **Executive power** resides in the **Presidency**. Presidential and Vice Presidential candidates always run as a team, so there is no practical way they could be of different parties. They are the only officials elected by all the people, and are thus presumed to have a mandate to govern along the lines of their campaign programs. While the people vote for presidential candidates by name, they are voting for a slate of electors pledged to the candidate.

Each state has electoral votes equal to the sum of its two Senators and all its Representatives. This is called the **electoral college**. The electors vote not in proportion to the popular vote in their states, but all vote for the candidate receiving a majority. Consequently, Presidential elections focus on closely contested states, especially on the large states. Presidents and Vice-Presidents are limited to **four-year terms**, and each can be re-elected once for a total of eight years in office.

The President proposes a program of legislation to Congress and Congress are expected to act on it. When the same party controls both branches, this can go smoothly. In recent decades, there has been a division in the government, with mostly Republican Party Presidents and Democratic Party Congresses. This produces one of three results: compromise on the issues, trading off a win on one for yielding on another, or stalemate and inaction.

The President's best-known role is in the foreign policy area, negotiating treaties, and in moments of international tension, as the **Commander-in-Chief of the Armed Forces**. The Congress, however, must ratify the treaties and has the power to declare war, so as international relations have become increasingly complex and events break more rapidly, there has been a great deal of contesting which branch can actually do what.

The Executive is charged with enforcing laws and implementing legislation. The President appoints members of the **Cabinet**. They are the leaders of the executive departments such as the Departments of State (the foreign office), Justice, Treasury, Agriculture, Labor, Commerce; and some new departments created by changing times, like Energy and Transportation. Each of these appointments must receive the approval of the Senate.

When Congress passes legislation to the President for enactment, it can be signed into law or vetoed. A veto stands unless the Congress can then muster a **two-thirds vote** in each house to override it.

The third branch is the **Judiciary**. Members of the Supreme Court, the Appeals **Courts**, and the lower-level federal courts are appointed for life by the President but require confirmation by the Senate. The courts interpret the Constitution and laws passed by Congress and the President when their meanings are not clear in a specific case. A **Supreme Court** ruling establishes a general precedent lower courts are expected to follow.

A by-product of the split between the parties has been that much legislation emerges from revision and compromise with ambiguous meaning and ends up being adjudicated by the Supreme Court. Since the Constitution and most of its amendments were written and ratified before this century, there is always a debate on their proper application in the very different economic, technological, and cultural environment of today. The court can

invalidate a law by determining that it violates the Constitution. But Congress and the President can usually enact the main parts of such laws by amending them to delete the parts found unconstitutional. **Justices** and the **judges** of Federal Courts, like the President and Vice President, can be impeached and tried by Congress if they are found to have committed certain high crimes. Although this is infrequent, it serves as a check on this unelected branch.

There is another *de facto* branch consisting of semi-autonomous regulatory groups, charged with watching over securities markets, foods and drugs, interstate commerce, telecommunications, and other fields. These groups are established by Congressional acts and their leaders are presidential appointees requiring Congressional confirmation. They are the career civil servants who are meant to be non-political in the sense of party membership.

The American system is complicated and not as efficient as a more authoritarian one would be. It requires much balancing and compromise to get anything done, and it is often frustrating to the citizenry. But in a modern, complex, multi-racial society, it is essential to have broad consensus on major issues, and this is what the system, regardless of its other problems, achieves. As a result there has been no genuine crisis in American government since the end of the Civil War in the 1860s.

Planning The Trip

What To Bring

Electricity

The electricity used in Washington homes is called standard, which is 110 volts. European appliances will require a voltage adaptor because most European countries use 220–240 volts. Although some hotel bathrooms have suitable electrical outlets, an adaptor is useful to have.

What To Wear

Washington's long, hot and humid summer means you should dress in clothing light enough to cope with sightseeing in comfort. Comfortable shoes are also essential for all museum and Mall walking.

But even if the weather is more appropriate to the beach, this is a capital city, and Washington's major hotels and restaurants will expect you to wear suitable clothing. Some restaurants require men to wear jackets and ties. Air conditioning is often so high in public places like, restaurants, theaters and cinemas that a light jacket is advisable. In winter, and temperatures usually drop sharply from November through February, warm coats are a necessity.

Entry Regulations

Visas & Passports

Visa regulations: A passport, a passport-size photograph, a visitor's visa, evidence of intent to leave the United States after your visit and, depending upon your country of origin, an international vaccination certificate, are required for entry into the United States by most foreign nationals. Visitors from the United Kingdom staying less than 90 days no longer need a visa. Vaccination certificate requirements vary, but proof of immunization against smallpox or cholera may be necessary.

Canadian and Mexican citizens, as well as British residents of Canada and Bermuda, are normally exempt from these requirements but it is always wise to check for specific regulations on international travel in your home country.

Extension Of Stay

Most visitors are given a six-month visa. If after six months you wish to stay longer, contact the immigration office. Obtaining a six-month extension is usually no problem. The immigration office is located 425 I Street NW, tel: 202 514 2000.

Customs

If you are 21 or over, you can take into the US 200 cigarettes, 50 cigars, or 3 lbs of tobacco; 1 US quart of alcohol and duty-free gifts worth up to $100. You are not allowed to bring in meat products, seeds, plants, or fruits. Don't even think about bringing in narcotics. Customs agents in the US are tough and efficient, and sniffer dogs routinely check luggage.

Health

In the United States health care is very expensive. If you get sick or need medical attention, the average cost for one night in a hospital in a semi-private room is astronomical. If you live in a foreign country and do not have private health insurance, try to obtain insurance for your stay before coming to Washington. For medical care and an ambulance in a serious emergency, tel: **911**.

Money Matters

American visitors: Credit cards are accepted almost everywhere, although not all cards at all places. They can also be used to withdraw money at ATMs (automatic teller machines) marked with the corresponding stickers (i.e. Visa, Mastercard, American Express, etc.). Out of state bank cards work, too, provided you find out what the corresponding system in Washington is before you leave home.

Overseas visitors: Several Washington banks and most of their branches will change currency, like: **Riggs National**, **Sovran**, **Crestar** and **First American**. **Deak International Ltd** change foreign currency at three locations: 1800 K Street NW (tel: 202 872 1427), 3222 M Street NW (tel: 202 338 3325) and 50 Massachusetts Avenue, NE (tel: 202 371 9219). Changing travelers checks at banks usually requires a passport.

Thomas Cook also have three outlets, at Union Station, 1800 K Street NW, and Georgetown Park shopping mall, 3222 M Street NW. **Sovran Bank** has an outlet at Dulles Airport. At National Airport money can be changed at **Teletrip**.

Public Holidays

The US has gradually shifted most of its minor public holidays to the Mondays closest to the actual dates, thus creating a number of three-day weekends.

Most federal, state and municipal offices, and banks will be closed on the following holidays:

January – New Year's Day and Martin Luther King Day
February – President's Day
March or April – Easter Sunday
May – Memorial Day
July – Independence Day (4th July)
September – Labor Day
October – Columbus Day
November – Thanksgiving Day and the day after
December – Christmas Day

Getting There
By Air

There are three airports serving Washington – **Washington Dulles International** (IAD), 26 miles west of the city, for international destinations and some national cities, **Washington National Airport** (WDA), sited almost in the heart of the city and only serving destinations inside the United States, and **Baltimore Washington International** (BWI), 9 miles south of Baltimore and 29 miles north of Washington, owned and operated by the state of Maryland.

Washington Dulles International Airport major international carriers:
Aeroflot, tel: 202 429 2922.
Air France, tel: 800 237 2747.
All Nippon Airways, tel: 800 235 9262.
American Airlines, tel: 800 433 7300.
Bahamas Airlines, tel: 800 222 4262.
British Airways, tel: 800 247 9297.
Continental Airlines and Continental Express, tel: 800 525 0280.
Delta Airlines, tel: 800 221 1212.
Lufthansa German Airlines, tel: 800 645 3880.
Northwest Airlines, tel: 800 225 2525.
Qantas Airways, tel: 800 227 4500.
Saudi Arabian Airlines, tel: 800 472 8342.
Trans World Airlines, tel: 800 221 2000.
United Airlines-United Express, tel: 800 241 6522.
US Air, tel: 800 428 4322.

There are **two information desks** covering transportation, hotels, language problems and paging. The first is immediately after passengers clear customs and immigration in the International Arrivals Area, when it is open 10am–7pm daily to meet all interna-

tional arrivals (tel: 703 661 6732). Travelers Aid is in the east end of the Main Terminal, on the lower level, open 10am–9pm every day but Saturday, open 10am–6pm (tel: 703 661 8636). Baggage claim is on the lower level of the terminal, leading straight out to the transportation area.

The **Washington Flyer taxis** are operated by the Airport Authority, as is the **Washington Flyer bus service** to three destinations: the central downtown terminal, Washington National Airport, and West Falls Church Metro station which leads right into Washington's metro rail system.

Washington National Airport carriers:
America West, tel: 800 247 5692.
American Airlines, tel: 800 433 7300.
Continental Airlines, tel: 800 525 0280.
Delta Airlines, tel: 800 221 1212.
Eastern Airlines, tel: 800 327 8376.
Midwest Express Airlines, tel: 800 452 2022.
Northwest Airlines, tel: 800 225 2525.
Trans World Airlines, tel: 800 221 2000.
United Airlines, tel: 800 241 6522.

Baggage claim is on the ground level, along with stops for taxis, **WDA shuttle buses** and the **National Airport shuttle** that goes to the city terminus at 1517 K Street NW. The **National Airport station** on the Metro Rail system is found across the North Concourse.

Baltimore-Washington Airport carriers:
Air Jamaica, tel, tel: 800 523 5585.
American Airlines, tel: 800 433 7300.
American West Business Express (Delta Connection), tel: 800 345 3400.
Delta Airlines, tel: 301 768 9000.
Continental Airlines, tel: 800 525 0280.
KLM Airlines, tel: 800 777 5553.
Northwest Airlines, tel: 800 225 2585.
Trans World Airlines, tel: 800 221 2000.
United Airlines, tel: 800 241 6522.
US Air, tel: 800 428 4322

Baggage claim is on the lower level, as are the exits to transportation. BWI operates a **bus shuttle service** into the downtown Washington terminus at 15th and K streets NW. As for taxis, there is an **Amtrak train service** (tel: 800 872 7245). Information booths are found throughout the airport.

By Bus

Greyhound-Trailways Bus Lines connects Washington DC with cities throughout the United States. Its downtown terminus is at 1005 First Street NE, a short walk to the metro at Union Station.

For fares, schedules, information on bus passes, tel: 202 565 2662.

By Rail

Union Station, only a few blocks north of the Capitol, reopened in 1990 in full splendor after extensive restoration and redecoration. It is now worthy of a visit whether you have a train to catch or not. Above and on the main ticket concourse are attractive shops and boutiques, while on the lower level are 9 movie theatres and one of Washington's largest food halls. **Amtrak** provides transportation from Washington anywhere across the United States. Tel: 800 872 7245 for information on inter-city services, motor vehicle transportation and sleeping car facilities. Union Station is on the Metro Rail system.

By Road

Offices of the American Automobile Association can advise on routes to and from Washington. Call your local office or tel: 202 222 9000 for North American Auto Travel Trip-Tiks maps and tour books. Washington is circled by the **Capital Beltway** formed by two interstates, I-495 and I-95, from which radiate seven major highways.

Interstate 95 heads north to Baltimore, Philadelphia and New York, and south to Richmond, Virginia.

The Gladys Spellman Parkway links South East Washington with Baltimore.

Interstate 50 heads east to Annapolis, the Chesapeake Bay and beaches.

Interstate 66 leads from Washington west into Virginia.

The Dulles Access road is for quick traffic to Dulles International Airport.

Interstate 270 heads north west to Frederick, Maryland and beyond.

Useful Addresses

Tour Operators

The following private operators provide regular, scheduled sightseeing tours to the general public, with some schedule variations during the high season. If you would prefer to tackle Washington's enormous variety of attractions on a more personal level, these and many other tour companies provide specialty tours for individuals and groups. Contact: WCVA, tel: 202 789 7000 for a complete list.

All About Town, 519 6th Street NW, Washington DC 20001. Tel: 202 393 3696. Complete guided tour routes of Washington, with accompanying lecture, via air-conditioned buses. Free pickup at major downtown hotels.

Spirit Cruises, Pier 4, 6th and Water streets SW (a short walk from the Waterfront Metro station), tel: 202 554 8000. Open daily – reservations recommended. Spirit Cruises offers a unique opportunity to "do it all" while visiting the nation's capital. Two-hour lunch cruises, three-hour dinner cruises, weekend afternoon cruises or 4½-hour sightseeing cruises to Mount Vernon. For something really different, try the Caribbean Escape Theme Cruises, offered Wednesdays, May–August.

Gold Line Inc., Gray Line Terminal, Union Station, 50 Massachusetts Avenue NE. Tel: 202 289 1995. Guided tours of Washington, plus tours to surrounding destinations, in new air-conditioned buses. Lectures are provided on each tour route. Free pickup at major downtown hotels.

DC Ducks, 2640 Reed Street NE, 20018 Washington, DC, tel: 202 832 9800. Tours depart 10am, noon and 2pm from Union Station. April–October, 7 days a week. Washington's first combined land and water tour company features four, 33-passenger amphibious sightseeing carriers that provide individual, family and group clientele with entertaining, yet educational adventure. The unique 90-minute tour focuses on the capital city's military and historic landmarks while traveling both on land then back up to the city via the Potomac River.

Tourmobile Sightseeing, 1000 Ohio Drive SW, Washington DC 20024. Tel: 202 554 7950. Tours to 18 historic sites aboard a narrated sightseeing shuttle tram (Washington Monument, White House, Lincoln Memorial, Smithsonian museums, Arlington Cemetery), free reboarding. Separate tours to Mount Vernon and the Frederick Douglass Home.

Wheels Across Washington, 2704 Warrenton Road, Hartwood, VA 22405. Tel: 703 752 4763. Horse and carriage tours. Depart from the Willard Intercontinental Hotel. Hours: daily April–November, some evening hours (depends on weather). Cost depends on number of people on the tour.

Water Cruises

Potomac Party Cruises Inc., *Dandee* Restaurant Cruise Ship, Zero Prince Street, Alexandria, VA 22314. Tel: 703 683 6090.

Potomac Riverboat Co., The *Cherry Blossom* and the *Admiral Tilp*, 205 The Strand, Alexandria, VA 22314. Tel: 703 684 0580.

Other Cruises, The *Spirit of Washington/Spirit of Mount Vernon*, Pier 4, 6th and Water streets SW, Washington DC 20024. Tel: 202 554 8000.

Useful Numbers

Washington, DC treats visitors well, with lots of brochures, information sheets and lists of events available from the following centers:

Washington, DC Convention and Visitor's Association, 1212 New York Avenue NW, 20005. Tel: 202 789 7000 for general inquiries. You can listen to a weekly recording of local events by dialing 737 8866.

Visitor Information Center, 1455 Pennsylvania Avenue NW, which is open Monday–Saturday 9am–5pm. Personal callers only.

International Visitors Information Service, 733 15th Street NW, Suite 300. Tel: 202 783 6540. Open Monday–Friday 9am–5pm.

Travelers Aid Society, 1015 12th Street NW. Tel: 202 347 0101 gives emergency attention to visitors. Branches can be found at Dulles and National airports, and at Union Station.

Other Helpful Numbers

Handicapped Visitor Information – 472 6770

Handicapped Services – 962 1245

Doctor Referral Service – 466 2870

Dental Referral Service – 686 0803
AAA Emergency Road Service – 222 5000
Public Transportation Information – 637 7000

Practical Tips

Emergencies

Security & Crime

Washington has the highest murder rate of any city in the United States. For the most part, the city is perfectly safe. But check with friends or hotel staff on arrival which parts of Washington are inadvisable for wandering round. It is wise not to travel alone late at night. Of course, there are areas where this rule does not apply, but it's a good rule to live by. If you do happen to run into trouble, pick up the phone and **dial 911**. The operator will connect you with the agency you require: police, ambulance or fire department.

Loss Of Belongings

If you happen to lose anything valuable, report it to the local police department. You will have to file a report, and if your lost goods are turned in, they will return them to you as soon as possible. This report is invaluable for insurance claims purposes.

Lost or stolen credit cards:
American Express, tel: 1-800 528 4800.
Visa, tel: 1-800 227 6800.
Carte Blanche/Diners Club, tel: 1-800 525 9135.
Master Card, tel: 1-800 826 2181.

Medical Services

To locate a doctor or a pharmacist consult the *Yellow Pages* of the phone book, or seek advice from your hotel staff. (*See also "Useful Addresses".*) Most hospitals have a 24-hour emergency room. Here are some of the larger hospitals:
DC General Hospital, 19th and Massachussetts Avenue SE. Tel: 675 5400.

The George Washington University Medical Center, 901 23rd Street NW. Tel: 994 1000.
Georgetown University Hospital, 3800 Reservoir Rd NW. Tel: 784 2000.
Sibley Memorial Hospital, 5255 Loughborough Rd NW. Tel: 537 4000.
Children's Hospital, 111 Michigan Avenue NW. Tel: 745 5000.

Pharmacies: There is a 24-hour drug store at Peoples Drug on Dupont Circle, the junction of Massachusetts and Connecticut avenues NW.

Lost Luggage

Most of the airlines and other transportation companies have insurance for lost customer luggage. Ask when purchasing your ticket about an insurance policy. Make sure all your luggage has identification tags. If you leave your luggage at the airport and it is turned in to the lost and found department, someone from that department will usually bring it to your hotel if you are unable to pick it up.

Weights & Measures

The US uses the Imperial system of weights and measures. Metric is rarely used. Below is a conversion chart.

1 inch	=	2.54 centimeters
1 foot	=	30.48 centimeters
1 yard	=	0.9144 meters
1 mile	=	1.609 kilometers
1 quart	=	1.136 liters
1 ounce	=	28.4 grams
1 pound	=	0.453 kilograms

Business Hours

Most businesses are open 9am–5pm, though many government-related offices open and close earlier. Major stores and shopping malls open at 10am, closing as late as 9pm. Many large supermarkets and drug stores stay open 24 hours. In general, banking hours are from 9pm–3pm, Monday–Thursday, and until 6pm on Friday. Some banks are open for limited hours on Saturday. All are closed on Sunday.

Tipping

Tipping is voluntary; gratuities are not automatically added to the bill. Here are a few tipping guidelines: Waiters are usually given 15 percent of the bill.

For above-average service, tip 20 percent.

Taxi cab drivers usually get 15 percent of the fare.

Tips to doormen, skycabs and porters 50–75 cents per bag. Hairdressers, manicurists and masseurs usually receive 10–15 percent of the total charge.

Media

Newspapers & Magazines

The *Washington Post* is the capital's oldest daily and Sunday newspaper, with a liberal editorial bent. The *Washington Times* was established in 1982 with money from the Reverend Sun Yong Moon, and has a conservative slant. It also publishes on Sundays. Almost every suburban Washington neighborhood has its own free newspaper, delivered weekly.

The *City Paper* is a free weekly news, arts, and information sheet, available from street corner machines and in some outlets like ice-cream parlors, book stores, restaurants and cafés.

The *Washingtonian* is a glossy monthly magazine, covering local news, politics, and gossip, with reviews of new art and culture presentations, restaurants and special interest shops. It carries feature articles on a broad range of issues, and entertainment listings.

Foreign news publications are available through many libraries. Central Washington newsstands, like the one at the corner of Connecticut Avenue and K Street NW, carry a wide range of foreign daily newspapers and journals. The newsstand at the National Press Building, 14th and F streets, NW, carries a wide range of US regional dailies.

Radio

There are over 27 AM and 26 FM stations serving the DC and suburban area. Below are some of the major ones:

News:/WTOP/1500 AM
News:/WAGE/1200 AM
Arts/Classical Information (NPR):/ WAMU/88.5 FM
Arts/Classical Information (NPR):/ WETA/90.9 FM
Business News:/WPGC/1580 AM
Latin Music/News:/WMDO/1540 AM

Jazz/Information:/WDCU/90.1 FM
Urban Contemporary:/WKYS/93.9 FM
Talk Radio:/WWRC/980 AM
Rock:/WWDS/101.1 FM
Rock:/WCXR/105.9 FM
Top 40 Pop:/WAVA/105.1 FM
Oldies:/WXTR/104.1 FM
Oldies:/WCPT/730 AM

Television

There are more than 15 television stations, and over 20 cable and movie channels serving the Washington area, giving round-the-clock TV viewing. There are three major television networks, ABC, CBS, and NBC. The Public Television service, PBS, has no commercials and supports itself with grants and donations.

Here are the local TV stations available without cable television:

Channel	Station
2 and 4	NBC
5 and 45	FOX
7 and 13	ABC
9 and 11	CBS
22, 26 and 32	PBS
50	IND WFTY Washington
54	WNUV Baltimore
66	WTKK North Virginia

Postal Services

Stamps can be purchased at any post office, from 8am–5pm Monday–Friday, and 8am–noon Saturday. Stamps are also available in vending machines located in airports, hotels, stores and bus and train stations. They are also available through the check out branches of Giant supermarkets and pharmacies, and Safeway supermarkets. For more postal information, including zip codes, tel: 202 682 9595.

Telephone, Telex & Fax

Coin-operated phones can be found anywhere in Washington and its suburbs: from public restrooms and gas stations to virtually any street corner. To operate, deposit the coins, listen for the dial tone, then dial your desired number.

Local calls inside Washington are seven digits only. The Washington DC prefix 202 is only applicable when calling into the capital from outside it. For numbers from Washington to Maryland the prefix is 301, for Virginia numbers,

703. All out-of-Washington numbers are preceded by dialing "1" – unless you are dialing a Maryland or Virginia suburb of Washington. To make a call through the operator, dial "0." Directions for using the telephone are usually printed on pay phones and can always be found in the front of the telephone book.

Telegraph services are available through Western Union, telephone toll free: 1-800 325 6000 or consult the telephone directory for the service nearest you.

Fax machines can be found at most hotels. Public fax companies are located throughout the city, so check the phone book *Yellow Pages* under "Facsimile" for the fax service nearest you.

Getting Around

Orientation

Washington is an extraordinarily clearly laid out city, once you understand the ground plan. It is divided into four basic sections: Northwest, Northeast, Southwest and Southeast. Numbered streets run north-south, beginning on either side of the Capitol, with East 1st Street to the map's right of the Capitol Building and West 1st Street to the map's left. Lettered streets run east-west, becoming name streets in alphabetic order as you go farther from the center. Avenues, named after states, dissect the city at angles across the grid, often meeting at traffic circles, such as Dupont Circle. **Maps:** available at major bookstores and some street vendors.

Public Transportation

Transport between Washington's three airports and downtown hotels is good. **National Airport**, the airport closest to the center of town, is on the metro system. The metro station is a short walk from the arrivals lounges, but can also be reached by regular shuttle buses. National Airport shuttle buses run to the downtown terminus at 1517

K Street NW. Taxi fares into downtown Washington are reasonably priced. **Dulles International** has a shuttle bus service to the downtown terminus at 1517 K Street NW, as well as shuttles to West Falls Church metro station, which feeds right into the metro system, and to National Airport. The Washington Flyer is a taxi service operated by the Dulles Airport. Trips into downtown Washington cost just over double the amount from National Airport. **BWI Airport** runs a shuttle service into the downtown terminus at 15th and K Street NW. Taxis to central Washington are also available. **Amtrak** runs a service from BWI into Union Station.

Taxis

Long-distance taxi fares are steep, but traveling inside Washington is cheaper than in other American cities and much cheaper than in some European capitals. This is because Washington cabs operate on fixed sums for each zone of the city they have to go through, and the zones were designed by the US Congress for maximum convenience and minimum expense to themselves. So a 2½-mile ride from Dupont Circle to Capitol Hill counts as one zone, and is a very reasonable fare.

Although you save money, you gain confusion. Drivers often speak little English, and once away from "Tourist Washington" rarely seem to know where they are going. Most do not carry maps.

The boundaries of each fare zone are not clearly displayed (there is occasionally, but not always, a zone map dangling on a chain from the back seat) so passengers have no way of knowing how many zones have been traveled or how much the fare should be. It must be said, however, that fares into central Washington from the airports are clearly marked, and most drivers are relatively honest. Besides, the city is not large enough for much "clockable" extra driving.

Taxis tend to be decrepit and usually without air-conditioning. Washington is one of the few Western cities in the world in which it is perfectly acceptable for drivers to pick up several fares during the course of one journey – an alarming practice if you are unaware it might happen or are in a hurry. This occurs mainly during rush hours, so leave plenty of time to arrive at your destination.

For planned trips, reserve a taxi at least an hour in advance of departure. Some of the major taxi cab companies are:

Taxi Transportation Service, tel: 398 0500

Barwood Taxi, tel: 301 984 1900

Checker Cab Company, tel: 270 6000

Taxi cabs outside DC are all the same price – a fixed fare to get in the cab, then additional fees for every mile (or part of) there after. If you are going a long distance, you can usually negotiate with the cab driver to give you a fixed rate.

Private Transportation
Limousine Services

For a more comfortable, luxurious form of transportation, try limousines. The price of limousine service does not vary much from company to company, with a two-to-three-hour minimum and a 15 percent mandatory tip for the driver.

Capital City Limousine, tel: 667 7900.

Congressional Limousine, tel: 468 6460.

Exclusive Limousine Inc., tel: 565 0009AC.

Limousine Service, tel: 907 9765.

American Pullman, tel: 340 2712.

Car Rentals

One way to get around Washington – particularly if you are interested in some of the worthwhile day trips – is to rent a car. You can do this at the airport, your hotel, or any car rental agency, checking the phone book under "Automobile Renting." Cars can often be delivered to you. Car rental companies all charge roughly the same price. Most hotels (but not all) offer free parking for their guests; if staying in the city for any lenth of time, leave your car in the garage. Parking around DC is difficult on the street and expensive in car parks.

Some of the bigger companies are Avis, Budget, Hertz, Alamo and Dollar. All have numerous offices around the city, so consult the phone directory for the one nearest you. Most rental agencies require you be at least 21 years old and possess a valid driver's license. If you are insured in the US, you should not have to purchase insurance from the agency. If uninsured, read the rental agency's insurance policy carefully before purchasing the car insurance.

Where To Stay

Reservations

It is imperative to make reservations at hotels and popular restaurants all year round, but especially during high season, April to September. However, not all restaurants take reservations, so call ahead to find out how long the wait will be.

Should you have no idea where you want to stay, contact Capitol Reservations, 1730 Rhode Island Avenue, NW, Suite 320, Washington DC 20036, tel: (202) 452 1270 or toll-free 1-800 VISIT-DC; fax: (202) 452 0537. They will find you a hotel in the price range or area you want.

If you are happy to stay outside the city center, it is not entirely necessary to reserve rooms in advance. There are plenty of modest chain motels and hotels inside the DC line but away from busy downtown. But it's wiser to reserve ahead in the high May to September season. If you reserve by telephone many hotels and motels will expect your credit card number to guarantee the room, or will require a deposit by cheque, so be sure to find out what their refund policy is like on cancellations.

Hotels

Hotels in Washington generally offer rooms in three categories – standard, superior, and deluxe – for single and double rooms, so check in which category you are being quoted a price when making a reservation. In Washington, rates are negotiable. They also vary considerably with the season, and most hotels run regular discount room rates, particularly at weekends and off season, so make inquiries.

Most double rooms offer two queen-size beds, so that you should inquire what charge is made if you want to occupy one of the beds with one or two children, the adults taking the other bed. King-size beds, only one per room, are sometimes available on request. "Single Occupancy" means one person to one room. Double Occupancy means two people, one bed. Unless indicated differently, all rooms will include a bathroom.

"All major credit cards" means Visa, Master Card, Carte Blanche and Diners Club. American Express is generally, but not always, acceptable. Some companies also accept the Discover Card and Japan Credit Bureau card.

Most major hotels and motel chains have toll free numbers for making reservations. When dialing the 1-800 number from within America, the call is free.

Top Hotels

The Willard Inter-Continental, 1401 Pennsylvania Avenue NW, Washington DC 20004. Tel: 202 628 9100. Steeped in Washington history, this is the grandest of the capital's grand hotels, with sumptuous rooms and scrupulous service. Amenities: 2 restaurants, café, bar, exercise equipment, laundry, parking, in-room video check-out, pets accepted. Credit cards: all major.

The Jefferson, 1200 16th Street NW, Washington DC 20036. Tel: 202 347 2200 or toll free 1-800 368 5966. A relatively small hotel, offering discreet and sensitive service in elegant surroundings. Amenities: restaurant, Saturday jazz, high tea, bathrobes, hair dryers, exercise and swimming facilities at University Club opposite, laundry, one-hour pressing, valet parking, pets accepted. Credit cards: all major except Discover.

The Hay-Adams, One Lafayette Square, Washington DC 20006. Tel: 202 638 6600 or toll free 1-800 424 5054. Old fashioned values are presented in modern-day comfort at this elegantly aristocratic, long-established hotel. Amenities: 3 restaurants, complimentary limousine, full butler service, valet parking, full valet service, arrangements can be made for exercise facilities at a neighborhood club. Credit cards: all major.

The Ritz-Carlton, 2100 Massachusetts Avenue NW, Washington DC 20008. Tel: 202 293 2100 or toll free 1-800 424 8008. Good taste abounds, from the restaurant to the interior decoration, and in the thoughtfulness of the service. Amenities: restaurant, light fare lounge, 24-hour room service, bathrobes, valet parking, dry cleaning and laundry, pets accepted. Credit cards: all major.

The Stouffer Mayflower, 1127 Connecticut Avenue NW, Washington DC 20036. Tel: toll free 1-800-HOTELS-1. On the National Register of Historic Places, this hotel is a repository of 20th-century political history, though its charm is reminiscent of a less abrasive time. Amenities: 2 restaurants, paid parking, dry cleaning and laundry, affiliation with a local health club, complimentary coffee and newspaper with wake-up call. Credit cards: all major.

The Four Seasons, 2800 Pennsylvania Avenue NW, Washington DC 20007. Tel: 202 342 0444 or toll free 1-800 828 1188. Opened in 1979, this attractive hotel, with views over Rock Creek Park and the C&O Canal, has been host to many of the world's more glamorous public figures. Amenities: 2 restaurants, valet and self parking, dry cleaning and laundry, exercise room, swimming pool, small pets accepted. Credit cards: all major.

The Madison, M and 15th streets NW, Washington DC 20005. Tel: 202 862 1600 or toll free 1-800 424 8577. Owned by art collector Marshall B. Coyne, this graceful hotel, with its many pieces and furnishing from the Coyne collection, has an imposing air of elegance that suggests it must be far older than its 30-years plus. Amenities: 2 restaurants, valet parking, dry cleaning and laundry, use of two local health spas. Credit cards: all major.

The Sheraton Carlton, 923 16th NW, Washington DC 20036. Tel: 202 638 2626 or toll free 1-800 325 3535. Designed in 1926 to lure the aristocrats of Washington society to its doors, this is a hotel of high luxury and old traditions with possibly the most impressive lobby in the capital. Amenities: restaurant, valet parking, dry cleaning and laundry, exercise room, use of the Sheraton Washington's pool. Credit cards: all major cards.

The Omni Shoreham, 2500 Calvert Street NW, Washington DC 20008. Tel: 202 234 0700 or toll free 1-800 228 2121. Built in 1930 and extravagantly restored at the end of the '80s, this has been the setting for an inaugural

ball ever since Franklin Delano Roosevelt was elected. A stately hotel of 800 rooms, located next to Rock Creek Park. Amenities: restaurant, light fare lounge, gourmet takeout shop, garage, Marquee Cabaret for evening entertainment, dry cleaning and laundry, fitness center, tennis courts and outdoor pools. Credit cards: all major.

J.W. Marriott, 1331 Pennsylvania Avenue NW, Washington DC 20004. Tel: 202 393 200 or toll free 1-800 228 9290. Marriott's flagship hotel offers a traditional atmosphere in an up-to-date setting close to the White House. Amenities: 4 restaurants, lounge and cocktail bar, valet parking, sauna, jacuzzi, indoor pool, weights and exercise room, dry cleaning and laundry, and a walk-through to the shops of National Place. Credit cards: all major.

The Capital Hilton, 16th and K streets NW, Washington DC 20036. Tel: 202 393 1000 or toll free 1-800-HILTONA. Comfortably appointed, elegantly understated hotel two blocks from the White House. Amenities: 2 restaurants, valet parking, fitness center and sauna, dry cleaning and laundry, buses to all airports. Credit cards: all major.

The Canterbury Hotel, 1733 N Street NW, Washington DC 20036. Tel: 202 393 3000 or toll free 1-800 424 2950. Soothingly restrained hotel with a European feel at the spot on which Theodore Roosevelt's house once stood. Amenities: restaurant, pub, valet parking, use of the YMCA health and fitness facilities, dry cleaning and laundry. Rooms are small suites with kitchenette, sofa, dressing room, minibar. Credit cards: all major.

The Marbury House, 3000 M Street NW, Washington DC 20007. Tel: 202 726 5000 or toll free 1-800 368 5922. In the heart of Georgetown, Washington's chic boutique and restaurant area, this hotel has a light and calm atmosphere. Amenities: restaurant, lounge, rooftop swimming pool, VCR rental and video library, valet parking, dry cleaning and laundry. Each room has fully stocked mini-bar and refrigerator. Credit cards: all major.

Good Value

The Quality Inn Downtown, 1315 16th Street NW, Washington DC 20036. Tel: 202 667 9827 or toll free 1-800 368 5689. Located at Scott Circle, within

easy walking distance of downtown Washington, the White House, and Georgetown. Amenities: each room is a fully equipped efficiency unit, complete with cooking facilities, dining area, sofa, TV, restaurant, free parking, coin-op basement laundry, use of nearby YMCA pool. Credit cards: all major.

The Ramada, 1600 New York Avenue NE, Washington DC 20002. Tel: 202 832 3200 or toll free 1-800 446 6900. A comfortably decorated, simple hotel away from the center. Amenities: coffeeshop, indoor pool, parking.

The Ramada Inn Central, 1430 Rhode Island Avenue NW, Washington DC 20005. Tel: 202 462 7777 or toll free 1-800 368 5690. A comfortable, family-feel hotel, close to the White House and the Mall's attractions. Amenities: 166 out of the 186 rooms are fully equipped with cooking facilities, dining areas, and TV. Informal restaurant, cocktail lounge, rooftop pool, coin-op laundry, video games, indoor parking, ironing equipment available on request. Credit cards: all major.

The Holiday Inn Central, 1501 Rhode Island Avenue NW, Washington DC 20005. Tel: 202 483 2000 or toll free 1-800-HOLIDAY. A straightforward, functionally efficient hotel, not far from Washington's museums and central shopping. Amenities: restaurant, lounge, outdoor pool, exercise room, dry cleaning and laundry, underground car park. Credit cards: all major.

Days Premiere, 1201 K Street NW, Washington DC 20005. Tel: 202 842 1020 or toll free 1-800 562 3350. Located close to Metro Center subway, a pleasantly decorated hotel. Amenities: good restaurant and bar, parking, outdoor pool, exercise room, dry cleaning and laundry. Credit cards: all major.

Howard Johnson's Motor Lodge, 2601 Virginia Avenue NW, Washington DC 20037. Tel: 202 965 2700 or toll free 1-800 654 2000. An attractively decorated hotel, two blocks from the Kennedy Center. Amenities: Bob's Big Boy restaurant, outdoor pool, free parking, dry cleaning and laundry. Credit cards: all major.

The Channel Inn, 650 Water Street NW, Washington DC 20024. Tel: 202 554 2400 or toll free 1-800 368 5668. Washington's only waterfront hotel, close to the marina restaurants, with large and simple but comfortable ooms. Amenities: good seafood res-aurant, coffeeshop, outdoor pool, plus the Arena Stage, golf course, in-loor and outdoor tennis courts are close by. Credit cards: all major.

Budget

Jost Inn, 1917 Bladensburg Rd NE, Washington DC 20002. Tel: 202 832 3600 or toll free 1-800 251 1962. Ad-joining the US National Arboretum, this modest two-story motel runs twice daily sightseeing buses into town. Amenities: Chinese/American restau-rant, parking, outdoor pool, free VCR movies. Credit cards: all major.
Allen Lee Hotel, 2224 F Street NW, Washington DC 20037. Tel: 202 331 1224. Simple but clean hotel – some rooms share baths. Great for the young. Amenities: free coffee and cookies in lobby on Sunday mornings, maid service daily. All rooms have TV; some have baths. Credit cards: Not accepted.

Youth Hostels

Washington International Youth Hos-tel, 1009 11th Street NW, Washington DC 20001. Tel: 202 737 2333. Lo-cated one block north of the Conven-tion Center, with common areas for meeting other travelers, information desk, ride board, free tours and mov-es, tight security, large kitchen avail-able for groups.
Bears Den Hostel – American Youth Hostels, Route 1, Box 288 Bluemont, VA. Tel: 1-703 554 8708 for details.

Campgrounds

Capitol KOA Campground, 768 Cecil Avenue, Millerville Md 21108. Tel: 301 923 2771. Sixteen miles from Wash-ngton metro system.
Cherry Hill Park, 9800 Cherry Hill Road, College Park, Md 20740. Tel: 301 937 7116. Just off Interstate 95 in Maryland. Full hook-up sites for vans, tents welcome, metro bus to entrance, guided tours of the city, group rates, swimming pool.
Duncan's Family KOA Campground, 5381 Sands Rd, Lothian, Md 20711. Tel: 301 627 3909. Twenty miles SE of DC. Wooded campground, family owned and operated, open March 15–October 31. City tours from camp-ground, van service to metro.

Eating Out

Where To Eat

The benefit of Washington as a mag-net to political refugees and other im-migrants from around the world is that there is almost no cuisine that is not represented somewhere in the city and its surrounding suburbs. Everything from Ethiopian cooking to Nepalese, from British high tea to the best French cuisine, can be found somewhere.

Some of Washington's (currently) most popular or interesting restau-rants, listed by ethnic origin. Reserva-tions are strongly recommended:

Afghan

Bamiyan, 3320 M Street NW. Tel: 338 1896. Good service and relaxed at-mosphere. Be sure to try the *aushak*, homemade stuffed noodles topped with yoghurt and tomato-meat sauces, either as an appetizer or an entree. A second Bamiyan is located in Old Town Alexandria on King Street. Open: lunch Monday–Friday 11.30am–2.30pm, din-ner Monday–Sunday 5–11pm.

American

Hard Times Café, 1404 King Street, Old Town Alexandria, VA. Tel: 703 683 5340. You must be a true chili con-noisseur to get full enjoyment from this establishment. A wide variety of chilies, both meaty and vegetarian are offered, some very spicy. Helpings are huge. Open: Monday–Saturday 11am–11pm, Sunday 4–10pm.
Joe & Mo's, 1211 Connecticut Avenue NW. Tel: 659 1211. A bit pricey but worth it if you have an appetite for slab-sized steaks and lunching with the powerful. Open: breakfast Mon-day–Friday 7.30–10am, lunch and din-ner Monday–Friday 11.30am–10pm, dinner Saturday 6–10pm.
Market Lunch, 225 7th Street SE. Tel: 547 8444. It's no surprise there's a fight to get in here for Saturday break-fasts. The crabcakes and homemade bread are superb, and the prices are cheap. You have a better chance of

getting a seat for a weekday lunch. Don't expect to pay with plastic. Open: Tuesday–Saturday 7.30am–2.30pm.
Morton's of Chicago, 3251 Prospect Street NW. Tel: 342 6458. Classic steakhouse with enormous portions of excellent beef or lamb, as well as fish and lobster, all displayed by the waiter in their uncooked state, along with the day's selection of vegetables, on a pre-meal trolley show. Entrees can be expensive, so choose carefully. Open: Monday–Saturday 5.30–11pm, Sun-day 5–10pm. Credit cards: all major.
The Palm, 1225 19th Street NW. Tel: 293 9091. Caricatures of the famous line the walls and some of the locally famous can be seen among the pa-trons. The atmosphere is decidedly clubby while the fare is simple but fill-ing. Be sure to make a reservation. Open: Monday–Friday 11.45am–10.30pm, Saturday 6–10.30pm.
Potowmack Landing, Washington Sail-ing Marina, George Washington Park-way, 2 miles south of National Airport. Tel: 703 548 9027. Although the food may not be particularly memorable, the view of the Potomac and DC itself is. If the season is right, you can watch people sailing and windsurfing on the river. Afterwards it's just a short, beau-tiful drive down the parkway to Mount Vernon. Open: daily lunch 11.30am–2.30pm, dinner 5.30–10pm.
Sam & Harry's, 1200 19th Street NW tel: 296 4333. A relaxed steak and seafood restaurant, serving vast slabs of grilled beef, lamb, chicken and fish, with good and generous side dishes. Open: lunch Monday–Friday 11.30am–2.30pm, dinner Monday–Saturday 4.30–11pm. Credit cards: all major.
Two Quail, 320 Massachusetts Av-enue NE. Tel: 543 8030. While the mismatched furniture and table set-tings are a bit peculiar, the atmos-phere is cozy and the cooking is inven-tive. Save room for the homemade desserts, especially the Key lime cheesecake. Open: lunch Monday–Fri-day 11.30am–2.30pm, brunch Sunday 10.30am–3.30pm, dinner Monday–Fri-day 5.30–10.30pm, Saturday 5.30–10.30pm, Sunday 5.30–10.30pm.

New American

Bistro 2015, Embassy Row Hotel, 2015 Massachusetts Avenue NW. Tel: 939 4250. Features often dazzling, sometimes experimental, but invariably interesting modern cooking in a traditionally decorated formal restaurant. Only the finest fresh ingredients used in the dishes served. Open: lunch Monday–Friday 11.30am–2pm, dinner Monday–Saturday 6–10pm, Sunday 6–9.30pm, Sunday brunch 11.30am–2.30pm. Credit cards: all major. Fixed-price menus are available.

New Heights, 2317 Calvert Street NW. Tel: 234 4110. Under the influence of its Indian owner, this distinctive and inventive restaurant takes "new cooking" farther by the subtle introduction of intriguing oriental and Asian spices and ingredients to Western produce. Dishes are lifted to often new but cunning contrasts of flavor and texture, presented in a calm, gently lit dining room. Open: Sunday–Thursday 5–10.30pm, Friday and Saturday 5–11.30pm, Sunday brunch 11am–2.30pm. Credit cards: all major.

Nora, 2132 Florida Avenue NW. Tel: 462 5143. Sometimes trying a little too hard to be original, Nora's is nonetheless worth a visit for its audacious balancing of seemingly incompatible ingredients, served in an intimate dining room (and outdoor dining area in clement weather). It declares its produce organic and biodynamic, but those bored by the thought need not expect a diminution of interesting flavors. Open: Monday–Thursday 6–10pm, Friday and Saturday 6–10.30pm. Credit cards: MC, V.

Tex Mex/Latin American

Rio Grande Café, 4919 Fairmont Avenue, Bethesda. Tel: 301 656 2981. You have to wait at least half an hour for a table at night, clutching a marguerita in the bar and munching on sublime taco chips, but the food is worth it – fresh lightly grilled fajitas, good tacos, tamales and enchiladas, as well as grilled fish and ribs. The restaurant is raucous with noise, so be in the mood. Open: lunch Monday–Friday 11am–3pm, dinner Monday–Thursday 3–10.30pm, Friday 3–11.30pm, Saturday 11.30am–11.30pm, Sunday 11.30am–10.30pm. Credit cards: All major. No reservations.

Austin Grill, 2404 Wisconsin Avenue NW. Tel: 337 8080. Cheerful rustic Texan decorated restaurant serving chunky chopped chili, fajitas, crab meat quesadillas, chili con queso, enchiladas and more. Open: Monday–

Thursday 11.30am–11pm, Friday and Saturday 11.30am–midnight, Sunday 11.30am–10pm. Credit cards: AE, DC, MC and V. No reservations needed. A second branch is located in Old Town Alexandria.

Terramar, 7800 Wisconsin Avenue, Bethesda. Tel: 301 654 0888. Slightly more expensive than the others, but good food. Open: lunch Tuesday–Friday 11.30am–2.30pm, dinner Tuesday–Sunday 5–10pm. Credit cards: AE, MC, V, Discover.

Chinese

Full Kee, 509 H Street NW. Tel: 371 2233. Cantonese stir-fried dishes, dumplings and noodles. Open: Sunday–Thursday 11–1am, Friday and Saturday 11–3am. Cash only.

Mr Yung's, 740 6th Street NW. Tel: 628 1098. Cantonese dishes and dim sum, plus idiosyncratic dishes such as frogs steamed with ham in lotus leaf, dried cabbage steamed with side pork, and shellfish with yellow leeks. Open: daily lunch Monday–Friday 11am–3pm, dinner 3pm–1am. Credit cards: AE, MC, V.

Ethiopian

Meskerem, 2434 18th Street NW. Tel: 462 4100. Try for a table on the top floor, with basket tables under a tented ceiling. Best with a large group, so that many dishes can be ordered. For two, try the combination platter to sample an array of items presented on the curious gray spongy pancake bread that is ripped off and used as the utensil for the food. Open: Monday–Thursday 5pm–midnight, Friday–Sunday, noon–12.30am. Credit cards: all major.

Red Sea, 2463 18th Street NW. Tel: 483 5000. In the heart of Adams Morgan, this is the first of the area's many Ethiopian restaurants. Concerned less with appearance than its neighbor Meskerem, it hails its ethnic cuisine as an event for the open-minded and gastronomically adventurous. In Ethiopia, a meal is a communal event, and it becomes so here with everyone in your party eating off the same plate, scooping up the meat and vegetable stews and sauces with *injera*, the flat spongy bread. The staff is happy to show you how to do it if you're uncertain. Open: Sunday–Thursday 11.30am–midnight, Friday–Saturday 11.30am–1am.

French

La Brasserie, 239 Massachusetts Avenue NE. Tel: 546 6066. The emphasis here is on the food and it's excellent. The menu ranges from luxurious lobster to a variety of thick quiches to devilishly rich creme brulee. In warm weather, the terrace makes a nice backdrop to the gastronomic delights. Open: daily 11.30am–11.30pm.

Le Caprice, 2348 Wisconsin Avenue NW. Tel: 337 3394. A tiny yet ambitious restaurant, focusing on elaborate presentations of classic and modern French dishes, with reduced stocks and sauces, and complex juxtaposition of unexpected ingredients. Open: lunch Tuesday–Friday 11.45am–2pm, dinner Tuesday–Thursday 6.30–10pm, Friday 6.30–10.30pm, Saturday 6–10.30pm, Sunday 6–9.30pm. Credit cards: all major. Three- or four-course fixed price menu is available for both lunch and dinner.

Le Gaulois, 1106 King Street, Alexandria. Tel: 703 739 9494. A large, traditional bistro-style restaurant, serving classic hearty bistro dishes like onion soup and daubes, as well as cuisine minceur and seasonal dishes. Open: Monday–Saturday 11.30am–10.30pm. Credit cards: all major.

Le Lion d'Or, 1150 Connecticut Avenue NW (entrance on 18th Street). Tel: 296 7972. A grand restaurant in the old style, offering classic and original dishes of supreme elegance and luxury, in splendid surroundings. Open: lunch Monday–Friday noon–2pm, dinner Monday–Saturday 6–10pm. Credit cards: all major.

Italian

Bice, 601 Pennsylvania Avenue NW (entrance on Indiana Avenue). Tel: 638 2423. Upmarket and discreet dining room, subtle traditional cooking. Excellent pastas and risottos, good grills with polenta or delicious vegetable concoctions. Open: lunch Monday–Friday 11.30am–2.30pm, dinner Monday–Thursday 5.30–10.30pm, Friday and Saturday 5.30–11.30pm, Sunday 5.30–10pm. Credit cards: AE, MC, V.

Galileo, 1110 21st Street NW. Tel: 293 7191. Elegant and spacious restaurant offering the fine cooking of Roberto Donna. Impeccable and complex seasonal pasta dishes, grilled fishes and meats in intriguing sauces

Open: lunch Monday–Friday 11.30am–2pm, dinner Monday–Thursday 5.30–10pm, Friday and Saturday 5.30–10.30pm Sunday 5–9pm. Credit cards: all major.

Ricchi, 1120 19th Street NW. Tel: 835 0459. A traditional Tuscan restaurant serving fresh, simple and hearty rustic cooking. Bread, meat and fish are cooked and grilled in the dining room's wood-burning stove. Wonderful sage and ricotta-stuffed tortellini, flavorful sauces for pastas and risottos, and excellent seafood. Open: lunch Monday–Friday 11.30am–2.30pm, dinner Monday–Thursday 5.30–10.30pm, Friday and Saturday 5.30–11.30pm. Credit cards: all major.

Notte Luna, 809 15th Street NW. Tel: 408 9500. A relaxed Italian/American restaurant, with a view of the bustling kitchen, serving inventive pizzas, imaginative pasta and salads, and excellent grilled meat and fish dishes. Open: Monday–Thursday 11am–11pm, Friday 11am–midnight, Saturday 5pm–midnight. Credit cards: all major.

Obelisk, 2029 P Street NW. Tel: 872 1180. An intimate restaurant, offering a daily changing four-course menu of simple fresh foods that include homemade breads and pastas, grilled vegetables, sophisticated soups, and grills in intriguing marinades. Open: Monday–Saturday 6–10pm. Credit cards: MC, V. Four-course fixed price dinner available.

Paolo's, 1303 Wisconsin Avenue NW. Tel: 333 7353. The food may be Italian, but the atmosphere is distinctly American. The decor is modern and bright, the service fast and friendly. Pizzas, pastas and salads are all good selections. The breadsticks are not to be missed. Open: Monday–Thursday 11.30am–midnight, Friday–Saturday 11.30–3am, Sunday 11am–midnight.

Japanese

Tako Grill, 7756 Wisconsin Avenue, Bethesda. Tel: 301 652 7030. A Japanese restaurant that as well as *sushi* and traditional Japanese dishes offers a robata menu of grilled meats, vegetables and fish cooked over charcoal. Open: lunch Monday–Friday 11.30am–2pm, dinner Monday–Thursday 5.30–9.45pm, Friday and Saturday 5.30–10.15pm. Credit cards: AE, MC, V. No reservations.

Seafood

Fish Market, 105 King Street, Old Town Alexandria, VA. Tel: 703 836 5676. Close to the waterfront, the Fish Market is a large restaurant made up of small, intimate rooms. The food is good and the helpings generous; their clam chowder is especially noteworthy. On weekend nights it's a popular bar where everyone comes to enjoy oyster crackers and huge schooners of beer. Although you may have to pay an extra charge to sit (and sing) in the piano bars upstairs, they're fun and definitely worth it. Open: daily 11.15am–midnight.

Spanish

Taberna del Alabardero, 1776 I Street NW (entrance on 18th Street). Tel: 429 2200. An authentic Spanish restaurant offering a wide variety of elegant tapas (appetizers) as well as paellas, grills, aromatic casseroles, and fish. Open: lunch Monday–Friday 11.30am–2.30pm, dinner Monday–Thursday 6–10.30pm, Friday and Saturday 6–11pm. Credit cards: all major.

Thai

Duangrat's, 5878 Leesburg Pike, Falls Church. Tel: 703 820 5775. Lengthy menu of classic Thai dishes, as well as some less familiar, in attractive pink surroundings. Open: lunch Monday–Friday 11.30am–2.30pm, Saturday and Sunday 11.30am–5pm, dinner Sunday–Thursday 5–10.30pm, Friday and Saturday 5–11pm. Credit cards: AE, DC, MC, V.

Attractions

Excursions

The following is a list of excursions detailed in full in the appropriate chapter of this guidebook.

The Mall East

Boundaries: 14th Street to Independence Avenue to 3rd Street to Constitution Avenue.
Smithsonian Institution Building
Freer Gallery
S. Dillon Ripley Center
Enid Haupt Garden
Sackler Gallery
National Museum of African Art
Arts and Industries Building
Carousel
Hirshhorn Museum and Sculpture Garden
National Air and Space Museum
National Gallery of Art, West and East Buildings
National Museum of Natural History
National Museum of American History

The Mall West

Boundaries: Rock Creek Parkway and Theodore Roosevelt Memorial Bridge east to Constitution Avenue to 17th Street; north to E Street; east to 15th Street; south to Constitution, including the Ellipse; east to 14th Street; south to Route 1 to Ohio Drive; following the coastline of East Potomac Park around the peninsula and up to Parkway and Memorial Bridge.
Ellipse
Washington Monument
Sylvan Theatre
Bureau of Engraving and Printing
United States Holocaust Memorial Museum
Tidal Basin
East Potomac Park
Cherry Blossom Festival
Jefferson Memorial
Hains Point
"The Awakening" sculpture

West Potomac Park
Lincoln Memorial
The Reflecting Pool and The Rainbow Pool
Constitution Gardens
Memorial to the Signers of the Declaration
of Independence
Vietnam Veterans Memorial and vigil sites

Around Logan Circle & Northeast

Boundaries: from Scott Circle, 16th Street north to Maryland line; southeast to Anacostia River west shore to Benning Road; west to Florida Avenue to North Capitol Street; south to Massachusetts Avenue; west to Scott Circle.
Logan Circle
Bethune Museum-Archives for Black Women's
History
Studio Theatre
Woolly Mammoth Theatre
Source Theatre
Meridian Hill Park
House of the Temple
Howard University
Trinity College/Chapel of Notre Dame
Catholic University/Hartke Theatre
Basilica of the National Shrine of the Immaculate Conception
Dance Place
Franciscan Monastery
St Anselm's Abbey
Gallaudet University
National Arboretum

Downtown

Boundaries: From Scott Circle, Massachusetts Avenue east to North Capitol Street; south to Louisiana Avenue; south to Constitution Avenue; east to 15th Street; north to E Street; west to 17th Street; north to N Street; east to Scott Circle.
Duke Zeibert's
Joe and Mo's
The Palm
Mayflower Hotel
St Matthew's Cathedral
B'nai B'rith Klutznick Museum
Sumner School Museum and Archives
National Geographic Society
Jefferson Hotel
Metropolitan AME church
Madison Hotel
Washington Post Building
Lafayette Park

Hay-Adams Hotel
St John's Church and Parish House
Decatur House
Blair House
Renwick Gallery
Sheraton Carlton
Treasury Building
Old Executive Office Building
Pershing Park
Freedom Plaza
Willard Hotel
Hotel Washington
National Theatre
Warner Theatre
Federal Triangle
National Aquarium
Old Post Office Pavilion
FBI
Ford's Theatre
House Where Lincoln Died
Navy Memorial/Market Square
National Archives
National Building Museum/Pension Building
Jewish Historical Society of Greater Washington
Government Printing Office and Bookstore
Washington Project for the Arts
d.c. space
Chinatown
National Museum of American Art
National Portrait Gallery
National Museum of Women in the Arts

Dupont Circle, Kalorama & Adams Morgan

Boundaries: From Scott Circle, 16th Street north to Piney Branch Parkway and Rock Creek; trace creek south to N Street; east to Scott Circle.
Kramerbooks
Sulgrave Club
St Thomas' Episcopal Church park
Church Street Theatre
National Trust for Historic Preservation
Iron Gate Inn
Historical Society of Washington DC (Heurich Mansion)
Embassy Row
Anderson House
Friends Meeting House
Brickskeller
Phillips Collection
Ritz-Carlton Hotel
Fonda del Sol Visual Arts Center
Holography Museum
Letelier Memorial/Sheridan Circle

Alice Pike Barney Studio House
Woodrow Wilson House
Textile Museum
Mitchell Park
Decatur Terrace
Islamic Center
Farmers' Market
Meridian
House International

Virginia

Monticello, Route 53, Box 316, Charlottesville, VA 22902. Tel: 804 295 8181/2657. 2˘ hours by car from Washington. Open: daily March–October, 8am–5pm. Off season: 9am–4.30pm. Admission: charge. The lines build up quickly, so try to arrive early in the day. Tours last 15 minutes. The gardens, the servant quarters and storerooms are open to the public, but not the upper floors of the house. Also open is **Jefferson's Grove**, an 18-acre park on the northwest slope of the hilltop. From the Visitor's Center, go south on Route 20, then left on Route 53.
The Skyline Drive: The Drive is inside the Shenandoah National Park – there is a small admission fee per car. Ask for a free copy of *Overlook*, the park newspaper, which lists what is happening and other interesting information.
Luray Caverns. Tel: 703 743 6551. Tours leave every 20 minutes from mid-March until mid-November, the first at 9am, the last at 6pm except for the period mid-June to Labor Day, when the first is at 9am, and the last at 7pm. From mid-November until mid-March it is open from 9am, last trip at 4pm. The admission fee includes a tour of an antique car museum. Take warm clothing for the caves.
Skyline Caverns. Tel: 703 635 4545. Tours run from end–May until Labor Day 8.30am–6.30pm. Off-season: 9am–5pm. Admission: charge. Take warm clothing for the caves.
Fredericksburg and Spotsylvania National Military Park, Lafayette Boulevard, PO Box 679, Fredericksburg, VA 22404. Tel: 703 373 4461. Open: daily 9am–5pm, except for Christmas and New Year's Day.
Fredericksburg Visitors' Center, 706 Caroline Street, Fredericksburg, VA 22401. Tel: 703 373 1776. Open: July–August 9am–7pm, rest of year 9am–5pm.

Manassas (Bull Run) National Battlefield Park, Interstate 66 and Route
234S, Manassas, VA 22110. Tel: 703
754 7107. Open: mid-June to Labor
Day 8.30am–6pm, rest of year
8.30am–5pm.

New Market Battlefield Park, Box
864, New Market, VA 22844. Tel:
703 740 3102. Open: daily 9am–
5pm. Admission: charge. Closed:
Thanksgiving, Christmas and New
Year's Day.

Endless Caverns, PO Box 859, New
Market, VA 22844. Tel: 703-740
1993. Open: mid-June to Labor Day
9am, last tour 7pm; Labor Day–November 14 9am, last tour 5pm; November 15–March 14 9am, last tour
4pm, March 15–June 14 9am, last
tour 5pm. Take a warm jacket as it can
become chilly and damp.

Bedrooms of America Museum, 9386
Congress Street, New Market, VA
22844. Tel: 703 740 3512. Open:
Memorial Day to Labor Day 9am–8pm,
rest of the year 9am–5pm. Admission:
charge.

Colonial Williamsburg, Colonial Williamsburg Travel Department, PO Box
, Williamsburg, VA 23185. Tel: 1-800-
HISTORY. Coming into Williamsburg on
Interstate 64, take the exit signed "Colonial Williamsburg," driving west to
the Visitor's Center. The grounds are
open 24 hours all year, the buildings
open from 9am–5pm. Basic admission
ticket is to 13 different buildings (except Governor's Palace, Bassett Hall,
the Wallace Gallery of Decorative Arts)
plus free hop-on, hop-off shuttle bus
transportation. The excepted buildings
will need extra tickets. A Patriot's Pass
gets you into all the properties and is
valid for one year; other ticket combi-
nations are available.

Busch Gardens, Route 60, 5 miles
east of Williamsburg. Tel: 804 253
3350. Open: Memorial Day to Labor
Day 10am–midnight; weekends only
mid-March to mid-May 10am–8pm.
Admission: charge.

Maryland

National Aquarium, Pier 3, Pratt
Street, Baltimore MD 21202. Tel: 301
576 3800. Open: May–September
Monday–Friday 9am–5pm, Saturday–
Sunday 9am–8pm; October–April Saturday–Thursday 10am–5pm, Friday
10am–8pm. Times can change, so call
first. Admission: charge.

Maryland Science Center & Davis
Planetarium, 601 Light Street, Baltimore MD 21202. Tel: 301 685 2370.
Open: Memorial Day–Labor Day, Monday–Saturday 10am–6pm, Sunday
noon–6pm; rest of the year, Monday–
Friday 10am–5pm, weekends 10am–
6pm. Tickets admit to everything.

Tourism Council of Annapolis & Anne
Arundel County, City Dock, Annapolis,
MB 21401. Tel: 301 268-TOUR. His-
toric Annapolis Inc. Tel: 301 267 8149.

Paca House and Gardens, 186 Prince
Street. Tel: 301 263 5553. Open:
Tuesday–Saturday 10am–5pm, Sun-
day noon–5pm. Admission: charge.

The Hammond-Harwood House, 19
Maryland Avenue. Tel: 301 269 1714.
Open: April–November, Tuesday–Saturday 10am–5pm, Sunday 2–5pm; November–April Tuesday–Saturday 10am
–4pm, Sunday 1–4pm. Admission:
charge.

The Chase Lloyd House, 22 Maryland
Avenue. Tel: 301 263 2723. Open: for
20-minute guided tours Tuesday–Saturday 2–4pm. Donations welcome.

The United States Naval Academy
Visitor Center, Gate 1, Ricketts Hall.
Tel: 301 263 6933. One-hour tours
start on the hour from March–May between 10am and 3pm; June 1–Labor
Day, weekends half hourly between
9.30am and 4pm; Labor Day weekend–Thanksgiving hourly between
10am and 3pm. Admission: charge.

THE BAY BEACHES

Sandy Point State Park, 800 Revell
Highway, Rt 50, Annapolis. Tel: 301
757 1841. Open: for picnicking, fishing and swimming from 6am–9pm,
Memorial Day–Labor Day. Admission:
charge, half price Wednesday.

Rocky Point Waterfront Park, Back
River Neck and Barrison Point roads,
Back River. Tel: 301 887 0217. Open:
Memorial Day–Labor Day 10am–7pm.
Admission: charge.

Bay Ridge Beach, Herendon Avenue,
Bay Ridge, Annapolis. Tel: 202 261
2298. Open: Memorial Day–Labor Day
Monday–Friday 10am–7pm, Saturday–
Sunday 9am–8pm. Admission: charge.

THE EASTERN SHORE

Cambridge-Dorchester Chamber of Commerce, 203 Sunburst Highway, Cambridge, MD 21613. Tel: 301 228 3575.

Blackwater National Wildlife Refuge,
MD 335, Cambridge, MD 21613.

Annie Oakley House, Hambrook Boulevard, Cambridge, MD 21613.

Meredith House & Neild Museum,
LaGrange Avenue, Cambridge, MD
21613. Tel: 301 228 7953. Open:
Thursday–Saturday 10am–4pm.

Brannock Maritime Museum, 210
Talbot Avenue, Cambridge, MD 21613.
Tel: 301 228 1245. Open: Saturday
and Sunday 1–4.30pm. Limited hours
January–February.

The Chesapeake Bay Maritime Museum, Mill Street, St Michaels MD
21663. Tel: 301 745 2916. Open:
daily April–mid-October 10am–5pm;
late-October–December 10am–4pm;
January–March weekends and holidays
only 10am–4pm. Admission: charge.

The Crab Claw, Navy Point, St Michaels, MD 21663. Tel: 301 745 2900.

The Inn at Perry Cabin, Watkins Lane,
St Michaels MD 21663. Tel: 301 745
5178.

The Town Dock Restaurant, 305 Mulberry Street, St Michaels, MD 21663.
Tel: 301 745 5577.

Longfellow's, Mulberry Street, St
Michaels, MD 21663. Tel: 301 745
2624.

Oxford, via the Tred Avon Oxford-
Bellevue Ferry.

Tilghman Island, off Route 33.

The Historical Society of Talbot
County, PO Box 964, Easton MD
21601. Tel: 301 822 0773. Open:
Tuesday–Saturday 10am–4 pm, Sun-
day 1–4 pm. Closed: Sunday January–
March.

Third Haven Meeting House, 405 S
Washington Street, Easton MD 21601.
Tel: 301 822 0293.

Other Attractions

Rehoboth Beach/Dewey Beach
Chamber of Commerce, PO Box 216,
Rehoboth Beach, DE 19971. Tel: 302
227 2233.

Bethany Beach – Fenwick Area
Chamber of Commerce, PO Box 1450,
Bethany Beach, DE 19930. Tel: 302
539 2100.

Deep Creek Lake – Garret County
Promotion Council. Tel: 302 334
1948.

The Cumberland-Frostburg Train. Tel:
1-800-TRAIN-50. Open: from the first
weekend in April–December 1, the
train leaves at 11.30am Tuesday–Friday, 11.30am and 3.30pm Saturday–
Sunday. Admission: charge.

Antietam National Battlefield, Route 65, Sharpsburg, MD 21782. Tel: 301 432 5124. Visitor's Center. Open: June–August 8am–6pm; September–May 8.30am–5pm. Admission: charge.

Exploring With Kids

Bureau of Engraving and Printing, 14th and C Streets SW. Tel: 447 9916. Hours: 9am–2pm Monday–Friday. The ticket office is located on 15th Street and opens at 8am (tickets are required late-May through August).

Capital Children's Museum, 800 3rd Street NW. Tel: 543 8600. Hours: 10am–5pm. Admission: charge.

Chesapeake & Ohio Canal Barge, 30th Street and the Canal NW (Georgetown). Tel: 472 4376 or 11710 MacArthur Boulevard Potomac, Maryland. Tel: 301 299 2026.

Federal Bureau of Investigation (FBI), J. Edgar Hoover Building 10th Street and Pennsylvania Avenue SW. Tel: 324 3447. Hours: daily 8.45am–4.15pm. Tours leave every 15 minutes.

Ford's Theatre, 511 10th Street NW. Tel: 426 6924 (museum). Hours: daily 9am–5pm. Theater closed on matinee days but museum may be reached through side entrance.

House Where Lincoln Died, 516 10th Street NW. Tel: 426 6830. Hours: daily 9am–5pm.

Marine Corps Museum, Washington Navy Yard, 9th and M streets SE. Tel: 433 3534. Hours: Monday–Saturday 10am–4pm, Sunday and holidays noon–5pm; May–September Friday 10am–8pm.

National Aquarium, Lower Lobby of Department of Commerce, 14th Street between Constitution and Pennsylvania Avenue NW. Tel: 377 2825. Hours: daily 9am–5pm. Admission: charge.

National Geographic Society Explorers Hall, 17th and M streets NW. Tel: 857 7000. Hours: Monday–Saturday and holidays 9am–5pm, Sunday 10am–5pm.

National Zoological Park, Rock Creek Park. Enter at 3001 Connecticut Avenue NW. Tel: 673 4800. Hours: daily 9am–6pm (summer hours); September 16–April 30, closes: 4.30pm.

Navy Museum, Washington Navy Yard, 9th and M streets SE. Tel: 433 4882. Hours: Monday–Friday 9am–5pm, weekends and holidays 10am–5pm; September–May, closes: 4pm.

Culture

Museums & Galleries

The Smithsonian Institution. The world's largest museum complex, was established over 100 years ago for "the increase and diffusion of knowledge among men." It comprises the **National Zoological Park** and 15 museums, most of which are grouped around the National Mall, and each of which is listed below. All museums are open 10am–5pm daily, unless otherwise indicated, and admission is free. Museum shops and dining facilities remain open until 30 minutes before closing time. For recordings on daily events in each museum, call Dial-A-Museum at 202 357 2020. For more information, including services for the disabled, tel: 202 357 2700.

Air & Space Museum, Independence Avenue, between 4th and 7th streets NW. The Smithsonian's largest museum, housing the nation's aerodynamic treasures from the Wright Brothers' 1903 Flyer to moon rocks and rockets. A fee is charged for admission to the film and planetarium shows.

Anacostia Museum, 1901 Fort Place, SE. Devoted to African-American heritage and located in Anacostia, a historic section of Washington named for the American Indian tribe which once lived there.

Arthur M. Sackler Gallery, 1050 Independence Avenue between 10th and 11th streets NW. Asian and Near Eastern art works span 6,000 years and include jades, bronzes, sculpture, paintings, furniture and lacquerware. Open: 10am–5.30pm.

Arts and Industries Building, Independence Avenue at 9th Street NW. Exhibits in the second oldest Smithsonian building recapture the spirit of the 1876 Philadelphia Exposition and the Victorian era. Open: 10–5.30pm.

Hirshhorn Museum & Sculpture Garden, Independence Avenue and 7th Street NW. Houses the extensive modern art collection of Joseph H. Hirshhorn, including works in every medium by European and American masters. Open: 10am–5.30pm.

Museum of African Art, 950 Independence Avenue SW. The collection study and exhibition of the art of sub Saharan Africa. Open: daily 10am–5.30pm.

Museum of American History, 14th Street and Constitution Avenue NW. Displays that include the flag that inspired "The Star-Spangled Banner" First Ladies' gowns and other political and cultural artifacts.

Museum of Natural History, Constitution Avenue at 10th Street NW. Anthropology, zoology, dinosaurs, insects minerals and gems, including the legendary Hope Diamond.

National Gallery of Art/East Building Pennsylvania Avenue between 3rd and 4th streets NW. A fine collection of modern European and American paintings, sculpture and graphic art housed in I.M. Pei's illustrious modern building.

National Gallery of Art/West Building, Constitution Avenue between 4th and 7th streets, NW. European paintings and sculpture of the 13th–19th centuries and American art, chronologically displayed.

Renwick Gallery, 17th and Pennsylvania Avenue NW. Changing exhibition from the museum's permanent collection highlight the American craft movement. Open: 10am–5.30pm.

Other Museums & Galleries

Art, Science and Technology Institute, 800 K Street NW. Exhibits include the largest hologram made and holographic equipment. Open 11am–6pm.

B'Nai B'rith Museum, 1640 Rhode Island Avenue NW. Twenty centuries of Jewish life.

Capital Children's Museum, 800 3rd Street NW. Hands-on museum with tasteful displays of arts, sciences and humanities.

Corcoran Gallery of Art, 17th Street and New York Avenue NW. Washington's oldest art collection, with a wide range of American art, Dutch and Flemish masterpieces, impressionists and post-impressionists. Open: 10am–4.30pm.

National Building Museum, F Street NW, between 4th and 5th streets. A celebration of America's architecture featuring the world's tallest Corinthian columns. Open: 10am–4pm.

National Museum of Women in the Arts, 1250 New York Avenue NW. More than 200 works by women from 29 countries.

The Octagon, 1799 New York Avenue NW. Displays of architectural exhibits in this home of the American Institute of Architects. Open: 10am–4pm.

Phillips Collection, 21st and Q streets NW. The permanent collection of the country's first museum of modern art.

Textile Museum, 2320 S Street NW. A display of Third World and American Indian textiles from antiquity to the present.

Washington Dolls' House and Toy Museum, 5236 22th Street NW. Small collection of antique dolls' houses, dolls, toys, games and playthings.

Washington Navy Yard, 9th and M Street SE. The nation's oldest naval facility.

Exhibits

Folger Shakespeare Library, 201 East Capitol Street SE. This world-famous library and Elizabethan-style theater has many exhibits on William Shakespeare and the Renaissance. Open: 10am–4pm.

National Geographic Society, 17th and M streets NW. Exhibits on early humans, weather stations, material from expeditions, and the world's largest unmounted globe.

Music & Opera

Check the *Washington Post* and the *Washington Times* for listings of current performances and recitals.

Kennedy Center Concert Hall, 2700 F Street NW. Tel: 202 467 4600.

National Symphony Orchestra, The Kennedy Center Concert Hall. Tel: 202 467 4600. The National Symphony's permanent home, featuring guest conductors, artistes and soloists.

Washington Opera, Kennedy Center. Tel: 202 416 7800. Classical and contemporary opera staged in the Kennedy Center's grand Opera House or the more intimate Eisenhower Theatre, complete with English subtitles.

Wolf Trap for the Performing Arts, 1624 Trap Road, Vienna, VA. Tel: 703 255 1868. A good mix of all types of performing productions including symphony, musicals, ballet, dance, pop and comedy.

Free Military Band Concerts. Concert hotline, tel: 202 433 4011.

Center for the Arts, George Mason University, 4400 University Drive, Fairfax, VA. Tel: 703 993 8877.

Dance

For a complete list of current events, check the *Washington Post* and the *Washington Times*.

Washington Ballet, Eisenhower Theatre, Kennedy Center, 2700 F Street NW. Tel: 202 467 4600. Also: 3515 Wisconsin Avenue NW. Tel: 202 467 4600. The company presents three repertory series of contemporary and classical ballet in Washington each October, February and May.

Dance Place, Avant-garde dance, 3225 8th Street SE. Tel: 202 269 1600.

Theater & Cabaret

Check the *Washington Post* and the *Washington Times* for a list of current productions.

Arena Stage, 6th and Maine Avenue SW. Tel: 202 488 3300. A three-theater complex featuring world classic and contemporary plays, new works, musicals and American drama.

Burn Brae Dinner Theatre, Route 29 at Blackburn Lane, Burtonsville MD. Tel: 301 384 5800. Features professionally-produced Broadway musical productions and a lavish buffet.

Capitol Steps, Chelsea's, 1055 Thomas Jefferson Street NW. Tel: 202 298 8222. A group of Congressional Staffers who perform political satire, featured regularly on National Public Radio.

d.c. Space, 7th and E Street NW. Tel: 202 347 4960. Cabaret dinner theater with American cuisine.

Discovery Theatre, Smithsonian Arts & Industry Building, 900 Jefferson Drive SW. Tel: 202 357 1500. Productions with young people in mind.

Folger Shakespeare Theatre, 201 E. Capitol Street SE. Tel: 202 546 4000. Classical theater with American flair and energy. Three masterworks by Shakespeare and plays chosen from a classical repertory are produced each season.

Ford's Theatre, 511 10th Street NW. Tel: 202 347 4833. Live, contemporary performances in the beautifully restored 19th-century theater, the site of President Lincoln's assassination.

John F. Kennedy Center for the Performing Arts, Virginia and New Hampshire Aves NW. Tel: 202 467 4600. The nation's cultural center and only Presidential memorial dedicated to the performing arts. Five magnificent theaters present a wide variety of entertainment.

National Theatre, 1321 Pennsylvania Avenue NW. Tel: 202 628 6161. The nation's oldest theater in continuious operation. It features national tours of Broadway favorites, pre-Broadway shows, and American premieres.

Nightlife
Clubs & Discos

Anton's 1201 Club, 1201 Pennsylvania Avenue NW. Tel: 202 783 1201. Local and national artists Tuesday–Saturday, playing pop, jazz and rock. Somewhat of a tourist trap.

The Bayou, 3135 K Street NW. Tel: 202 333 2897. Live music most nights. Good entertainment for an older, hip crowd.

The Birchmere, 3901 Mt Vernon Avenue, Alexandria VA. Tel: 703 549 5919. Some of the most outstanding local bluegrass music.

Blues Alley, 1073 Wisconsin Avenue NW. Tel: 202 337 4141. Local and national jazz artists, plus dinner menu.

Cities, 2424 18th Street NW. Tel: 202 328 7194. New American Cuisine downstairs, dancing to current top 40 DJ music upstairs.

Deja Vu, 2119 M Street NW. Tel: 202 452 1966. Nostalgic but lively dance club featuring DJ music from the '60s to the present day, and the area's largest dance floor.

Jonathan's, 1520 K Street NW. Tel: 202 638 6800. Dancing to DJ music of the '50s, '60s, and top 40. Karaoke machine Wednesday and Friday.

Joe and Mo's, 1211 Connecticut Avenue NW. Tel: 202 659 1211. Dancing at this restaurant on Saturdays from 9pm to live orchestra playing swing and '20s and '30s standards.

Kilimanjaro, 1724 California Street NW. Tel: 202 328 3838. Restaurant and night club offering reggae and African sounds.

9.30 Club, 930 F Street NW. Tel: 202 393 0930. Underground rock acts, blues and funk performers.

Bars

There are bars and cocktail lounges at most of the major hotels, and many of Washington's restaurants, particularly those in Georgetown, have bar stool and cocktail table space at Happy Hour. Listed below, however, are specialty bars.

Champions, 1206 Wisconsin Avenue NW. Tel: 202 965 4005. A sports fan's paradise, featuring sports memorabilia and a satellite dish, dance floor and DJ.
Penalty Box, 111 King Street, Alexandria, VA. Tel: 703 683 0323. Team banners, sports photos and major televised sporting events, via satellite, saloon fare.
Third Edition, 1218 Wisconsin Avenue NW. Tel: 202 333 3700. A famous Georgetown saloon, with full and light-fare menus.

Festivals

For listings of festivals and other celebrations while you are in Washington, check the Weekend Section of the *Washington Post* or the *Washington Times*.

Listed here are some of the more popular events:

January

Robert E. Lee's Birthday Celebration. Held at Lee's former home, Arlington House, in Arlington National Cemetery. Open house featuring 19th-century music, samples of period food and exhibitions of restoration work.
Martin Luther King Jr's Birthday Observance. Wreath-laying ceremony at the Lincoln Memorial, accompanied by the presentation of King's "I have a dream" speech, local choirs, guest speakers and military color guard salute.

February

Chinese New Year Parade. Firecrackers, lions, drums and dragon dancers make their way through Chinatown.
Abraham Lincoln's Birthday. Wreath-laying ceremony and reading of the Gettysburg Address at the Lincoln Memorial.
George Washington's Birthday Parade. Parade through Old Town Alexandria, plus special activities at George Washington's home, Mount Vernon.

March

St Patrick's Day Parades. Parades through Old Town Alexandria, and downtown along Constitution Avenue: dancers, bands, bagpipes and floats.
Smithsonian Kite Festival. Kite makers and flyers gather at the Washington Monument to compete for prizes and trophies.

April

National Cherry Blossom Festival. The Cherry Blossom Festival Parade celebrates the blooming of 6,000 Japanese cherry trees, with princesses, floats and VIPs. Events include fireworks, a fashion show, free concerts in downtown parks, the Japanese Lantern Lighting Ceremony, the Cherry Blossom Ball and an annual Marathon Race.
Imagination Celebration. A festival of the performing arts for young people, with national children's theater companies at the John F. Kennedy Center for the Performing Arts.
Thomas Jefferson's Birthday. A wreath laying ceremony and military drills held at the Jefferson Memorial.
Duke Ellington Birthday Celebration. Musical celebration of this native Washingtonian's contribution to American music.
Potomac International Regatta. US college teams compete with Britain's Oxford and Cambridge Universities on the Potomac.
William Shakespeare's Birthday. A day of music, theater, children's events, food and exhibits at the Folger Shakespeare Library.
Easter – White House Easter Egg Roll. Children eight and under accompanied by an adult gather on the White House South Lawn for the traditional Easter Egg Roll.

May

Filmfest DC. Premieres dozens of international and American films, in theaters across the city.
Gross National Parade. A zany, unorthodox parade to benefit the Police Boys and Girls Clubs of DC. Travels along M & 18th streets NW to Wisconsin Avenue.
Crystal City Festival. A weekend of food, fun and physical feats to benefit charity.
Greek Spring Festival. Food, music, dancing, games and entertainments at Saints Constantine and Helen Greek Orthodox Church.
Memorial Day Weekend Concert. The National Symphony Orchestra performs on the West Lawn of the US Capitol.
Memorial Day Jazz Festival. Big band music by local bands, in Old Town Alexandria.
Memorial Day Ceremonies at Arlington Cemetery. Wreath laying at the Kennedy gravesite, at the Tomb of the Unknowns, and services at the Memorial Amphitheater with military bands and a presidential keynote address.
Memorial Day Ceremonies at the Vietnam Veterans Memorial. Wreath-laying, speeches, military bands and a keynote address.

During The Summer Months

Marine Corps Tuesday Evening Sunset Parades. Featuring the US Marine Drum and Bugle Corps and Silent Drill team at the Iwo Jima Memorial.
Marine Corps Friday Evening Parades. At the Marine Barracks, 8th and I streets SE.
Carillon Saturday Evening Recitals. At the Netherlands Carillon on the grounds of the Iwo Jima Memorial.
"Music Under The Stars" Wednesday Evening Concerts. Big Band sounds at the Sylvan Theater on the Washington Monument grounds.
Noon Hour Concerts. Local performers provide light lunchtime entertainment Tuesdays at Farragut Square and Thursdays at Pershing Park.
Washington National Cathedral's Summer Festival of Music. Concert series.
Sunday Polo. Matches every Sunday afternoon on the field east of the Lincoln Memorial.

C&O Canal Barge Rides. Take a step back in time on one of the mule-drawn barges up the canal in Georgetown and in Great Falls Maryland.

Military Band Summer Concert Series, at the US Capitol West side, the Sylvan Theatre on the Washington Monument grounds and the Navy Memorial Plaza.

"The American Sailor." Multimedia presentation show-casing the history and character of the US Navy, at the Washington Navy Yard waterfront.

US Navy Memorial "Concerts on the Avenue." Delightful program each Thursday and Saturday at 8pm at the US Navy Memorial on Pennsylvania Avenue.

Twilight Tattoo Series each Wednesday at 7pm on the Ellipse grounds between the White House and the Washington Monument.

June

Philippine Independence Day Parade. Parade and fair, food, crafts and music in downtown Washington, along Pennsylvania Avenue from 4th Street to 13th Street NW. **Fair**: Freedom Plaza on Pennsylvania Avenue.

Festival of American Folklife. American music, crafts, ethnic foods, and folk heritage on the Mall.

July

National Independence Day Celebration. American music, dramatic reading of the Declaration of Independence and a demonstration of colonial military manoeuvres held on the Constitution Avenue steps; parade down Constitution Avenue; plus free concerts and an evening fireworks display over the Washington Monument.

DC Free Jazz Festival. Top national and international jazz performers in free concerts at Freedom Plaza.

Civil War Life Re-enactment. Union and Confederate troops camp, drill and skirmish; music, dancing and tour of the 1794 historic home, Sully Plantation, near Dulles International Airport.

Latin-American Festival. Food, music, dance and theater at the National Mall on the Washington Monument grounds.

August

Georgia Avenue Day. Parade, carnival rides, live music and foods on Georgia Avenue at Eastern Avenue NW.

National Frisbee Festival. On the National Mall near the Smithsonian's National Air and Space Museum.

September

Annual International Children's Festival. Three-day outdoor arts celebration at Wolf Trap Farm Park for the Performing Arts.

African Cultural Festival. Food, music, dance and crafts are on display at Freedom Plaza, 14th Street and Pennsylvania Avenue NW.

DC Blues Festival. Celebration of the blues, featuring top performers at Anacostia Park in SE Washington.

Black Family Reunion. Weekend-long celebration, offering fun, food, exhibits and performances on the National Mall.

Labor Day Weekend Concert. National Symphony Orchestra in concert on the West Lawn of the US Capitol.

Adams Morgan Day. Lively street festival with live music, crafts and cooking, down 18th Street, Columbia Road and Florida Avenue NW.

Elderfest. Annual festival for older Americans at Freedom Plaza, with fun, food and entertainment.

Constitution Day Commemoration. On the anniversary of its signing, the original US Constitution is displayed in its entirety at the National Archives, plus various military honor guard ceremonies.

Rock Creek Park Day. Music, activities, food, arts and crafts.

October

US Army Band Fall Concert series. Tuesday and Thursday, Bruckner Hall at Fort Myer in Arlington Va.

American Discoveries Festival. Top performers, music and cooking of a different American city each year. Freedom Plaza.

Columbus Day Ceremonies. The Knights of Columbus and other groups in a tribute to Christopher Columbus at the Columbus Memorial Plaza in front of Union Station, with wreath laying, speeches and music.

Theodore Roosevelt's Birthday Celebration. Festivities at Theodore Roosevelt Island and Reserve.

November

Armistice Day Celebration. Tour of home of President Woodrow Wilson, with music from the World War I period.

Veteran's Day Ceremonies. Service in the Memorial Amphitheater at Arlington National Cemetery and wreath laying at the Tomb of the Unknown soldier.

December

Festival of Music and Lights. More than 80,000 tiny lights sparkle on the trees and shrubs of the Washington Mormon Temple in Kensington, MD, with live nativity scene and concerts at 7.30pm.

"Holidays at Mount Vernon." The recreation of an authentic 18th-century holiday season, with a tour of the third floor of the mansion, usually closed to the public.

Carol Singing. The US Marine Band and local choirs at Wolf Trap Farm Park.

National Christmas Tree Lighting/Pageant of Peace. In a special holiday celebration with seasonal music, military bands, and caroling, the giant National Christmas Tree near the White House is lighted by the president of the United States. From then until New Year's Day, the Ellipse is the site of nightly choral performances, a Nativity scene, a burning yule log and a display of lighted Christmas trees representing each state and territory in the United States.

US Botanic Gardens' Christmas Poinsettia Show. Over 3,000 red, white and pink plants amidst a display of Christmas wreaths and trees, at the US Botanic Gardens.

Washington National Cathedral Christmas Celebration and Services. Christmas carols and seasonal choral performances.

White House Christmas Candlelight Tours. Evening tours of the White House Christmas decorations.

New Year's Eve Celebration at the Old Post Office Pavilion. Live entertainment.

Shopping

This table gives a comparison of American, Continental and British clothing sizes. However, it is always best to try on any article before buying it as sizes can vary.

Women's Dresses/Suits

American	Continental	British
6	38/34N	8/30
8	40/36N	10/32
10	42/38N	12/34
12	44/40N	14/36
14	46/42N	16/38
16	48/44N	18/40

Women's Shoes

American	Continental	British
4ˇ	36	3
5ˇ	37	4
6ˇ	38	5
7ˇ	40	6
8ˇ	41	7
9ˇ	42	8

Men's Suits

American	Continental	British
34	44	34
—	46	36
38	48	38
—	50	40
42	52	42
—	54	44
46	56	46

Men's Shirts

American	Continental	British
14ˇ	37	14ˇ
15	38	15
15ˇ	39	15ˇ
16	40	16
16ˇ	41	16ˇ
17	42	17

Men's Shoes

American	Continental	British
6ˇ	—	6
7ˇ	40	7
8ˇ	41	8
9ˇ	42	9
10ˇ	43	10
11ˇ	44	11

Where To Shop

Shopping ranges from the downtown and Chevy Chase outlets of international fashion names, to small specialty shops located all over town and the glitzy new shopping complexes and malls that have mushroomed both in the center and in the suburbs.

One of the most individual of these in design is the renovated **Old Post Office Pavilion** at 1100 Pennsylvania Avenue NW. A glass-enclosed elevator carries visitors to the Observation Tower for a magnificent view over the city. **Connecticut Avenue**, south of Dupont Circle, is the place for the Washington outlets of European stores, such as Burberry's of London, at 1155 Connecticut Avenue NW, and, on K Street, Bally of Switzerland, Hugo Boss, Louis Vuitton and Pampillonia, and US fashion names Raleigh and Rosendorf/Evans. North of **Dupont Circle** are two terrific bookstores – Kramerbooks & Afterwords, at 1517 Connecticut Avenue NW, where you can read and eat (in Afterwords café) in a relaxed atmosphere. Mystery Books, at 1715 Connecticut Avenue NW, offers Washington's largest selection of thriller, mystery, spy and suspense novels.

In **Georgetown**, along Wisconsin Avenue and M Street, are smaller specialty fashion and accessory boutiques, like Hugo Boss, while the **Georgetown Park** shopping Mall on the corner of both streets is a new and glamorous outlet for upmarket clothes, accessories and furnishings. The Shops at **Metro Center** offer a more affordable selection, from outlets such as The Limited, Dolcis, and Sharper Image. Around the Metro Center area are the Chanel Boutique, Harriet Kassman, Fahrney's Pens, and Hecht's department store. **Union Station's** concourses are home to a large complex of shops, food stalls, major restaurants and movie theaters.

Top European designers, such as GianFranco Ferre, Giorgio Armani, Byblos, and Gucci can be found at the **Watergate complex**, the **Mazza Galerie** mall in Chevy Chase and on **Wisconsin Avenue** at Chevy Chase. Particularly popular in the casual market for their quality, their fashion appeal and their price are the chain stores of the Gap, the Limited, Limited Express – each offering clothes for children as well as adults – Banana Republic and Britches. Check the telephone directory for the nearest branch. Ann Taylor, another chain, sells good-quality, reasonably priced working and dressy clothes for women.

Upscale department store Saks Fifth Avenue is found at **2051 International Drive**, McLean, VA; the **Galleria** at Tyson's II in VA and on Wisconsin Avenue in Chevy Chase, MD. I Magnin and Lord & Taylor, at the **White Flint Mall** on Rockville Pike, MD, Nordstrom's at Montgomery Mall, Democracy Boulevard, MD and Tyson's Corner, VA, are fashion specialty stores catering to men, women and children. Woodward & Lothrop, at Metro Center and Montgomery Mall is a full line, mid-level department store.

Montgomery Mall has recently undergone a complete overhaul to bring it up to the glitzy standard of the White Flint Mall and Tyson's Corner, a mall that because it has more shopping outlets than there are days in the year also provides hotel accommodation on the territory, for those who *do* want to shop until they drop.

Sports

The Dow Jones-sponsored Information Network gives sports results and other information daily over the telephone. Check the *Yellow Pages* for details.

For events at the **RFK Stadium**, home of the Redskins, tel: 202 547 9077, or the ticket office on 202 546

2222/3337. Free information on events at the **Capital Centre**, home to the NHL Washington Capitals and the NBA Washington Bullets, can be heard by dialing 816 1616 and when asked, entering 2714 on the dial. Free information on events at **Memorial Stadium**, home of the Baltimore Orioles, at 1000 E 33rd Street, Baltimore, MD 21218 can be had by dialing 816 1616 and when asked, entering 2708.

Bike Rentals

Big Wheel Bikes, Georgetown, 10034 33rd Street NW. Tel: 337 0254.
Fletcher's Boat House, 4940 Canal Road NW. Tel: 244 0461.
Swains Lock, MD on the C&O Canal, 4 miles above Great Falls. Tel: 301 299 9006.
Thompson's Boat House, Rock Creek Park and Virginia Avenue NW. Tel: 333 4861.

Boat Rentals

Thompson's Boat Center, Rock Creek Park and Virginia Avenue NW. Tel: 333 4861.
Jack's Boats, 3500 K Street NW. Tel: 337 9642.
Fletcher's Boat House, 4740 Canal Road NW. Tel: 244 0461.
Swain's Lock, MD on the C&O Canal, 4 miles above Great Falls. Tel: 301 299 9006.
Swan Boats (pedal boats), Tidal Basin Boat House, Jefferson Memorial. Tel: 484 0206.

Ice Skating

National Sculpture Garden, 7th Street and Constitution Avenue NW. Tel: 889 3800.
Pershing Park, Pennsylvania Avenue between 14th and 15th streets NW. Tel: 737 6937.

Further Reading

Many books have been written about this delightful city and its people. Here are a few considered to be essential reading for the traveler looking to understand more about Washington, DC.

Capitol Losses, James Goode. Washington, DC: Smithsonian Books, 1958.
The Concierge's Guide to Washington, McDowell Bryson and Adele Ziminski, Wiley.
A Museum Guide to Washington, DC, Betty Ross. Washington, DC: Americana, 1988.
Natural Washington: A guide for hikers, bikers, birders and others lovers of nature, Richard L. Berman and Deborah Gerhard. McLean, VA: EPM Publications, 1991.
Smithsonian Guide to Historic America, Henry Wiencek. New York: Stewart, Tabori and Chang, 1989.
Spring in Washington, Louis J. Halle. Baltimore and London: John Hopkins University, 1988.
Washington DC Access, Richard Saul Wurmau, New York: Access Press, 1987.
Washington DC At Its Best, Robert Skane, Passport Books.
Washington Itself, E.J. Applewhite. New York: Knopf, 1986.
The Washington Post Guide to Washington, edited by Robert L. Price, New York: McGraw-Hill, 1989.

Other Washingtoniana

Beautiful Swimmers: Watermen, Crabs and the Chesapeake Bay, William W. Warner. New York: Penguin, 1976.
The following murder mysteries, published by Fawcett of New York, were written by Margaret Truman, daughter of the 33rd president of the United States:
Murder in the Smithsonian
Murder in Georgetown
Murder at the FBI
Murder on Capitol Hill
Murder in the White House
Murder on Embassy Row
Murder in the Supreme Court
Murder in the CIA
*Murder at the Kennedy Center*History
Alexandria on the Potomac: The Portrait of an Antebellum Community, Harold W. Hurst. Lanham, Maryland: University Press of America, 1991.
Capital Image: Painters in Washington 1800–1915, Andrew J. Costentino and Henry H. Glassie. Washington, DC: Smithsonian Books, 1983.
The Creation of Washington, DC: The Idea and Location of the American Capital, Kenneth R. Bowling. Fairfax, VA: George Mason University, 1991.

Old Washington, DC in Early Photographs 1846–1932, Robert Reed. New York: Dover, 1980.
Through a Fiery Trail: Building Washington 1790–1800, Bob Arnebeck. Lanham, MD; New York; and London: Madison, 1991.
Two Hundred Years: Stories of the Nation's Capital, Jeanne Fogle. Arlington, VA: Vandamere, 1991.
Washington, DC: A Guide to the Nation's Capital. Reproduction of 1939 edition compiled by Works Progress Administration (Federal Writers Project American Guidebook Series). Detroit, Michigan: Omnigraphics Inc., 1991.
Washington, DC: Capitol City 1879–1950 (Vol. II), Constance Mclaughlin Green. Princeton, New Jersey: Princeton University Press, 1976.
Washington Behind the Monuments, Bruce I. Bustard. Washington, DC: National Archives and Records Administration.

Travel Guides For Kids

While there are plenty of books about touring with your children, two special ones, available locally, have been written for children 8 years and older to read themselves:
Washington DC Guidebook for Kids, Carol Bluestone and Susan Irwin. Noodle Press. This guide is filled with historical facts, trivia, puzzles and games about the city's top attractions.
Washington! Adventures for Kids, Marti Weston and Florri DeCell. Vandamere Press. This book takes a "scavenger hunt" approach to the top sights and is useful as a focus for museum visits.

There more than 190 books in the *Insight Guides* series which cover every continent, including 29 titles devoted to the United States, from Alaska to Florida, from Seattle to Boston.

Two titles which are also relevant to the present volume are *Insight Guide: Crossing America* and *Insight Guide: Old South*.

Index